Magnificent Obsession

Lloyd C. Douglas

Magnificent Obsession

A MARINER BOOK
Houghton Mifflin Company
Boston · New York

First Mariner Books edition 1999

www.houghtonmifflinbooks.com

Library of Congress Cataloging-in-Publication Data
Douglas, Lloyd C. (Lloyd Cassel), 1877–1951.
Magnificent obsession / by Lloyd C. Douglas. —
1st Mariner Books ed.
p. cm.
ISBN-13: 978-0-395-95774-5 ISBN-10: 0-395-95774-5
I. Title.
PS3507.07573M3 1999
813'.52—dc21 99-20071 CIP

Printed in the United States of America

DOC 10 9

To Betty and Virginia

I

IT HAD LATELY BECOME COMMON CHATTER AT BRIGHTWOOD Hospital — better known for three hundred miles around Detroit as Hudson's Clinic — that the chief was all but dead on his feet. The whole place buzzed with it.

All the way from the inquisitive solarium on the top floor to the garrulous kitchen in the basement, little groups — convalescents in wheeled chairs, nurses with tardy trays, lean internes on rubber soles, grizzled orderlies trailing damp mops — met to whisper and separated to disseminate the bad news. Doctor Hudson was on the verge of a collapse.

On the verge? . . . Indeed! One lengthening story had it that on Tuesday he had fainted during an operation — mighty ticklish piece of business, too — which young Watson, assisting him, was obliged to complete alone. And the worst of it was that he was back at it again, next morning, carrying on as usual.

An idle tale like that, no matter with what solicitude of loyalty it might be discussed at Brightwood, would deal the institution a staggering wallop once it seeped through the big wrought-iron gates. And the rumor was peculiarly difficult to throttle because, unfortunately, it was true.

Obviously the hour had arrived for desperate measures.

Dr. Malcolm Pyle, shaggy and beetle browed, next to the chief in seniority, a specialist in abdominal surgery and admiringly spoken of by his colleagues as the best belly man west of the Alleghenies, growled briefly into the ear of blood-and-skin Jennings, a cynical, middle-aged bachelor, who but for his skill as a bacteriologist would have been dropped from the staff, many a time, for his rasping banter and infuriating impudences.

Jennings quickly passed the word to internal-medicine Carter, who presently met eye-ear-nose-and-throat McDermott in the hall and relayed the message.

"Oh, yes, I'll come," said McDermott uneasily, "but I don't relish the idea of a staff meeting without the chief. Looks like treason."

"It's for his own good," explained Carter.

"Doubtless; but . . . he has always been such a straight shooter, himself."

"You tell Aldrich and Watson. I'll see Gram and Harper. I hate it as much as you do, Mac, but we can't let the chief ruin himself."

Seeing that tomorrow was Christmas, and this was Saturday well past the luncheon hour, by the time Pyle had tardily joined them in the superintendent's office each of the eight, having abandoned whatever manifestation of dignified omniscience constituted his bedside manner, was snappishly impatient to have done with this unpleasant business and be off.

When at length he breezed in, not very convincingly attempting the conciliatory smirk of the belated, Pyle found them glum and fidgety — Carter savagely reducing to shavings what remained of a pencil, Aldrich rattling the pages of his engagement book, McDermott meticulously pecking at diminutive bits of lint on his coat sleeve, Watson ostentatiously shaking his watch at his ear, Gram drumming an exasperating tattoo on Nancy Ashford's desk, and the others pacing about like hungry panthers.

" Well," said Pyle, seating them with a sweeping gesture, " you all know what we're here for."

" Ab-so-lute-ly," drawled Jennings. " The old boy must be warned."

" At once! " snapped Gram.

" I'll say! " muttered McDermott.

" And you, Pyle, are the proper person to do it! " Anticipating a tempestuous rejoinder, Jennings hastened to defend himself against the impending din by noisily pounding out his pipe on the rim of Mrs. Ashford's steel waste basket, a performance she watched with sour interest.

" Where do you get that 'old boy' stuff, Jennings? " demanded Pyle, projecting a fierce, myopic glare at his pestiferous crony. " He's not much older than you are."

Watson tilted his chair back on its hind legs, cautiously turned his red head in the direction of Carter, seated next him, and slowly closed one eye. This was going to be good.

" Doctor Hudson was forty-six last May," quietly volunteered the superintendent, without looking up.

" You ought to know," conceded Jennings drily.

She met his rough insinuation with level, unacknowledging eyes.

" May twenty-fifth," she added.

" Thanks so much. That point's settled, then. But, all the same, he wasn't a day under a hundred and forty-six when he slumped out of his operating room, this morning, haggard and shaky."

" It's getting spread about too," complained Carter.

" Take it up with him, Doctor Pyle," wheedled McDermott. " Tell him we all think he needs a vacation — a long one! "

Pyle snorted contemptuously and aimed a bushy eyebrow at him.

"Humph! That's good! 'Tell him we all think,' eh? It's a mighty careless, offhand damn that Hudson would give for what we all think! Did you ever . . ." He pointed a bony finger at the perspiring McDermott, ". . . did you ever feel moved to offer a few comradely suggestions to Dr. Wayne Hudson, relative to the better management of his personal affairs?"

McDermott rosily hadn't, and Pyle's dry voice crackled again.

"As I thought! That explains how, with so little display of emotion, you can advise somebody else to do it. You see, my son," — he dropped his tone of raillery and became sincere — "we're dealing here with an odd number. Nobody quite like him in the whole world . . . full of funny crotchets. In a psychiatric clinic — which this hospital is going to be, shortly, with the entire staff in strait-jackets — some of Hudson's charming little idiosyncrasies would be brutally referred to as clean-cut psychoses!"

The silence in Mrs. Ashford's office was tense. Pyle's regard for the chief was known to be but little short of idolatry. What, indeed, was he preparing to say? Did he actually believe that Hudson was off the rails?

"Now, don't misunderstand!" he went on quickly, sensing their amazement. "Hudson's entitled to all his whimsies. So far as I'm concerned, he has earned the right to his flock of phantoms. He is a genius, and whosoever loveth a genius is out of luck with his devotion except he beareth all things, endureth all things, suffereth long and is kind."

"Not like sounding brass," interpolated Jennings piously.

"Apropos of brass," growled Pyle, "but — no matter.

. . . We all know that the chief is the most important figure in the field of brain surgery on this continent. But he did not come to that distinction by accident. He has toiled like a slave in a mill. His specialty is guaranteed to make a man moody; counts himself lucky if he can hold down his mortality to fifty per cent. What kind of a mentality would *you* have " — shifting his attention to Jennings, who grinned, amiably — " if you lost half your cases? They'd soon have you trussed in a big tub of hot water, feeding you through the nose with a syringe! "

" You spoke of the chief's psychoses," interrupted McDermott, approaching the dangerous word hesitatingly. " Do you mean that — literally? "

Pyle pursed his lips and nodded slowly.

" Yes — literally! One of his notions — by far the most alarming of his legion, in so far as the present dilemma is affected — has to do with his curious attitude toward fear. He mustn't be afraid of anything. He must live above fear — that is his phrase. You would think, to hear his prattle, that he was a wealthy and neurotic old lady trying to graduate from Theosophy into Bahaism. . . ."

" What's Bahaism? " inquired Jennings, with pretended naïveté.

" Hudson believes," continued Pyle, disdainful of the annoyance, " that if a man harbors any sort of fear, no matter how benign and apparently harmless, it percolates through all his thinking, damages his personality, makes him landlord to a ghost. For years, he has been so consistently living above fear — fear of slumping, fear of the natural penalties of overwork, fear of the neural drain of insomnia. . . . Haven't you heard him discoursing on the delights of reading in bed to three o'clock? . . . fear of that little aneurism he knows he's got — that he has driven himself at full gallop with spurs on his boots and burrs under his saddle, caroling about his freedom, until he's ready to drop. But whoever cautions him will be warmly damned for his impertinence."

Pyle had temporarily run down, and discussion became general. Carter risked suggesting that if the necessary interview with the chief required a gift for impertinence, why not deputize Jennings? Aldrich said it was no time for kidding. McDermott again nominated Pyle. Gram shouted, "Of course!" They pushed back their chairs. Pyle brought both big hands down on his knees with a resounding slap, rose with a groan, and sourly promised he'd have a go at it.

"Attaboy!" commended Jennings paternally. "Watson will do your stitches, afterwards. He has been getting some uncommonly nice cosmetic values, lately, with his scars; eh, Watty?"

The disorder incident to adjournment spared Watson the chagrin of listening to the threatened report of Jennings' eavesdropping, an hour earlier, on the dulcet cooing of a recently discharged patient, back to tender her gratitude. Emboldened by his rescue, he dispassionately told Jennings to go to hell, much to the latter's faunlike satisfaction, and the staff evaporated.

"Let's go and eat," said Pyle.

As they turned the corner in the corridor, Jennings slipped his hand under Pyle's elbow and muttered, "You know damned well what ails the chief, and so do I. It's the girl!"

"Joyce, you mean?"

"Who else?" Jennings buttoned his overcoat collar high about his throat and thrust his shoulder against the big front door and an eighty-mile gale. " Certainly, I mean Joyce. She's running wild, and he's worrying his heart out and his head off! "

" Maybe so," Pyle picked his footing carefully on the snowy steps. " But I don't believe it's very good cricket for us to analyze his family affairs."

" Nonsense! We're quite past the time for indulging in any knightly restraints. Hudson's in danger of shooting his reputation to bits. Incidentally, it will give the whole clinic a black eye when the news spreads. If the chief is off his feed because he's fretting about his girl, then it's high time we talked candidly about her. She's a silly little ass, if you ask my opinion! "

" Well, you won't be asked for your opinion. And it's no good coming at it in that mood. She may be, as you say, a silly little ass; but she's Hudson's deity! "

Jennings motioned him to climb into the coupé and fumbled in his pockets for his keys.

" She wasn't behaving much like a deity — unless Bacchus, perhaps — the last time I saw her."

" Where was that? "

" At the Tuileries, about a month ago, with a party of eight or ten noisy roisterers, in the general custody of that good-for-nothing young Merrick — you know, old Nick Merrick's carousing grandson. Believe me, they were well oiled."

" Did you — did she recognize you? "

" Oh, quite so! Came fluttering over to our table to speak to me! "

" Humph! She *must* have been pickled! I thought she was getting on, all right, at a girls' school in Washington. . . . Didn't know she was home."

Jennings warmed his engine noisily, and threw in the clutch.

" Maybe she was sacked."

Pyle made some hopeless noises deep in his throat.

" Too bad about old Merrick. . . . Salt of the earth; finest of the fine. He's had more than his share of trouble. Did you ever know Clif? "

" No. He was dead. But I've heard of him. A bum, wasn't he? "

" That describes him; and this orphan of his seems to be headed in the same direction."

" Orphan? I thought this boy's mother was living — Paris or somewhere."

" Oh yes, she's living; but the boy's an orphan, for all that. Born an orphan! " Pyle briefly reviewed the Merrick saga.

" Perhaps," suggested Jennings, as they rolled into the club garage, " you might have a chat with old Merrick, if he's such a good sort, and tell him his whelp is a contaminating influence to our girl."

" Pfff! " Pyle led the way to the elevator.

" Well, if that proposal's no good, why don't you go manfully to the young lady herself and inform her that she's driving her eminent parent crazy? Put it up to her as a matter of good sportsmanship."

" No," objected Pyle, hooking his glasses athwart his nose to inspect the menu, " she would only air her indignation to her father. And he likes people to mind their own business — as you've discovered on two or three occasions. He keeps his own counsel like a clam, and doesn't thank anybody for crashing into his affairs, no matter how benevolent may be the motive. . . . It would be quite useless, anyway.

Joyce can't help the way she's made. She is a biological throwback to her maternal grandfather. You never knew him. He was just putting the finishing touches to his career as a periodical sot when I arrived in this town, fresh from school. Cummings was the best all 'round surgeon and the hardest all 'round drinker in the state of Michigan for twenty years; one of these three-days-soused and three-weeks-sober drunkards. This girl evidently carries an overplus of the old chap's chromosomes."

" You mean she is a dipsomaniac? "

" Well — that's a nasty word. Let's just say she's erratic. Ever since she was a little tot, she has been a storm center. Sweetest thing in the world when she wants to be. And then all hell breaks loose and Hudson has to plead with the teachers to take her back. Oh, she's given him an exciting life; no doubt of that! And lately it's booze! "

" Hudson knows about that part of it, of course! "

" I presume so. How could he help it? She makes no secret of it. At all events, she's no hypocrite."

Jennings sighed.

" Rather unfortunate she has this one embarrassing virtue; isn't it? But, that being the case, I dare say she'll have to go to the devil at her own speed. We must persuade Hudson however to clear out and take a long leave of absence. He can take her along. Lay it on with a heavy hand, Pyle. Be utterly ruthless! Tell him it affects us all. That ought to fetch him. I never knew anybody quite so sensitive to the welfare of other people. Save that card for the last trick: tell him if he doesn't clear out, for a while, he will do up the rest of us! "

◇ ◇

For the first half hour of their conference, which was held in the chief's office the following Tuesday, Pyle stubbornly held out for a trip around the world, Joyce to accompany her father. Indeed, the idea had seemed so good that he had armed himself with a portfolio of attractive cruise literature. He had even made out an intriguing itinerary — Hawaii, Tahiti, ukeleles — Pyle was a confirmed land-lubber with a dangerously suppressed desire to lie on his back, pleasantly jingled, under a trans-equatorial palm, listening to the soft vowels of grown-up children unspoiled by civilization — the Mediterranean countries, six months of hobnobbing with brain specialists in Germany. The latter item had been included as a particularly tempting bait. Hudson had often declared he meant to do that some day.

The chief listened preoccupiedly; tried to seem grateful; tried to seem interested; but as Pyle rumbled on with his sales-talk the big man grew restless, refilled his fountain-pen, rearranged his papers in neater piles, had much difficulty hunting a match-box. Then he shook his head, smiling.

No, much as he appreciated Pyle's friendly concern, he wasn't going around the world; not just now. Of course he had been sticking at it too steadily. Lately he had had it on his mind to build a little shack in some out of the way place, not too far off, and put in there from Friday afternoon to Tuesday morning, at least in decent weather, tramp, fish, botanize, read light novels, sleep, live the simple life. He would begin plans on such a place at once. Spring would be along soon.

" And — meantime? " persisted Pyle, gnawing at the tip of his uptilted little goatee.

Hudson rose, slammed a drawer shut with a bang, swung a leg over the corner of his desk, folded his arms tightly, and faced his counsellor with a mysterious grin.

" Meantime? . . . Pyle, I hope this won't knock you cold. I'm going down to Philadelphia, week after next, to marry my daughter's school friend, Miss Helen Brent."

Pyle's eyes and mouth comically registered such stunned amazement that the Hudson grin widened.

" And then the three of us will be spending a couple of months in Europe. I've arranged with Leighton to come over from the university and take care of such head cases as Watson can't handle. Watson's a good man; bright future. Oddly enough, I was on the point of asking you in to talk this over when you said you wished to see me."

Pyle bit off the end of a fresh cigar and mumbled felicitations, not yet sufficiently recovered to pretend enthusiasm.

" Doubtless you think me a fool, Pyle."

Hudson took a turn up and down the room, giving his colleague an opportunity to deny it if he wished. Pyle puffed meditatively.

" Seventeen years a widower," mused Hudson, half to himself. He paused at the far corner to straighten a disordered shelf of books.

" A man accumulates a lot of habits in seventeen years." He returned to his desk-chair. " Sounds like the wedding of January and June, eh? "

Had Jennings been in Pyle's place, his eyes would have twinkled as he replied, " *January!* What! You? January? Nonsense, Chief! Not a day over October, at the farthest! "

Pyle smiled wanly, and shifted his cigar to the other corner of his mouth.

"I came by this valuable new friendship early last year when Miss Brent was made Junior advisor to my Joyce."

Something of sympathetic comradeship in Pyle's reviving interest, now that he was partially coming to, encouraged Hudson to toss aside what remained of his reticence and tell it all.

To begin with — Miss Brent was an orphan; parents reputable Virginians; most interesting French background on her mother's side; same kind of blood that the guillotine spilt in 1789. . . . "Quite pronouncedly Gallic, she is — at least in appearance."

Jennings, had he been there, would have been audacious enough to suggest, slyly chuckling, "Oh — in that case we should amend June to *July!*" Then he would have watched the chief's face intently.

But Pyle, who had no traffic with psychoanalysis, attached no significance whatever to the fact that the young lady's probable temperament was somewhat on the chief's mind.

"About Thanksgiving," Hudson was saying, "Miss Brent, after a brief encounter with influenza, left the school and spent a few days at home. No sooner was she gone than Joyce slipped out, one night; attended a party, down in the city; defied some house rules as to hours; flicked all her classes next day; stormed until the shingles rattled when they rebuked her; and, in short, contrived to get herself suspended, notwithstanding that her record — thanks to Miss Brent's influence — had been quite above reproach ever since she matriculated, a year ago last September."

The story went forward rather jerkily. Hudson was not

given to confiding his perplexities to anybody. Pyle discreetly remained silent.

"Well — she came home and plunged immediately into a series of hectic affairs; out every night; in bed most of the day; nervous, testy, unreasonable. I can't tell you, Pyle, how thoroughly it did me in. . . . She's all I have, you know.

"At my wit's end, I suggested that she invite Miss Brent up to visit us through the holidays. Twice before had she been our guest for a few days, and I had seen something of her on my occasional visits to Washington. Believe me when I tell you that this charming girl was no more than across our threshold last week, than Joyce was another creature, poised, gracious, lovable — a lady!"

He paused to take his bearings before going further; impelled to explain how the swift movement of events, that first evening at dinner, amply accounted for his decision to ask Helen to marry him; reluctant, even in the interest of plausibility and self-defence, to give words to the memory of that occasion. It had all been so natural; so unimpeachably right; so precisely as it ought to be! He had remarked — perhaps a bit more ardently than he intended, for his heart was full — how happy it had made him — and Joyce — that she had come. "I don't see how we can ever let you go!" he had said; to which Joyce had added impetuously, "Why need she ever go? She's happier here than anywhere else; aren't you, darling?"

Pyle recrossed his legs and cleared his throat to remind the chief that he was still present.

"As a matter of fact, Miss Brent is certain to be happier with us than she was at home. Since childhood, she has lived with an uncle, her father's elder brother, an irascible, penurious, not very successful old lawyer. There are no women in the family. And I have reason to suspect that her cousin, Montgomery Brent, is a bit of a rake, though she has idealized him out of all proportion; calls him 'Brother Monty,' thinks him vastly misunderstood by his father and everybody else . . . that kind of a girl, Pyle . . . espouses the cause of homeless cats, under dogs, misunderstood cousins, my flighty, wilful Joyce . . . and now — thank God — she has promised to join forces with *me!* I think she's making something of a mission of it, Pyle. I was quite willing to wait until she had finished school in June; had some serious misgivings, indeed, about that; but she dismissed the thought lightly. If I needed her, I needed her *now*, she said. . . . I hope to God it works out! "

Pyle said he believed it would; moved to the edge of his chair; looked at his watch; asked if this was a secret.

Hudson stroked his jaw, his eyes averted.

" I don't object to their knowing. . . . Let's consider it sufficient, for the present, that I'm going to Europe with my daughter." He mopped his broad forehead vigorously. " The rest of it they can learn in due time. Report to Aldrich and Carter and the others that I'm off on a vacation."

" Any special word for Mrs. Ashford, Chief? " Pyle paused with his hand on the door-knob.

Hudson thrust his hands deeply into his trouser pockets and walked to the window, staring out.

" I'll tell her myself, Pyle," he answered, without turning.

◇ ◇

Doctor Hudson named his isolated retreat Flintridge. It was quite remote from the beaten trail of travel. A mere acre had been tamed to serve the cottage for which his hasty sketches, before leaving, were elaborated and executed in his absence by his loyal friend, Fred Ferguson, the best architect in town.

It was an inhospitable bit of country, thereabouts. Sheer cliffs, descending abruptly to the black water (a long flight of wooden steps led to the little boat-house and adjacent wharf) had discouraged such colonization as had long since developed the western shore, two miles distant. Deformed pines clawed the rocks, sighing of their thirst in summer, shrieking of nakedness in winter.

Almost from the first, Flintridge never knew certainly, for there was no telephone, when its master would appear for a week-end. It anticipated, made forecasts, baked ineffable angel food cakes, caught vast quantities of minnows for bait, and held itself in instant readiness to welcome the big man with the ruddy face (just a shade too ruddy, any heart diagnostician could have told him), silver-white hair, gray eyes with deep crows-feet, and expressive hands eloquent of highly developed dexterity.

When and if he came, it would be on Saturday, late afternoon. Once only had he brought Joyce and Helen — strangers, passing them, presumed they were both his daughters — but that was merely temporizing with his promise to seek a retreat. And he now needed days off, if ever; for his young wife's gregarious disposition and charming hospitality had multiplied his social obligations in the city.

How easily she had adjusted herself to his moods! How proud he was of her, not quite so much for her exotic beauty, as because of her exquisiteness of personal taste and the tact with which she met the rather exacting problems of fitting neatly and quickly into his circle of mature acquaintances. It delighted him that she chose the right word, wore the right costume, intuitively knew how to manage a dinner-party without seeming concerned as to what misadventures might have occurred in the kitchen. Yes; the affair was "working out" — how often he used that phrase! — immeasurably better than he had dared hope.

Even the women liked her! They had accepted her on approval at first; but when it became evident that she had no intention of taking on airs because their grizzled spouses fluttered about her with the broad compliments privileged to fifty addressing twenty-five, they admitted she was a dear.

But, however pleasant it was for Hudson to note his wife's growing popularity, certified to by the increasing volume of their social activities, his new duties contributed little to the reinvigoration of that fatigued aorta which had worried Pyle.

"The chief's in better fettle — think?" said Jennings.

"Temporarily," conceded Pyle. "But you don't mend an aneurism with late dinners, three a week. I'm afraid he'll crash, one of these days."

Not infrequently some visiting colleague — for Brightwood now not only attracted patients from afar but had become a mecca for the ambitious in the field of brain surgery — would be driven out into the country to rusticate for a day or two. They seemed singularly alike, these brain-tinkers from otherwhere; moody, abstracted men, in their late forties and early fifties, most of them; seldom smiling, ungifted with small talk, not unusually inclined to be somewhat gruff. Hudson preferred to hold conferences with them at the lake, for their conversation would be tiresomely technical. And anyhow, men who trafficked daily with Death could not be expected to enliven a house party.

A devoted pair of middle-aged twins served as caretakers at Flintridge. What time Perry Ruggles, of the stiff knee, hairy throat, and Airedale disposition, was not tinkering the boat engine with greasy wrenches or trolling in and out of season for bass, he was teaching little patches of apathetic soil to take a maternal interest in iris and petunias. On Saturdays about five o'clock, he would put on his other coat and limp down to the gate that admitted from the narrow ridge road; and, having opened it, would flick little stones off the driveway with his good foot.

Martha, his buxom sister, wrought ingenious quilts, concealed from the taciturn Perry the vandalisms of an impertinent, bottle-fed fawn; was silly over a pair of tame pheasants whose capacity for requiting her affection was as feeble as her need was great; scratched her plump arms gathering early berries in anticipation of some high moment when her pie would be approved with a slow wink, of which the learned guest, profoundly discoursing of surgical mysteries to his celebrated host, would be entirely unaware.

On Saturdays, about four-thirty, having again made sure she had laid out the doctor's pajamas on the bed, and turning the vase of roses on his chiffonier a little more to the advantage of the tallest, Martha would take her stand before the window in the sun-parlor, her knuckles pressed hard against her pretty teeth, devoutly praying for a swirl of yellow dust and a flash of glittering nickel at the bend of the ridge road, visible through an open lane of dwarf spruce.

At the sound of gravel crunching under heavy tires, she would dash to the door and fling it open, always hoping — and hating herself for it — that the doctor had come alone or, if not alone, accompanied by another man. She had been uneasy, abashed, and awkward in the presence of young Mrs. Hudson, whose beauty had stirred remembrance of a certain pre-Christmas shopping excursion when she was nine. . . . There had been a French doll, so beautiful it had made Martha's little throat ache with longing. Her wistful eyes had gushed sudden tears, and she had put out a hand, tentatively.

"No, dear," her mother had cautioned. "You may look at her, but you mustn't touch."

◇ ◇

On the broad mantel in the "gun room" (there had been a bit of chaffing about the "gun room," seeing there was only one gun in it among all the miscellaneous instruments of sport — golf clubs, fishing tackle, and the like) an impressive row of silver cups testified that Wayne Hudson was no less expert at play than with the more important implements of surgery.

It was a frequent remark of his intimates that Hudson possessed an almost uncanny capacity for projecting the sensitiveness of his cognitive fingers to the very tips of whatever tools he chose to manipulate. There were nerves in his niblick, in his casting-rod, in his scalpel.

"A lucky devil!" bystanders used to remark when he had successfully made a long putt up-grade on a sporty green.

"An uncommonly good guesser!" his confrères agreed occasionally, when some quite daring prognosis — probably defining the exact location of a brain tumor on such cryptic evidence as the arc of an eyebrow, the twitch of a lip, the posture of a hand in repose, or the interjection of an unbecoming phrase into casual conversation — was verified.

Among the trophies on the mantel — whose inscriptions

always amazed a visiting colleague, marvelling at his distinguished host's diversity of proficiencies — there was a tarnished triple-handled aquatic prize won by Doctor Hudson when, in the early days of his interneship, he had taken a First in a mile swim.

" Still swim? "

" Regularly."

" Enjoy it? "

" Well — it's good for me."

" Keeps your weight down? "

" Perhaps. But, in any event, it's good for me."

Some time in the course of his visit, the visitor would rag his athletic host upon the excess of his prudence; for the most conspicuous article of furniture in the " gun room " was an elaborate but not very decorative inhalator of the super-type used by life-savers at busy wharves and crowded beaches, equipped with nickeled oxygen tanks and a complication of mechanical mysteries.

" What's that thing? "

Hudson would tell him, briefly, brusquely.

" What do *you* want with it? "

" Oh, somebody might fall in. The water's deep out here."

It was clear enough to the guest, if he ventured to press his queries, that Doctor Hudson did not enjoy any talk about aquatics. The guest found himself wondering why. Perry Ruggles could have explained, had he been disposed. There had once been a very anxious hour at Flintridge, down on the narrow pier. Not even Martha knew. The next time he had come out, Doctor Hudson had brought the inhalator, and had explained its use to the terrified Perry who thereafter stood in dread of the thing. It became a grim specter that haunted his life. Some day, he suspected, he would be obliged to experiment with it. The responsibility constituted a steady, remorseless threat that tortured him and kept him awake nights. Some sharp, man-to-man candor had been handed to the surgeon, that afternoon, by his uncouth caretaker. It had been a long time since anybody had called Wayne Hudson a fool to his face. He accepted the degree with dignity.

"Perhaps I am, Perry," he replied soberly. "You probably wouldn't know. But, however that may be, the thing you're to keep in mind is that this top valve controls the oxygen; and if you have occasion to use it, don't get excited and forget."

Not a few men of importance to the surgical world, resident in widely-spaced cities, recalled having had brief and somewhat disquieting conversations about swimming, while guests at Flintridge, when, one Sunday morning in early August, they read the front-page dispatch which reported that Doctor Wayne Hudson, widely known brain surgeon of Detroit, had drowned, the late afternoon before, near his summer place on Lake Saginack.

At their breakfast table in Seattle, Doctor Herman Bliss read the shocking headlines to his wife, and when she had commented sympathetically, he added:

"Not only very sad, my dear, but very strange!"

Pressed for explanation, he reviewed for her the incidents of a visit he had paid to his friend at the lake cottage, and the heavy constraint which had fallen upon their conversation when he had made some inquiries about his host's enjoyment of the water.

"Do you suppose," conjectured Mrs. Bliss, "that there

could have lurked in his mind some vague mirage of the fate that waited for him? "

Her husband pursed his lips and shook his head. " I don't take much stock in such theories," he declared, almost too vehemently to be convincing.

" But you told me once that Doctor Hudson was ' prescient '! "

" Only a form of speech, Grace. Nobody is prescient. However, Hudson was extraordinarily sentient; psychic, to an uncommon degree."

" But why did he persist in swimming," inquired Mrs. Bliss, " if he was afraid of it? "

" For that very reason, unquestionably. I never knew a man so impatient of normal people's timidities, or more passionately eager to make himself independent of fear. Doubtless this was the one thing that gave him anxiety, and he was resolved to master it."

" But — by the same logic," objected Mrs. Bliss, " he might have jumped off a precipice, if he found himself afraid of that."

" Not quite the same thing! Here was something he had been able to do with ease, skill and safety. Now, for some reason, he had suddenly become afraid of it. An experience of cramp, perhaps. . . . Might happen again. The fear filtered through his thinking. . . . Had prided himself on living in complete mental liberty. . . . Knew now that he was housing a dread! So long as he gave that phobia the hospitality of his mind, he would be, by that much, no longer his own man; so he decided to go to the mat with his antagonist. I fancy that explains."

The newspaper account further detailed that by a singular coincidence the inhalator which Doctor Hudson owned, and kept at his cottage, was in use on the other side of the little lake at the exact moment of his own tragic need of it.

A few hundred yards off shore, near his grandfather's estate, " Windymere," young Robert Merrick, alone in his sailboat, had been knocked unconscious by a jibbing boom and pushed into the water.

" Must have been drunk," indignantly commented Doctor Bliss. " Things like that don't often happen to sober people."

Excited bathers, informed that there was an inhalator at the Hudson cottage, had rushed a speed-boat across for it, and after an hour's heroic exertion, were successful in restoring the young man to partial consciousness. It was said that he would undoubtedly recover.

" Unquestionably! He would! " growled Bliss.

It was believed, said the dispatch, that had the inhalator been immediately available and promptly applied, Doctor Hudson's life might have been saved. The caretaker, Perry Ruggles, observing the evident distress of his employer, had rowed quickly to the spot, dived for him, dragged his limp body into the boat. Desperately, Ruggles had set forth with his unconscious passenger toward the Windymere beach, and had rowed until his strength failed. Small craft, attracted by his signals, hurried to him; found him huddled over the lifeless body of Doctor Hudson, weeping hysterically, while the little boat drifted in the middle of the lake.

" Never saw such dog-like devotion as old Perry's. I suppose he went in after him, clothes and all; bad leg too."

Robert Merrick, the paper continued to explain, was the only son of the late Clifford Merrick and Mrs. Maxine Merrick, now resident in Paris. He had only that day returned from an extended visit with his mother, having gone abroad immediately after finishing at the State University in the mid-year senior class. He was further identified as the grandson of Nicholas J. Merrick, retired founder and large stockholder of the Axion Motor Corporation, with whom he made his home at " Windymere."

" Hope this youngster will be able to realize how valuable a person he is," said Doctor Bliss, putting down the paper, " now that he has had his life handed back to him at such a price! "

There was still another coincidence connected with this event. The village physician, suspecting that Merrick's head injury might be in need of more skilful examination than he could give it, had sent him in a swift ambulance to Brightwood Hospital. At that moment he did not know that the man who had made Brightwood famous for its brain surgery would be unable to see his young patient.

" What do you suppose the boy said," speculated Mrs. Bliss, " when he learned what it had cost to save his life? "

" Well," reflected the doctor glumly, " from my own observation of the type of young cub whose father is dead, whose mother lives in Paris, whose doting grandfather is a retired millionaire, and who gets himself bumped off his boat by a boom in broad daylight, I should suppose he just scratched a match on the head of his bed and mumbled, ' Whadda yuh know about that! ' "

II

SLOWLY AND CAREFULLY — FOR HE WAS STILL LIMP FROM his battle with pneumonia, resultant from the prolonged use of a lung-motor in the inexperienced hands of excited people — two nurses had trundled young Merrick up to the well-appointed solarium.

"It won't hurt him a bit," Doctor Watson had said, "and there is at least the suspicion of a breeze upstairs."

Parking his chair in an alcove somewhat sequestered from the general assembly of convalescents, most of them white-turbaned like himself, his uncommunicative attendants had pattered quickly away as if relieved to be off to more pleasant undertakings.

Their scamper added to his perplexity. Yesterday he had tried to explain the prevailing taciturnity of the people who waited on him: it was the weather. The muggy, mid-August humidity accounted for it. If doctors were brief and brusque, nurses crisp and remote, it was because the patients were fretful . . . everybody out of sorts . . . naturally.

But, even so, something more serious than a low barometer ailed this hospital. Its moodiness was too thick to be interpreted by a murky yellow sky, the abominable rasp of cicadas in the dusty maples, or the enervating heat. Brightwood was in trouble; nor could Bobby shake off the feeling that he, himself, was somehow at the bottom of it; else why this conspiracy of mute glumness in their attitude toward him? My God! . . . He might as well have been some penniless bum, fished out of the gutter, and patched up for sheer humanity's sake. . . . Didn't they know who he was?

. . . Why, his grandfather could buy up the whole works, and never miss it!

It wasn't that they'd neglected him, he was bound to admit. Somebody had been always hovering over him. . . . God! . . . What a ghastly experience he had been through! . . . That fog . . . drifting in grayish-white, balloon-like billows across the road — impenetrable, acrid, suffocating — a damp, chilling, clinging cloud that pressed painfully against his chest, swathed his arms, clogged his feet. . . . That trip back from Elsewhere! . . . Would he ever live long enough to forget? It made him shudder to remember it! . . . That unutterable fatigue!

Sometimes it had been more than he could bear. After he had plodded, staggering, groping his way, for a few shaky steps, the Thing would rush him, with a roar like heavy surf, and hurl him incredible distances back toward oblivion. Then the violence of the storm would subside, followed by an ominous silence. . . . Was he really dead, this time? . . . Suddenly, the Thing would swoop him up again and pitch him deeper into the stifling fog. . . .

After years and years of that — he had grown old and stiff and sore with his hopeless struggle — the situation had begun to clear. Now and again there were ragged rents in the fabric of the fog through which certain landmarks might be fleetingly recognized, as steeples and spires come up, faintly, on an acid-touched plate. These hazy perceptions were, at first, exclusively olfactory. He had read, somewhere, that the nose was more integrally a part of the brain than the other sense organs. Perhaps the smelling faculty (he had taken more than a casual interest in physiology) was the oldest of all the perceptive organs; earliest to evolve. But no; that would be feeling . . . feeling first, then smelling. . . . It had amazed and amused him that part of his mind seemed to be trudging alongside, analyzing the predicament of the rest of his mind, wading through the fog.

Now there had come a much wider gap in the drifting cloud, and through it breezed a combination of identifiable odors; strong scents crushed hard against his face; smell of good wool, and, buried in the wool, iodoform, cigarette smoke, chlorides of this-that-and-the-other, anesthetics, antiseptics, laboratory smells, hospital smells.

A weight shifted about on his chest. It was warm. It throbbed. It pressed firmly, rested briefly, moved a little space, paused again, listened; went back to spots it had visited before; listened, more intently.

Then the weight had lifted and the medley of smells vanished. Through the next rift in the fog, voices were speaking from a vast distance; one of them calm, assured; the other bitter, unfriendly. . . . That had been the beginning of his perplexity. . . .

" I believe he's going to pull through! "

" Doubtless — and it's a damned shame! "

After that, there had been a complicated jumble of voices — one of them a woman's — before the fog closed in on him again. Occasionally, the cloud would tear apart, and he would take up his load . . . he seemed to be carrying some enormous weight . . . and plod on woodenly. He would have yawned, but deep breathing had gone out. They weren't doing it any more . . . quite too painful. One breathed in short, dry, hot gasps . . . glad to have them at the price. . . . Tom Masterson had confirmed that fact. . . . Tom — doubtless this was part of his delirium — Tom had sat by the bed; and, queried about the new style of breathing, remarked, "That's the way we're all doing it. . . . Not nearly so good as the old way, of course, but better than none."

Another smothering billow of fog had engulfed him; but the Thing wasn't in it. He didn't mind now, so long as the Thing was gone.

He opened his eyes and glimpsed a square of blue sky through a real window. The curtain fluttered. A motor churned in a court somewhere below; gears rasped, gravel scrunched. Ice tinkled in a glass, near at hand. A starched nurse, eyes intent on her watch, fumbled for his forearm. The sharp tip of a thermometer dug cruelly into the roots of his tongue. That was what ailed it, then — all this awkward gouging while he had been unconscious.

He had become aware of the steady drone of an electric fan, the metallic whir of a lawn-mower in parched grass; had dully explored his cracked lips with a clumsy tongue; had regarded with apathy the nurse who bent over him; and, after a few hoarse croaks, had contrived to ask where he was. She told him. Sluggishly, he surmised that his presence at Brightwood indicated there was something wrong with his head. There was; it ached abominably, and was bandaged. He felt of it gingerly, and inquired.

"A hard bump. But you are doing very nicely. Drink this, please!"

And then he had slept some more. A dim light was burning when he awoke. Everything was very quiet; so he decided to go to sleep again. Another day came . . . two or three of them, maybe . . . he couldn't remember.

A young, red-headed doctor, in a white coat, had appeared and asked some questions of the nurse. He seemed a friendly person . . . but young. Doctor Hudson was the big man at this place. If there was something the matter with his head, he wanted Hudson.

" I say," he had called, stiffly turning his eyes toward the doctor, " why doesn't Doctor Hudson look in? He knows me. I've been at his house. Does he know I'm here? "

" I'm Doctor Watson, Mr. Merrick. I'm looking after you. Doctor Hudson is not in the city. . . ."

After Doctor Watson had left the room, he had beckoned the nurse to the bedside. Had Miss Hudson called? . . . No; but that was because he wasn't seeing visitors yet . . . that is, not many. . . . Yes, his grandfather had been in . . . and a Mr. Masterson. . . . The accident? . . . Oh yes, they would tell him all about that, a little later. . . . What he needed now was sleep; lots and lots of it; no worry or excitement. . . . What we wanted now to make us well was sleep. . . . Then we could have visitors, and the visitors would tell us everything we wanted to know. . . . That kind of silly baby-talk! . . . Hell's bells!

This morning however he had grown impatient. These people were carrying their stupid silence strike too far! Obviously he had been in some sort of a scrape. Very well. . . . It was not the first time. There would be some way to settle it. There always had been. Was he not accustomed to paying for smashed fenders, broken china, splintered furniture, outraged feelings, and interrupted business? If anybody had a grievance, let him make a bill of it, and he would draw a check! It wasn't any of this hospital's business, anyway! Or . . . was it? . . . What could he have done to their damned hospital? . . . Run into it?

" Tell me this much, won't you, Miss . . . ? "

" Bates."

" . . . Miss Bates; just how did I get this whack on my head? . . . And I won't ask you any more questions."

" There was a mast or something flew around and knocked you off a boat."

" Thanks."

A mast had knocked him off a boat! He grinned; tried to remember. Well — that was that; but how did the hospital get in it?

◇ ◇

At noon, his nurse had been relieved for an hour by a no less important factotum than Mrs. Ashford herself, superintendent of the hospital.

She sat by the window with a trifle of needlework in her hands, apparently intent upon it; but quite aware of her patient's mood and expectant of an outburst.

Bobby studied her face and decided in its favor. It was a conclusion to which patients at Brightwood customarily arrived with even more promptness, but he was in no state of mind to lose his heart impetuously to anyone in this establishment where he was being treated with such contemptuous indifference.

He found himself guessing her age. Everybody indulged in such speculations on first sight of Nancy Ashford. Her maternal attitude toward the staff, the nurses, the patients, was premised solely upon her white hair. The fact that she had come by it in her early twenties, at the time of her husband's fatal illness, in no way discounted the matronly authority it gave her as the general counsellor at Brightwood. Notwithstanding her quite youthful face and slim, athletic figure, many people who outranked her in years called her mother — a perfect specimen of the type that instantly invites confidences. She had become a repository for a wider diversity of confessions than come to the ear of the average priest.

Doctor Hudson's tragic death had been a deeper sorrow to her than anybody connected with Brightwood was ever going to know certainly — whatever might be guessed; and the business of bearing it with precisely the right outward expression of regret was the most serious problem she had ever faced.

For fifteen years Mrs. Ashford had grown more and more indispensable to Doctor Hudson. Entering his experimental hospital as an operating nurse, shortly after the death of her husband — a promising young surgeon and protegé of the brain specialist — she had quickly and quietly transferred many an administrative responsibility from her chief's shoulders to her own, almost without his realizing how deftly she had eased him of an increasing volume of wearisome details. The time came when her decisions represented the opinions of Doctor Hudson, and went unquestioned. Nobody was jealous of her influence over him, or of her calm authority over the institution. Improvident young internes sought her counsel in their troublesome business affairs. Nurses told her their love stories. Patients laid their hearts bare to her; confided everything from minor domestic perplexities to major crimes; wrote to her after they had gone home; not infrequently proposed marriage to her; deluged her with Christmas gifts.

" Isn't she sweet? " the women patients would say. She was not. The word was silly, applied to her. She was understanding, tactful, and, above all, strong; with the face of a young woman, the mind of a man, and the white hair of a matron.

There were some other things about Mrs. Ashford which, had young Merrick known, might have changed his attitude toward her that morning, as she sat jabbing her needle into the bit of tapestry and waiting for him to blow up.

Doctor Hudson had taken her for granted. He had grown accustomed to confiding every difficulty to her, and only rarely was he disposed to debate any of her opinions. There was no phase of his professional life to which she was a stranger. Even some of the strictly private enterprises to which he gave himself with stealthy concern — thinking them effectively concealed — she had discovered, either by chance or shrewd guess; and from that knowledge she had long since deduced at least a vague and troublesome idea of the motive back of them. He would have been amazed — perhaps somewhat annoyed — had he known that Nancy Ashford almost knew the one important secret of his life.

How deeply she cared for him, and the nature of that affection, the surgeon suspected, but resolutely refused to recognize. Anything like a mutual admission of their actual dependence upon and attraction for each other would, he felt, lead to unhappy complications. He could not marry her. Joyce would have disapproved.

"A nurse? . . . Why, Daddy! . . . You wouldn't! . . . You mustn't!"

On the morning that he told Nancy he was to be married the next Tuesday to Joyce's college friend, she had said quickly, "A very sensible thing to do. She will make you happy. I am so glad for you."

"I had hoped you might think that," he replied, obviously relieved.

Luckily for both, they were not facing each other. He was tugging on his rubber gloves, in the little laboratory adjacent to his operating-room, and she was buttoning his long white coat down the back. He pretended not to notice how long it was taking her.

" All right, back there? " he sang out, with attempted casualness, glancing over his shoulder.

" Quite all right now," she had answered, in a tone that matched his for lightness; but — it was not quite all right. . . . Nothing would ever be quite all right again.

Bobby had felt his heart warming toward the lady of indeterminate age who busied herself with the needle, evidently unaware of the tumult of his mind. He decided to disturb her peace. He would ask a few questions which he had been at some pains to compose. They sounded a bit bookish, as if memorized. . . . It was clear enough, he said, that he had been in some kind of a mess. He was forever getting into messes. That appeared to be his occupation. It was customary with him, he recited, with what sounded more like silly bravado than he had intended, to be in a bad scrape and not know the full particulars until the next morning. What was this one about? Had anybody else been hurt? He could not recall. If there were damages, he would gladly pay.

It had turned out to be a surly speech, as it progressed; mostly because Mrs. Ashford did not look up from her work, or seem properly attentive to the petulant complaint. Mistaking her effort at self-control for but another exhibition of the indifference under which he had fretted, Bobby grew irascible. In the very middle of a spluttery sentence however he broke off suddenly and regarded her with perplexity. As she raised her eyes to meet his, he saw that they were brimming with tears. Her lips trembled.

" What have I done? " he demanded huskily. " It's

something very terrible. I can see that in your face. You've simply got to tell me. I can't stand this anxiety any longer! "

Mrs. Ashford put down her work on the table, came to the bedside, and taking one of Bobby's hands in both of her own said, " My friend, something has occurred here that makes us all very, very unhappy. It happened about the time that you came here. We are not recovered from it. But it was not your fault, and the damages cannot be settled. You need give yourself no further concern about it."

Not a bit satisfied, but assured by Mrs. Ashford's tone that their discussion was at least temporarily a closed incident, Bobby made no further effort to press his inquiries. He murmured his regrets that there had been any trouble and sank into his pillows, disquieted, but — whatever was the matter, it was no concern of his. That was good. That was ever so much better than he had feared.

It had been a very welcome diversion, an hour later, when Doctor Watson had suggested the solarium. In the rumbling elevator, Bobby had made a feeble effort to be jocular. It was impossible that the grief which had seemed to distress the matronly Mrs. Ashford would be equally experienced by so young and pretty a girl as the slender blonde who stood at his elbow, silently awaiting their arrival at the top floor.

" I'll bet you a box of candy against a pleasant smile," he said, grimly, " that we do less talking in our hospital than any place else on earth."

Instantly he realized it was the wrong thing to have said to her. She did not challenge his statement. It was not that she was offended. It was rather as if she had not heard him. She was in trouble. She was in the same kind of trouble that afflicted everybody else in this hospital. It plunged him again into the gloom from which he had partly extricated himself through the not very reassuring statements of Mrs. Ashford.

Squelched to a shamed silence by the girl's rebuff, he gazed steadily ahead, conscious of flushed cheeks, as they wheeled him into the alcove, adjusted his pillows, half-lowered the blind, moved the screen closer to isolate him from the others, and, without a word or a smile, hurried away.

He must have been there an hour or more before he learned what he thought he had wanted to know.

In the course of that hour, failing of scraping together enough remembered facts to be of any service in the solution of his problem, he had gone wool-gathering in all directions.

Perhaps it was his sense of utter desolation and loneliness that had set him going over the path of his singularly bitter childhood.

◇ ◇

Bobby Merrick had grown up about as independent of the normal restraints imposed upon children as could have been possible in civilized society.

When he was a little lad, his father, Clif Merrick, had been too much occupied with business — what time he was not yacht racing, deer hunting, or on other journeys not quite so clearly explained — to pay any attention to the sensitive child beyond an occasional pat on the head as he passed him on the stairs in tow of a governess; or a brief and clumsy tussle in imitation of paternal playfulness. The big man was always half drunk when he made these rough overtures of comradeship. The boy dreaded seeing his father approach, of a late afternoon, with a flushed face, suggesting a good romp together.

On such occasions, if she was present, Bobby's neurotic mother usually intervened.

"You're much too rough with him, Clif," she would expostulate. "He's only a little boy. You hurt him! Stop it, I tell you!"

"Nonsense!" his father would reply, glancing toward the governess for approval, "you don't know anything about boys. Does she, Bobby?"

In all truth, she didn't; but the lad would be distressed over the episode, hardly knowing what answer was expected of him.

Once — how vividly he remembered this! — his mother, upon being sarcastically scorned in his presence for the way she was "bringing up a soft little mollycoddle, with his hands full of dolls and dishes" (true enough), had shocked him by screaming, in a shrill falsetto, "Leave him alone; damn you! I won't have you bullying him any more when you're drunk! You touch him again and I'll call the police!"

The police! For his father! Bobby remembered that it had made him ill — nauseated. The governess had had to carry him upstairs, where he was awfully sick. He even remembered what it was he had eaten — currant pudding. He had never cared much for currants thereafter.

Clif Merrick so steadily ragged the child, after that, about his girlish toys and trinkets, that Bobby himself revolted against the soft program the women made for him and gratefully approved when his father suggested boxing lessons. Strangely enough, he found himself happy with the new sport. Eager to test the value of the instruction he was receiving, he occasionally slipped away from the big house about time for school to be out in the afternoon, attired in an immaculate black velvet suit with white lace cuffs, and waited at the corner for somebody to yell " Sissy! " When he returned home he would be very dirty and greatly in need of repair, but grinning from ear to ear.

When he was twelve, Bobby's father had died suddenly of pneumonia brought on by exposure while duck hunting in nasty weather. Young as he was, the boy realized that his mother's bereavement was accepted by her with a calm fortitude out of all proportion to her weakness for indulging in self-pity.

One of her remarks, upon their return from the cemetery that bleak afternoon, was chiseled indelibly upon her son's mind. None of the epitaphs he had regarded with childish curiosity, as they drove slowly along the narrow, winding roads, was carved deeper. Sometimes, when he thought of it, he winced; sometimes he grinned.

" Well," she said, handing Colleen her furs, " that's *that!* "

" Yes, ma'am," dutifully replied Colleen, accustomed to occasional outbursts of caste-forgetful confidences vouchsafed by her mistress, " it certainly is! "

And then, apparently dissatisfied with her rejoinder, which had taken an almost too casual view of the matter for one who entertained so wholesome a respect for death, Colleen added, sepulchrally, " It must have been very hard, ma'am, to leave him out there."

Upon which followed the memorable elegy spoken by his mother.

" Well; *I'll know now where he is!* "

Sometimes, when, as a collegian, Bobby was at that exact stage of intoxication where the tragic in a man's experience becomes distorted into broad, screaming farce, and even sacred memories make wry faces and put out their tongues in scorn of everything decent, he would recall his mother's elegiac comment, laugh uproariously, and pound his knee. "What a corking epitaph!" he had shouted once, and had instantly cursed himself for a drunken fool.

◇ ◇

Bobby could not remember precisely when he had become conscious that his father and mother despised each other. It must have been while he was still a mere baby. By the time he was eight, they had stopped quarreling, their mutual contempt too ponderous for so frail a vehicle as speech. Unquestionably she had suffered much; but it was no use trying to champion her cause. She was entitled to her son's pity, and had it. He would have been glad enough to have respected her, too, had that been possible.

Petulant, selfish, suspicious — Maxine Merrick was no end difficult. Her only proficiency was her skill as a pianist; and aware that it was the sole endowment she was in a position to transmit, she had begun to teach the child piano technique almost before he knew the letters on his building-blocks.

A restless soul, she was; temperamentally cursed with "floating anxiety"; pretty, after a fashion . . . a transparent blonde . . . always attracting attention at the opera where she quite took one's breath away with her beauty at thirty yards; given to fits of melancholy, for which there was plenty of excuse, God knew; dissatisfied with her own personality which she constantly endeavored to improve, either by tinkering with her face and figure, or by taking her disheveled mind to quack psychiatrists and will doctors for adjustments. She was on the sucker list of all the advertising mountebanks in town; talked seriously about palmistry;

had paid a considerable sum for a horoscope which related her affairs somehow with the movements of Arcturus; frequently had her fortune told.

She vibrated between institutions for the care of the body and the cure of the soul. Having spent a busy season of assiduous devotion to the business of being plucked, picked, dyed, frescoed, and massaged; sitting long and painful hours in the studios of beauty experts, Maxine would suddenly experience an unaccountable surge of disgust, and make off hurriedly to some sanatorium de luxe where, in seclusion almost conventual, she lived on unsalted insipidities, and listened of evenings in the lounge to mellifluous harangues on personality expression . . . nerves in order . . . the will to live . . . life at its utmost; followed by less sidereal comments by the chief of staff concerning the importance of internal purity — not of the conscience, which was out of his field, as the piracy of his bills attested — but of the colon, to which he referred with a bland candor somewhat disconcerting to the newer arrivals, still serving their novitiate in the by no means unexacting vocation of hypochondria.

During these spells of improving her health and personality, Maxine would lose many pounds and add as many new words to her pathological vocabulary. It suited her mood, during such retreats, to become as disdainful of her appearance as a Thibetan lama.

One day, for no apparent reason other than caprice, there would be a flurry of trunks and boxes, tickets and taxis, and a swift return home, to the utter consternation of yogis who had been fattening on her patronage, and the indignant amazement of pallid charlatans whose income would be alarmingly depleted by the sudden demobilization of her crusade for the Perpetual Light. It would be generally rumored among the patients that Mrs. Merrick was a brilliant social leader . . . " simply required, my dear, to stop and rest for a few weeks, now and then, if you know what I mean " . . . which was nonsense; for Clif Merrick never took her anywhere, and she could have numbered her friends on her fingers.

On these excursions in quest of youth, beauty, sweetness and light, his mother never took Bobby along. He remained at home in the custody of grafting servants and an endless procession of young governesses, none of whom ever stayed longer than a few weeks. The prettier ones were the quickest to go . . . sometimes on an hour's notice. He had put on quite a scene when Miss Newman had left without so much as saying good-bye to him, and had been slapped by his father for the racket he was making.

Shortly after Maxine had been assured that henceforth she would know exactly where Clif was, the big house on Piedmont Square was sold, and Bobby was taken to Europe where his mother rapidly improved in health and spirits. He was placed in a school for rich waifs at Versailles, where he fraternized with youngsters who had become an embarrassing liability to divorced parents. On brief vacations he joined " Maxine " — as he obediently called her — in Paris, scowling his distaste when, in the presence of her new friends, she chattered baby talk to him, to which he made sour replies in a voice that frequently skidded off the treble clef. She had filled her spacious apartment with wigged and bangled old harridans, who swapped dull prattle about their aristocratic relatives for caviar and champagne and was inordinately vain of her *ménage*, which Bobby impudently insisted would better be called her *menagerie*.

There were lonely summers at Brighton and Deauville,

lonely Christmases at Cannes; private schools and sycophantic tutors; trains and hotels; brief, dry, hard friendships with over-sophisticated, unwanted boys like himself, envious of their mothers' Pekineses, and not infrequently dizzy with pilferings from the decanter on the sideboard.

At seventeen, he had been sent back, alone, to enter a high-toned prep school in Connecticut where, for previous lack of a balanced intellectual ration and experience of steady discipline, he survived only until Thanksgiving. Headmaster Bowers saw him off on the train and returned to lead the chapel exercises. Ineffable calm sat on his brow, and his voice was vibrant with unfeigned gratitude as he announced, "We will stand and sing the Doxology."

Through the influence of old Nicholas, Bobby was then accepted, provisionally, in another preparatory school, a Military Academy not quite so close to salt water. . . . "It's just a ritzy reform school," he wrote, on his first day, to his perplexed grandparent, who replied, in substance, that, if that were so, it was quite the place for him. To his instructors there, he gave more bother than any other six, but contrived to stay on. Through these days, he renewed his abandoned taste for boxing, under a preceptor who cuffed him about, shamefully, until he discovered that the boy was game and thereafter took an interest in him. It was Mr. Bowman's boast, when Bobby finished with them, that albeit he was a bit frail in algebra, he could lick his weight in wildcats.

◇ ◇

It was at the State University, however, that Bobby had struck his stride. Neither a loafer nor a dunce, he easily ran circles around the average student in such classes as stirred his curiosity. Zoölogy? . . . He ate it up! Physiology . . . psychology . . . chemistry . . . he was constantly amazing his friends by his ardent boning, especially in chemistry, in the face of his utter indifference to scholastic credit in the courses he disliked.

His David-and-Jonathan friendship with Tom Masterson had been good for him; better for him than for Tom, a likable youngster with an insatiable ambition to be a short-story writer.

They had found each other as rushees at a luncheon for freshmen in the Delta Omega house, and decided on the spot to room together. Young Masterson, however eager to emancipate himself from the restraints of a rather severely disciplined household, was something of an idealist, and opened up a new world to Bobby who, listening at first because he liked Tom, and later because he liked what Tom said, learned from his youthful tutor a love for the classics which, in the original, he had despised.

But Masterson, not having been brought up on cocktails, was not much advantaged by the tardy instruction he received in exchange for his Greek and Roman mythology. Once he started — no matter what the hour, place, or circumstance — Tom could be depended upon to continue drinking until he was unconscious. Bobby, approximately sober, would get him home, somehow, and put him to bed with all the solicitude of a mother. Apparently it never occurred to him that he was jeopardizing his chum's future.

" Poor old Tommy! " he would say, unlacing his shoes. " I'm afraid you'll just never learn to drink like a gentleman! "

Nor was the Merrick influence much of a blessing upon the Delta Omega house into which he and Tom moved as sophomores. Had he been less lovable, he might have been less dangerous. His charming irresistibility was fatal to the good resolutions of many a chap who honestly wanted to stay sober and do his work. Even the seniors — by custom disdainful of juvenile society — once they were in debt to him for lavish hospitality which was at first reluctantly accepted, found themselves careening over the road in Bobby's big touring-car, late Friday afternoons, en route to his grandfather's home on Lake Saginack.

And the indulgent old man, believing they would all have a better time if they had the house to themselves — and eager to be out of the racket — would be driven in to the city to find sanctuary at the Columbia Club. The neighborhood used to protest, but old Nicholas always reminded them — when they complained of drunken demons, for whose conduct he was presumably responsible, driving recklessly with open mufflers and raucous sirens, at all hours of the night — that boys would be boys. When they smashed something, he paid for it.

Not infrequently Bobby's week-end guests went back to Ann Arbor on Monday morning without a nickel; wearing their very socks by permission of their host, who owned them after an all-day poker game on Sunday. How often they promised themselves, " Never again! " but it was hard to stand out against Bobby's insidious smile. Moreover, the food and service at old Nicholas' country palace was a tempting diversion from the near-starvation of fraternity fare and the discomforts of a crowded house where nothing ever received anxious thought and respect but the impending payments on the mortgage.

◇ ◇

For some time, Bobby had been conscious of a dull rumble of conversation just beyond the screen. It began to annoy him. Some stupid ass was airing his home-brewed philosophy.

"All this here talk about Providence . . . Providence; bah — I say! . . . Take this very case, for instance! . . . Here is a noted man who had made himself so useful that people came to him from thousands of miles for help that nobody could give them but him! . . . Look at me, for instance! . . . "

Bobby scowled, and muttered, "Yeah! . . . Look at you! . . . It's bad enough to have to listen to you!"

"Look at *me!* I came here clear from Ioway; and lucky enough I got here when I did. . . . Last operation he ever performed, they tell me! . . . And they might have saved his life too if that pulmotor thing, or whatever it was, hadn't been in use on that drunken young What's-his-name with the rich granddaddy! What right had he to be alive, anyhow . . . now I ask you?"

It may have been Bobby's sudden pallor that attracted the attention of the nurse who sat at the little desk by the door. She quickly crossed the room and asked if there was anything he wanted. Bobby swallowed with a dry throat, attempted a grateful smile, and replied weakly, "Perhaps I should go back . . . feel better in bed . . . not very strong yet. Tell them, will you?"

His exit from the solarium was effected with such promptness that the patients observed it. Who was this youngster? Questions were asked and answered. The man who had discoursed of the unseemly ways of Providence was deeply contrite. . . . Wished he'd known, he said.

Bobby's nurse stepped out into the corridor, after putting him to bed, and an interne passing by remarked, " So he knows all about it."

" Well, he had to find out sometime, didn't he? "

" Yes — but he's a pretty good scout. . . . And it was a rotten way to dish it up to him! "

" You should worry," snapped Miss Bates.

◇ ◇

For hours, Bobby Merrick lay with his eyes closed, motionless, but not asleep. At first, he was hotly indignant. What right had these saps from Ioway, or wherever, to pass judgment on what kind of people had a right to live? How could anybody be so small-minded as to hold it against him that his life had been saved, even if it could be shown that Doctor Hudson might have been rescued if the oxygen machine had been available? It wasn't his fault. He hadn't borrowed the damned thing! He hadn't asked to have his life saved at that price, or at all!

And then his resentment over this monstrous injustice gave way to steady thinking. Perhaps, after all, he was under a certain obligation to this dead man. Very good; he would show his appreciation of what it had cost to save his life. He fell to wondering whether Doctor Hudson had left his young wife and Joyce properly provided for. Joyce was extravagant. He knew what it must require to keep her going. He had had her in tow, occasionally, himself.

" See if Mrs. Ashford is free to come here for a moment," commanded Bobby. The nurse nodded stiffly, left the room, and, in a few minutes, Mrs. Ashford stood by the bedside.

Assuming what he believed to be a mature, conventional,

business tone — the tone of large capital about to indulge itself in a brief seizure of magnanimity — he inquired, without preamble, " What sort of an estate did Doctor Hudson leave? "

" I do not know," she replied; and after a pause added crisply, " Why? "

The dry crackle of that " why? " irritated him. She had given him reason to believe that she was sympathetic. Surely she might know he was not asking this question out of sheer curiosity.

" You seem to infer that it is none of my business," he retorted.

Nancy Ashford colored slightly.

" Well," she snapped, " is it? "

Bobby's face felt hot. He was at a serious disadvantage, and she was not helping him; not making the slightest attempt to understand him.

" You might at least credit me with an honest wish to do something about all this, if I can," he expostulated angrily.

" I am sorry if I offended you," — with forced composure — " You were thinking of giving some money to the family? "

" If they need it — yes."

" Whose money? "

Bobby raised up on one elbow and scowled.

" Whose money? Why, my own, of course! "

" Some you earned, maybe? "

For a moment, he was speechless with exasperation over the studied insolence of her query. Sinking back upon the pillow, he motioned to her to leave him. Instead, she took her stand at the foot of his bed, and, hands on hips, militantly began an address distinguished for its lack of polite ambiguity.

" You invited this," she said thickly. " You called me in

here to get some information about the Hudsons, and I'm going to tell you! And then you can pay them off . . . with your grandfather's money! Do you know what killed Doctor Hudson? . . . Worry! They said it was overwork that weakened his heart. I know better! The only thing that counted in his life, besides his profession, was Joyce. He saw her going to the dogs. Part of that was your fault! You've had a reputation for ruining all your friends! "

Bobby Merrick lay stunned under the attack, his eyes wide with amazement at the woman's audacity.

" The poor chap tried to pull himself together." Her voice wavered a little, but she went on with resolution. " Built that little house at the lake; went swimming when he wasn't able; knew he wasn't able; had provided a lung-motor for emergencies; and then, at the moment when he has to have it — *you're* using it! *You* — of all people! And now you casually suggest settling the bill with money! "

Something in his look — it was the look of a hurt animal — checked Nancy's passionate diatribe.

" Please forgive me," she muttered agitatedly. " But, as I say, you invited it. You wanted to know. I have told you."

Bobby swallowed awkwardly, and rubbed his brow with the rough sleeve of his cotton smock.

" Well," he muttered hoarsely, " you've told me. If you've said everything you have to say, I won't keep you."

She started toward the door, paused, turned about, walked slowly to the window and stood looking out, her left elbow cupped in her right hand, the slim fingers of the other tapping her shoulder, agitatedly, at first; then meditatively. Bobby watched the slowing tempo of her fingers, cleared his throat nervously, and decided to meet her half way.

" That was really all I had to offer; wasn't it? . . . just money? "

She returned slowly to the bedside, drew up a chair, sat down, and rested her plump arms upon the white counterpane close to his pillow.

" You have something very valuable besides money; but you'll never use it." Her tone was judicial, prophetic. " It's in you, all right, but it will never come out. Nobody will ever know that you had it. The money will always be blocking the way. . . . You were much disturbed today, because you overheard an impolite insinuation that your life wasn't worth saving at the price of Doctor Hudson's. Naturally, you resented that. Your indignation does you credit. . . . However — crude as that man was, what he said was true, wasn't it? . . . You admitted it was true when you decided to put uo a cash difference. But you can't justify yourself that way. It might make things more comfortable for the Hudson family; but it wouldn't help you to live with yourself again."

She had taken his hand in hers, maternally. Disengaging his eyes, she stared upward absorbedly, and murmured, as if quite alone, " He'd never do it, of course. . . . Couldn't! . . . Wouldn't! . . . Too much money. . . . It would be too hard . . . take too long . . . but God! . . . *What a chance!* "

Bobby stirred uneasily.

" I'm afraid I don't get you . . . if — if you're talking about me."

" Oh, yes, you do! " She nodded her head, slowly, emphatically. " You know what I mean . . . and you wish you were up to it . . . but —" pulling herself together resolutely, " you're not; so we won't talk about it any more. . . . Is there something I can get for you before I go?"

Bobby raised a detaining hand, and their fingers interlaced.

" I think I know now what you're hinting. But it's quite impossible, as you say. It's worse than impossible. It's ridiculous! Doctor Hudson was famous! Nobody can ever replace him! . . . Oh, I say, Mrs. Ashford; that's quite too bad! I didn't mean to say the wrong thing, you know! "

For Nancy's eyes had suddenly tightened as if wincing under sharp pain, and her white head bent lower and lower in a dejection strangely out of keeping with her aggressive personality. He ventured to touch her hair in a clumsy, boyish caress, murmuring again that he was sorry.

"That's all right, boy," she said thickly, regarding him with weary eyes, suddenly grown old. "You needn't worry about *me!* . . . *I'll* carry on! . . . My little problem is quite simple compared to yours."

She straightened up, patted his hand, and smiled.

Bobby raised on one elbow.

" You're a good sport, Mrs. Ashford! "

" Thanks! . . . You like people to be good sports; don't you? . . . So do I. I'd rather be a good sport than worth millions! . . . I expect you're a pretty good sport too: aren't you, Bobby? "

He relaxed on his pillow and studied the ceiling.

" Your — what you were talking about — would be a sort of sporting proposition; wouldn't it? "

" Quite! "

" Years and years! "

" For life! . . . There would be no discharge in that war! "

She extended her hand, as one man to another.

"I'm going now. . . . Sure you're not angry with me any more?"

He shook his head, with tightly closed eyes, and gripped her hand. The emotional tension of the past half hour was taking advantage of his physical weakness. Hot tears seeped through his lashes and trickled down his temples.

Nancy withdrew her hand, stood for a moment silently regarding him, her knuckles pressed hard against her lips; then turned away and quietly closed the door behind her.

III

"You say he's different," pursued Joyce interestedly. "How do you mean — different? Sober, perhaps?"

Masterson chuckled.

"Don't be a fool!" she growled. "You know very well what I meant."

He returned his empty glass to the silver tray on the table, settled himself comfortably into the cushions of the garden swing, and so frankly considered the slender shapeliness of the girl in the wicker chair that she shifted her position uneasily.

"Yes," he replied, reverting tardily to her question, "he's all of sober, and then some. He's owlish . . . morose . . . prowls the night like Hamlet . . . has an idea that people resent his having been saved from drowning."

"How absurd! Did he tell you that?"

"As much as."

She thumbed the pages of the novel that lay in her lap and frowned.

"Well — and what is he proposing to do about it? . . . Sulk?"

Young Masterson indicated by a slow shake of the head, eyes half closed, that the problem was too vast for him, and meditatively tapped the end of a fresh cigarette on the arm of the swing.

"You'll discover for yourself that Bobby is greatly altered since his accident. I can't quite make him out. Yesterday, when I saw him at Windymere, I expected to find him in better spirits. He is almost well now; has been walking about on the grounds for days. But he seems thoroughly preoccupied. I suggested it might improve his disposition if we threw together a little cocktail, and he said, 'You know where the makings are: help yourself.' I shook up enough for both of us, but he wouldn't join me; and when I ragged him about it, he replied, from about ten miles off, that he'd 'another plan in mind.'

"'Something that doesn't include gin, evidently,' I suggested; and he nodded cryptically.

"'Something like that,' he replied. You know about how little he discloses through that poker face of his, when he decides to be *incomunicado*."

"So — you dared him to tell you, I suppose."

"No; I just kidded him a little, but he didn't take it very nicely. Just sat — and posed for 'The Thinker.' 'What's the big idea?' I said. 'Gone over to Andy Volstead?'"

"What did he say?" demanded Joyce, as the pause lengthened.

"He said, 'Hell, no!' and then mumbled, down in his throat, that he'd gone over to Nancy Ashford."

"And who's Nancy Ashford?" she inquired, sharply, flushing with annoyance over her disclosure.

"You ought to know," smugly enjoying her vexation. "She is the superintendent of Brightwood Hospital."

"Oh — you mean *Mrs*. Ashford. I hadn't thought of her as Nancy. They must have become quite well acquainted. Why, she's an old lady."

"Well — so much the better; wouldn't you say?"

She met his banter with a grimace.

"You spend too much of your time thinking up story plots, Tommy. It's affecting your mind."

"Maybe so," agreed Masterson dryly. He stretched his

long arms over the back of the swing and regarded her with an inquisitive smile. "Your own story grows more exciting every minute. What else do you want to know about Bobby?"

Joyce offered him the concession of a crooked smile.

"Did he say whether he was coming in soon?"

"Nary a word on that. However, he may not feel himself quite up to it yet. . . . Rather awkward situation, you'll admit."

She nodded, and there was a moment's silence.

"You have Bobby and me all wrong, Tom. We were together pretty steadily . . . in December . . . before Helen came. . . ."

Masterson broke in with an unpleasant chuckle.

"I'm surprised that you remember anything about December," he teased. "My own recollection of it is very pale."

"Yes; I'll admit it was rather dreadful. Especially the evening we celebrated your birthday. That must have been a mighty rough night on the sea. Incidentally, I have not seen Bobby since. When he finished at the university in February, he sailed for France to visit his mother, without a line to me that he was going. I had two short letters from him later. Then he turns up at home; next day this dreadful thing happens to us."

She hesitated before going on.

"So — now you know exactly how thick we are. Does it sound — romantic like?"

"Of course, you're bound to keep it in mind," observed Masterson soberly, "that Bobby feels quite terribly about the — the thing that occurred out there at the lake. Never having met Helen, he is a bit shy about meeting her now.

He may fear she would be slightly prejudiced against him, under the circumstances."

"I'm afraid she is," agreed Joyce reluctantly. "Entirely natural that she would be."

"How is Helen, by the way?"

"Oh, she's steady — the darling! Want to see her? I'll tell her you're here."

She rose, handing Masterson her book.

"Helen has been entertaining a queer little lady for the past hour or more, but I think she is free now. The caller was one of father's patients, I presume. So many people have been here lately . . . all sorts . . . people we had never heard of who come with tearful gratitude to tell us what father had been to them. Really, it has kept us quite stirred up. I wish they wouldn't. . . . And letters? . . . Today there was a long one from a man in Maine hinting that father had saved his life, somehow, years ago. He didn't state the particulars. . . . Seemed rather secretive, as if there were some big mystery behind it; as if there were something he wanted to tell, but couldn't. Very queer. . . . I'll go and call Helen."

She turned toward the big white house with the green shutters, and Masterson's eyes appraisingly followed her graceful movements as she crossed the lawn. . . . Some girl! . . . He set the swing gently in motion and inhaled deeply from his cigarette. . . . A thoroughbred! So, she was Bobby's, then? What the devil did Bobby mean — trying to keep this a secret from him? Well, if she considered herself Bobby's property — and obviously she did — Bobby's pal must be loyal. However, a man could look at her, couldn't he? . . . And wish she belonged to him? . . . A compliment, in a way . . . perhaps . . . debatable question, probably. . . . But seriously, why shouldn't an artist in creative writing have as much license to admire beauty for its own lovely sake as a painter — no matter whose girl she thought she was? What a type! Not many blondes like that left in this dyed and painted world. . . . Original colors, these. . . . Pale gold and milk white; with the slinky-footed gait of some wild woods thing. . . . Some girl! But what made her think Bobby was interested in her? Or — was he? If so, he had kept his sentiments carefully concealed. . . .

Joyce's reappearance through the shrubbery, accompanied by her step-mother, interrupted Masterson's day-dreaming. The two offered a striking contrast. Mrs. Hudson was Latin in every feature and curve, in the glossy blackness of her shingled hair, the arch of her brows, the utter lack of self-consciousness in her posture and carriage. Joyce was perfect Saxon; slightly the taller. Leading the way, she seemed the older.

He strolled to meet them. Helen waved her hand, upon sight of him. She had adopted the rôle of being years his senior, much to his amusement. They had often made a little game of it — he, cast for the part of a spoiled nine-year-old, which he carried off with amazing skill; she, the exasperated but polite mother, endeavoring to keep her whelp in hand without making too much of a scene. They had done it, quite spontaneously, at the Byrnes, one evening. Laura Byrne, upon her own testimony, "had about passed out." Senator Byrne had said the skit was worth a fortune in vaudeville "big time." They had thought it not half bad. themselves.

The conventional uniform of the bereft had only accentuated her youth. It called attention to her girlish vitality, deepened her dimples, whitened her throat; as a severe frame on a bright etching will heighten its colors; emphasize its values.

She extended a small hand and smiled. Her recent experience had left traces. She was pale and a bit remote, her appearance suggesting convalescence from a serious illness.

The smile fluttered momentarily and was gone; but it was essentially the same smile that one waited for, plotted for, tried to recapture in memory, analyzed without success. Once Masterson had attempted to persuade one of his women in a story to smile like that; but she couldn't learn it. He had written, of " Gloria " —

" It was more than a smile. It was a little sonata, in three movements. It arrived first in her eyes, which gradually grew wider and bluer. Almost imperceptibly, but very disturbingly, the patrician brows lifted, ever so little, as if they asked permission. That was the *adagio* movement.

" Then, suddenly, the sonata played upon her lips, as when an organist seeks with one hand a lower bank of keys for the melody. They parted to disclose the smallest, straightest, whitest of teeth. That was the *scherzo* movement.

" Instantly, however, as if the lips had become alarmed at their own audacity, they closed, demurely. But the smile lingered in her eyes — in the outer corners of her eyes — long after her pretty mouth had done with it; and that was the *largo* movement. *Largo dolcemente.*

" And the beholder? What of him? Ah — but his pulse ran on into throbbing, pounding *strotto!* "

Masterson knew the description was silly. He had added, rather helplessly:

"— a vastly disquieting smile; a smile to be smiled with discretion, preferably among strong-minded, elderly men — relatives, if at all convenient to have relatives at hand."

Helen Hudson smiled. Today it was a sonatina. The movements were *adagio, andante, lento;* but it was no less stirring for its chastened mood.

◇ ◇

"It seems a long time since we saw you, Tom," she said, in her husky contralto, motioning him to a place beside her in the swing.

Joyce had remained standing.

"Tommy," said she, "I had promised Ned Brownlow I would go for a ride with him. He's out front now, waiting for me. . . . Mind if I go?"

"Depart in peace!" Masterson held up two fingers, pontifically. "I am in excellent hands."

Joyce's slim fingers trailed caressingly across her stepmother's shoulders as she moved away. "I'll not be long, dear," she said.

"Have you been getting out, at all?" inquired Masterson, with comradely solicitude.

Helen shook her head.

"Too busy! Callers come here at all hours; people one can't very well refuse to see; patients of Doctor Hudson's and others he appears to have befriended in one way or another. I presume you recall the quite unusual number of floral remembrances. . . ."

"I never saw so many!"

"Well, Tom, those flowers came at the direction of people from many places; from persons whose relation to us was very difficult to establish. Fully a score were unidentifiable by anyone at Brightwood. And these callers I am receiving daily are mostly unknown to us. They come to inquire if there is anything they can do for Joyce and me. Yesterday a queer old Italian turned up and tried to present me with a thousand dollars. That's just a sample. Their stories are quite different, what there is of them — for they are strangely reticent — but one fact is common to all . . . sometime, somewhere, Doctor Hudson had helped them meet a crisis — usually involving money loaned; though not always money; sometimes just advice, and the aid of his influence."

"He surely had a big heart!" said Masterson.

"Yes, certainly; but there's more to it than that. Lots of men have big hearts, and are generous with their money. This is a different matter. His dealings with these people were something other. They all act as if they belonged with him to some eccentric secret society. They come here eager to do something, anything, for me, because they want to express their gratitude; but when you pin them down and invite them to tell you by what process they got into our family's debt, they stammer and dodge. It's very strange.

"Since two o'clock, I've been listening to a story that perplexes me more than any of the others; probably because I prodded a little deeper into the mystery. An old lady I didn't know existed came to tell me what a wonderful man Doctor Hudson was, and could she be of any aid to me? . . . I'd like to talk it over with someone. Would it bore you?"

"Tell me — please!"

"Well — it all began, said Mrs. Wickes, with an operation on her husband. Doctor Hudson had warned them it was hopeless. The family was left destitute. She says there was no bill sent from the hospital; that Doctor Hudson found a good position for the older boy and sent the girl, who had some talent for drawing, to an art school. . . . She pointed to that lovely marine over the mantel in our living-room, and said, 'That's hers. She gave it to him. It was exhibited by the Architectural League in New York.' . . . Doctor Hudson had stood between them and disaster, she said, until they were able to look out for themselves; and when, a couple years later, she went to his office with a small payment on the debt they owed him, he refused to accept it; said, at first, that he had had enough joy out of it, and didn't want to be repaid any farther. She quite insisted; and he said, 'Did you ever tell anybody about our little transaction?' 'No,' she replied. 'You told me not to — and I didn't.' 'Then,' he declared stoutly, 'I *can't* take it back!'

"Of course, she was dissatisfied to leave it that way — she has all the instincts of a lady — but when she pressed him to take the money he explained, 'Had I considered this a loan, I could accept its repayment. I did not so regard it, when I invested it in your family. You have all been much more successful and prosperous than I thought you were going to be. So — since I believed I was giving it to you outright, I *can't* take it back now because, in the meantime, *I have used it all up, myself!*'"

"Pardon me," said Masterson, "I don't believe I quite understand. What was that last thing he said to her?"

Helen nodded, mysteriously, and repeated the inexplicable phrase.

"You may well inquire," she went on. "I asked Mrs.

Wickes what that meant, and she grew restless. 'I can't say that I rightly know,' she stammered.

"'But you have a suspicion!' I said.

"At that she hurriedly changed the subject by taking a bulky purse from her handbag. She pressed me to take the money. It had been invested, she said, and now she wished to restore it to us.

"I said to her, 'If Doctor Hudson refused to accept it, so shall I. You had best reinvest it. Put it back where it was, if it yielded a good rate.'

"'Oh, I can't do that,' she replied. 'They're quite done with it, you know.'

"Well, after that, I gave it up! She was over my head!"

"Perhaps she's a bit cracked," hazarded Masterson.

Helen was thoughtful.

"Yes; she would be cracked, and we could let it go at that, and smile over it, if she was the only one of her species."

"You mean that you've entertained some more like her?"

She nodded.

"Yesterday, a quite well-known merchant called on me. You would recognize his name. His affair with Doctor Hudson dated ten years back. He wanted to pay me a pretty large sum of money which he said was interest on a loan. I thought it odd that he was coming forward with it after so long a time, and he confessed that Doctor Hudson had refused it. So did I, of course.

"My curiosity had the better of me, and I pressed him to tell me about it. He said that about ten years ago he was on the rim of failure. He had started in business for himself; had over-reached; and, as if he was not having enough anxiety, his wife passed through a lengthy and expensive illness. He had built a beautiful home. It was more than half paid for. He decided to let it go at a cruel sacrifice to get cash to put into his tottering business. He listed the house with a real estate concern. It was worth thirty-five thousand dollars. He was offering it for twenty thousand. There was a temporary depression of real estate values. Well — next day, he said, Doctor Hudson came to see him.

" 'I understand you're selling your home for twenty thousand dollars. Why are you doing that? It's worth twice that much.'

" The young merchant explained that he must have money immediately, or his business would fail.

" 'I'll lend you twenty thousand," said Doctor Hudson. 'I haven't it, but I can get it. Pay me the principal of this loan when you are prospering again. I shall not expect any interest, because I have use for it, myself; and you are not to tell anyone, while I live, that we have transacted this business.' "

" What an odd deal," commented Masterson.

" Wait until you hear the rest of it," said Helen quietly. " Within three years, my caller said, he had returned the money, and was insistent upon paying interest on the loan. Doctor Hudson refused to take it. And what do you think he said when he declined to accept the money? "

" Give up! "

" He said, 'I can't take it, you see; for *I've used it all up myself!*' Now — that's five distinct times I've heard that phrase, in the past week! What do you make of it? "

" Queer! " said Masterson. " Couldn't have had something to do with his income tax, could it? You know . . . so much allowed for gifts, charity, and the like."

" Tommy, don't be foolish! "

" Well — have you a theory? "

" Not the faintest glimmer of one." Then, animatedly, " Did you ever hear the story of Doctor Hudson's early life? "

" No; does it offer a clue to these queer performances of his? "

" Not at all . . . at least, it offers no clue to me. Perhaps . . . to a psychologist, which I am not. . . . But, I think I'd like to tell you. . . . It's no secret.

" You see, Wayne's parents were very poor. They lived on a farm upstate somewhere. He had to look out for himself, early. As a boy he had wanted to be a surgeon. He came to Detroit, at fifteen, to enter high school, and worked in the home of a Doctor Cummings . . . "

" And married his daughter! I knew that much."

" You're going too fast. . . . In the Cummings' home, Wayne Hudson was errand boy, hostler, accountant, and, on occasion, nurse, cook, private secretary, and rescue squad."

" Rescue? How's that? "

Helen hesitated.

" This Doctor Cummings was a very capable man, with a large practice; but unfortunately he drank too much . . . periodically. At intervals of anywhere from three weeks to two months, he would disappear for days. It was Wayne's duty to track him down, clean him up, bring him home, and meantime invent excuses for his absence and serve as a shock-absorber between the doctor and all his interests — the hospitals, the patients, the family."

" Not a very pleasant occupation for a high school boy."

" No," agreed Helen, " but calculated to mature him early. And it was not by any means a thankless task. Doctor Cummings was of course deeply appreciative and in his repentant moments assured him of his lasting gratitude.

He sent Wayne to college later, and guaranteed his medical training with a life insurance policy, which, strangely enough, became accessible exactly when he had most need of it, for Doctor Cummings died when Wayne was a senior in college."

"Perhaps that helps to explain Doctor Hudson's marriage while he was still a medic," commented Masterson. "Doubtless the girl was fond of him. He felt under heavy obligations to the family. That . . . and the propinquity . . . so he married her."

"Not quite that," corrected Helen. "He was very fond of her; had given up everything to be in Arizona with her until she died. For more than four years, she was his chief concern. Naturally, he couldn't give proper attention to his work. He told me he had days of depression, while in the medical school, fearing he had mistaken his vocation, after all. His studies were hard, and he had much difficulty keeping up with them."

"One would hardly think that Doctor Hudson had ever found his studies difficult."

"He continued to find them so, for fully a year after his wife's death. Then, something happened! No; I do not know what it was. He did not tell me, and I did not insist; but something happened! One day he became conscious of a new attitude toward his books, his profession. He worked whole nights in the hospital laboratory, without fatigue. Then, soon after, through an odd circumstance, he was obliged to do a difficult operation at three o'clock one morning on an emergency case — a head injury. It attracted much attention. From then on he specialized in brain surgery. You know how well he succeeded."

Masterson closed one eye, and considered her thoughtfully.

"I can see," he said, measuring his words, "that it's

somehow in the back of your head that this rather remarkable change in him . . . this quite sudden step-up from depression . . . sense of failure . . . halfway notion to quit medicine and sell bonds or something . . . into prompt recognition and success . . . I think you suspect that it's all tied around this — this funny business of his charities? Am I right? "

She nodded.

" Mostly however because here are two mysteries about him. I suppose I have tried to relate them . . . unconsciously, perhaps. They may have no association, at all. . . . Maybe he would have told me all about it, had he lived. . . . But — we've talked enough about mysteries, Tommy. Let's go and look at the asters."

Masterson followed her through the garden, admiring her childish enthusiasm over the autumn flowers. It was as if she caressed them. He knew she expected him to go now, and toyed with his keys.

" Don't stay in too closely," he admonished. " These people will wear you out."

" I'm taking a few days off . . . going up into the country tomorrow, to see Martha, our caretaker's sister. She's not very well . . . dreadfully broken up, you know; and I haven't seen her since it all happened."

" Might I drive you up? I should like to! "

" Thanks; but I shall want my car while I am there.'

" We might tow it! "

" Oh — do you really want to go up there so badly as that? I'll tell you what you may do; drive Joyce up to Flintridge, Sunday afternoon. Probably I'll be lonesome by that time."

They strolled together to the gate.

" How fine it is that you and Joyce still have each other! "

" Yes; isn't it? "

He stepped into his car, waved a hand, and disappeared around the corner. Slowly Helen retraced her steps to the garden, sauntered along the narrow path, stooped to cup her pink palms around a garish dahlia. How fine it was that she and Joyce still had each other. . . . Or had they?

IV

AS OLD NICHOLAS AROSE FROM THE TABLE THAT SATURDAY night, he said, no more to his tall grandson than to himself, "I am glad I could live until now!"

The past eight years had been dreadfully unhappy for him. It was not that there had been fresh reasons for unhappiness, but leisure to realize how much of life's solider satisfactions he had missed.

From his 'teens until his retirement from the business he had organized, Merrick's consuming passion had been concerned with the development of a great industry; an enterprise singularly difficult in that it lacked the natural guidance of established precedents. There were rules to be made for it, but none to be followed. It was a business without an ancestry.

Men who dealt with any product in the field of ceramics had thousands of years of good tradition back of them. Weavers, tanners, jewelers, masons; builders of houses, ships, cathedrals; growers of grain, fruit, cattle — these people could plat their economic curve and determine future policies by past experience. It was not so of motors.

The rise of that industry had been meteoric, dramatic! A prosperous young bicycle factory turned its attention to the experimental manufacture of a horseless carriage, as a tentative sideline. Young Merrick's stockholders were frankly skeptical of the venture in the face of public hilarity over the noisy, undependable, cumbersome, dangerous gasoline buggy.

And then — one day — the power-driven vehicle was suddenly an accepted fact. But the distance between the fox-statured *eohippus* and the draft horse was no wider than that of the evil-smelling little rattle-trap of an automobile, when Nicholas Merrick first made its acquaintance, and the strong, swift, silent, streamline motor-car which eventually developed.

Its evolution involved hazards as foolhardy as investments at Monte Carlo. A bewildering succession of revolutionizing inventions made the business over, again and again, while investors wrung their hands and shrieked discordant counsel into the ears of apprehensive directors. Costly machinery, installed yesterday, would be scrapped today to be replaced by costlier tomorrow. Those were days when the man who bore the final responsibility for such a chaotic enterprise found that twenty-four hours' devotion to business was demanded by this unprecedented industry, plunging impetuously over an uncharted course, narrowly skirting ruin every few weeks, and turning sharp corners every day.

Responsive to general clamor, prophetic of great fortunes to be made, innumerable companies hastily entered the motor-mart where competition became merciless, unscrupulous. Disaster was inevitable for all but a few of the keenest, the bravest, the luckiest. Merrick experienced all the anxiety of a pioneer leading a long wagon-train of scared emigrants across a trackless desert without a compass. For fully thirty years, but little of his time or thought had been deflected from his exacting responsibility.

When, therefore, at seventy-two, he wearily dismounted from the tiger he had ridden — an event which called for a brilliant complimentary banquet at the Chamber of Commerce in the suburban town of Axion — he was a very tired old man with a fortune estimated at twenty millions, a high blood pressure, and a large stock of disquieting memories.

Clif. . . . God! — what a tragedy! . . . Clif's mother — a timid, brown thrush of a woman — had died when the boy was twelve. Nicholas had scarcely missed her. They had built the big shops, that year. He saw little of the boy. Occasionally there would be a brief and stormy session — Nicholas violently hortatory, Clifford calmly insolent — but nothing ever came of it beyond estrangement.

Nobody could say he had not done his utmost to surround his son with opportunities. Surely if money could have done it, Clif had a chance. Nicholas had always silenced his own misgivings with that reply.

"God knows I've spent enough on him! . . . I can't nurse him, myself!"

But now that enforced idleness had brought opportunity for serious reflection, Nicholas milled it all over, elbows on knees, empty hands dangling. The old alibi was no good.

Nor was there any reasonable expectation of better things to be expressed by the new generation. Bobby was a lovable youngster, to be sure. Nicholas rejoiced in his ready wit, his winning smile, his unfailing consideration of his grandfather's moods, but he gave no promise of success. Beyond the fact that he played the piano like a professional artist, possessed an unusual capacity for making and retaining friendships, and had contrived to finish his college course, Bobby held out no encouragement that he would ever do anything worth a thought. He would drive and drink, gamble and golf, hunt and fish, marry some dizzy, dissipated, scarlet-lipped little flapper and tire of her; he would summer in Canada, winter in Cannes, clip his coupons, confer with his tailor, subsidize the symphony orchestra, appear on the stationery of a few charities and on the platform when the Republican candidate for President came to town; and, ultimately, be pushed into a crypt in the big, echoing, gothic mausoleum alongside Clifford, the waster.

Oh, there had been an occasional ray of hope; a mere phosphorescence; just enough to make the darkness a little more dense when the flash was over.

On the last day of his grandson's senior year . . . it was a mid-year class, with ceremonies deferred until commencement . . . Nicholas had driven over to the little city of the State University, lunching with his old-time friend, the head of the Department of Chemistry. He had straightened and beamed when Professor Garland said, " I don't know whether you're aware of it, Merrick, but that wild young cub of yours has the making of a chemist."

" Honest? Speak to him about it; won't you, Garland? It would mean more — coming from you! "

Garland had made a lengthy rite of mixing his tea and hot water before replying, " Chemistry's hard work, old chap! Your boy knows he doesn't have to work! "

And when Nicholas' face fell, Garland added, consolingly, " You can't blame him. Why should he put on a rubber apron and puddle in nasty stews and noxious stinks when he can get some joy out of life."

◇ ◇

Tonight a great weight had been lifted from old Nicholas. He had not been prepared for the news of his good fortune, and though his spirit sang, his sagging shoulders testified to the gravity of the load he had now thrown off. He laid a brown, parchment-colored hand affectionately on Bobby's arm, and together they sauntered from the dining-room into the spacious library. This was the old man's sanctuary. The walls were covered, literally from walnut-beamed ceiling to Chinese rug, with cases filled with unexcelled and unexplored classic literature. The mental pabulum on which Nicholas fed, these days, consisted for the most part of mystery stories strangely alike in plot and technique. It was not that Nicholas had no mind for better reading. It was only that he was tired of thinking.

They strolled into the library, and the weary old fellow sank with a sigh into the depths of his favorite chair. A gaudy-jacketed detective story lay, face downward, on the table. Bobby took it up, read its title aloud, and grinned.

" Light, Grandpère? "

He offered a flame at the tip of the old man's cigar.

" Exciting yarn? "

Nicholas puffed energetically for a moment, like a leaky bellows, and replied, " The inspector is just questioning the cook, Bobby, and she says she knows the shot was fired at exactly eleven-ten, because that is the time she always puts out the cat."

" You should be pretty well acquainted with the kitchen habits of that cook, by this time, Grandpère. It's the same one, isn't it, in all these stories? "

" By no means, sir," protested Nicholas. " The last cook was a man! "

Bobby was restless to be by himself and eager to divert his grandfather to his novel so that he might escape. The emotional strain of the past hour had been decidedly wearing. The confidence he had extended to the old man represented many days of serious thought; and nights too when he had paced his room for hours considering his tentative decision from every possible angle of objection. Now that he had resolved upon his course, it was only fair that he should inform his grandfather. He had done so. He had made a conscious effort to avoid a dramatic moment. He hated scenes; he had been brought up on them. But old Nicholas had passed through quite too much despair and anxiety not to be raised to an exalted mood by the young fellow's calm announcement of a program committing him to a task at once expensively sacrificial and, as to duration, interminable.

For a moment, after Bobby had flung out the words, the old man had sat stupified and incredulous. He had put down his fork. His jaw sagged and his chin chopped up and down as in a shaking palsy. The deep wrinkles about his mouth had joined the wrinkles about his eyes, in a series of half-circles, as he peered across the table. He dug his gnarled old fingers into the snowy cloth, rested his weight on his elbows and demanded, in a rasping treble, " How's that, Robert? I don't believe I caught what you just said! Say that again! "

Bobby had said it again, slowly, calmly, convincingly. Old Nicholas' seamed face twitched, and he rubbed the corners of his cavernous eyes with the back of his mottled hand.

" You are a brave boy! " he said, his voice breaking.

Then, ashamed of his weakness, he violently cleared his throat, straightened his back, and declared with dignity, " I congratulate you, sir! I cannot remember when any member of my tribe has made a decision of greater moment than yours! May God — bless you! " The benediction was spoken with a quaver. . . . It was almost too much for both of them.

For an hour thereafter, Bobby had outlined his future

plans with a breadth of scope and clarity of detail certifying to the vast amount of time and thought he had spent on them, the old man following every word with eager nods of his leonine head, and occasional hard bangings of his fist upon the table to emphasize his approval. "Yes, sir," he would shout, tumultuously, "you can do it! You will do it! You have it in you! I always thought you had!" His mood was reminiscent of the good old days when it required a deal of table-pounding to convince the directors that a radical and immediate change of policy was necessary to meet new conditions, no matter what it cost.

Now that the first tidal wave of enthusiasm had broken and surfed, Bobby wanted the subject temporarily dismissed. He had lived with his problem—eaten it, dreamed it, walked the floor with it, gone to the mat with it, cajoled it, cursed it, for a month; and, having now brought it to something like a climax, he was ready to see it tabled.

Sensing his grandson's restlessness as he stood toying with a paper-weight, Nicholas deliberately located his place in the book, meticulously polished his glasses, and smiled a very obvious adieu.

"Think I'll step out for a little stroll, if you are to be reading, Grandpère," said Bobby.

Nicholas nodded several times; puffed noisily, contentedly; buried himself in his story.

Immediately Bobby's back was turned, however, he put down the book and stared after the receding figure, his old eyes wide with a new interest to which he had not yet become accustomed. Bobby looked back, as he passed through the doorway, and grinned. Nicholas caught up his book, frowned heavily over some abstruse passage he had just come upon, and puffed mightily on his long cigar.

◇ ◇

Changing his pumps for tennis shoes and his dinner coat for a light sweater, Bobby let himself out through the carriage door, upon the driveway. There was a half moon in an unclouded sky and a few fireflies. He trudged aimlessly on the drive, left it for the grass, wandered along the narrow path by the rose arbor, found himself near the huge twin pillars of the gate, strolled out upon the highway. It was not a busy thoroughfare, but a narrow, graveled motor-road serving chiefly the widely-spaced country estates fronting on the western shore of the lake.

It was very quiet tonight. Hands in pockets, head tilted forward in moody meditation, he strode along indifferent to his random journey, his eyes becoming accommodated to the gloom.

He was glad he had told his grandfather. Tomorrow he would drive down to Brightwood and tell Nancy Ashford. It was like having strong anchors to windward that these two people should share his secret. He hoped Nancy Ashford would be content to say, "Very proper! Much as I expected!" and let it go at that. He wasn't much of a success in moments crammed with sentimentality. It was all right in the case of Grandpère, of course. He was an old man, and a bit mellow. But he hoped Nancy would be sensible.

Bobby had walked a mile. A hundred yards ahead of him, at a sharp bend of the road, a pair of glaring headlights tilted at a precarious angle indicated that a car had listed heavily to starboard. . . . In the ditch, he surmised. He heard the sudden churning of the motor, as power was violently applied to impotent wheels. "Green driver," he reflected. Again the roar of the straining motor proclaimed that somebody was making a bad matter no better. " Fool! " he muttered; and quickened his steps.

Evidently the driver had sighted him, and, unsure of his intentions, was making a final effort at extrication before he reached the car; for, as he came within a few feet of it, the engine fairly bellowed with exasperation and the big coupé shuddered. There was a young woman at the wheel.

" My God, sister," shouted Bobby, when the racket had subsided, " don't do that any more! "

Sister accepted the admonition with wide eyes into which Bobby now gazed interestedly at close range. She smiled, and he reconsidered his earlier opinion of her. She was probably unaccustomed to driving in soft gravel; unacquainted with its treacheries; might be a most excellent driver almost anywhere else.

" Is it really down very deep? " she inquired, with anxiety.

There was a curious huskiness in her voice that gave it an intimate, just-between-us, confidential timbre.

Bobby walked to the rear and looked.

" Very! " he declared. " To the hub. Your differential is flat on the ground."

Her face was perplexed.

" I don't know what that is," she admitted, " but I'm sure it shouldn't be."

" No," said Bobby paternally, " they do better when they're up off the road."

She sighed, and dabbed at a warm neck with a trifle of lace.

" It's my fault, I suppose," ruefully, " I was driving rather fast; and at that sharp turn a car came whopping toward me with the sort of lights they use on aviation fields. I turned out, slipped off . . . "

" And here you are! " finished Bobby. " Lucky you didn't upset. You might have been badly hurt."

She searched his shadowed face, slightly stirred by the note of concern for her safety . . . might be safer without it. What she saw caused her no anxiety.

" Well, at least we have no broken bones to worry about. All I have to do now is to get this car back on the road. Anything to suggest? I'm awfully helpless about such things. Not meaning," she added quickly, " that I'm in the habit of ditching my car."

" I'm sure you're not," said Bobby encouragingly. " This gravel is very slippery."

" What do you think I'd better do? " she asked, in a tone that quite relinquished all further responsibility into his hands.

It was as if she had leaned her slight weight against him. For the past half hour, he had been thinking himself the loneliest, most utterly detached person on earth. His important resolution had quite cut him off from his habitual round of interests, but had not yet keyed him on to any new ones. Nobody had ever been so desperately in need of friendship.

He rested an elbow on the ledge of the open window and became whimsically didactic.

" In cases like this, when the local power-plant has proved insufficient, it is customary to seek aid. One calls in the neighbors. They, having suspected all along that their services might be required, have gone early to bed, and must be pounded out with loud noises and the offer of a king's ransom. Having bathed, shaved, dressed and breakfasted, they come, growling, with a snorting tractor . . . "

" And when they are all ready to pull, the tow-line breaks, and they must drive the tractor to town for another."

"Something like that," agreed Bobby.

"Your advice seems clear," she said, matching his mood. "First, one goes for the neighbors." She tallied the item on her fingers. "But which one?"

"Which one of the neighbors?" Bobby countered with a chuckle. "Or which one of us? . . . I'll go, of course, gladly. But," he added commandingly, "you're coming along! I won't have you out here alone in a stalled car!"

It was spoken spontaneously. Doubtless it meant nothing more than an unintentionally peremptory way of saying he considered it unsafe for her to be left by herself on this unfrequented road. But the fervent phrasing of it, the implied possessorship he had put into his "I won't have you out here alone" brought her a queer sensation. Nobody had ever used precisely that tone with her before. She felt . . . well . . . as if she were being absorbed . . . ever so little . . . just the tiniest mite of her; like the first almost invisible trickle of fine sand pouring through the needle-slim neck of an hour-glass; nothing to be alarmed about, surely. She could easily enough reverse the glass, whenever she wished. For the moment, it was not unpleasant to let it run; just for the novelty of it. It wouldn't be much. She would see to that. In a half hour, she and this delightful chap, with a clean-cut profile that might have graced a Grecian coin, would go their ways. If it pleased him to issue orders, she would humor him by coming to attention and clicking her heels.

Bobby opened the door and offered his hand. She took it without hesitation and stepped out upon the road.

"Should I have locked the gears?" she asked.

"No," drawled Bobby, "it'll be here when we come back." They both laughed.

Leaving the highway, they entered a thickly-hedged narrow lane, cut through a dense tract of tall firs.

"I hope you know where we're going," she said, as Bobby strode forward.

"Can't say that I do," he confessed. "I never was in here before; but I think it must be the private road to the Foster estate. Doubtless we will find one of the farmers' cottages presently."

The girl trudged along beside him, taking two steps to his one on high heels not meant for hiking in country lanes. A sheep scuttled out of the left hedge and dashed frantically across the road, a few feet ahead of them. Instinctively she caught at Bobby's sleeve.

"Oh — but that startled me!"

"Here! Take my hand!"

It was a small hand that she gave him, and he held it as if he were leading a little child. Absurd as he was bound to admit it, his attitude toward her was proprietary; and, incautious as she knew it to be, her response to it was spontaneous. She had a sensation that just the smallest imaginable emanation of herself was being quietly assimilated by the strong fingers of this dominating boy.

Mentally, Bobby tightened his grip; physically, he led her as one would a younger sister.

"We might encounter all sorts of adventures," she suggested. "Suppose we ran into a nest of — of counterfeiters!"

"There aren't any counterfeiters, any more," scoffed Bobby. "They're all bootlegging. . . . More profits and less risk."

"Oh — how I hate it!" she cried, passionately. "What a vulgar, beastly thing it's come to be! It never concerned me, one way or the other, until lately. But now . . . it's destroying my best friend! "

Bobby was annoyed at his sudden stab of jealousy. But what right had he to be jealous?

" I have good reason to hate it too," he rejoined bitterly; adding, with a growl, " but I believe I've got it licked! "

" Oh, I hope so! " she exclaimed, with a quick intake of breath. " It would be such a pity . . . "

Her sentence hung suspended, and for some time neither spoke.

" That's the first time anybody ever said to me that it would be — a pity."

So — the time had come now to reverse the glass. She would do it at once . . . presently . . . but not abruptly. . . . How did one up-end an hour-glass gradually, imperceptibly, she wondered. Perhaps the proper technique would occur to her. . . . Meantime . . . the silence was lengthening; and silence, at this juncture, was disturbing.

" You knew it — without being told, didn't you? "

" I'm not sure that I did. It wouldn't have mattered much to anybody."

" How silly! . . . No one concerned whether you fling yourself away? "

" That did sound melodramatic, didn't it? . . . as if I wanted to play Orphan Annie."

" You've been rather — down, haven't you? " Careful! . . . careful! . . . The glass couldn't be up-ended by any such process as this!

" Horribly! . . . But — I'm not now! "

" That's good! . . . Fresh grip? "

Neither of them knew just why there was a momentary tightening of their hand-clasp. Naturally, the word suggested it. The sudden pressure of his fingers about her hand was but an affirmative; perhaps an acknowledgment of her encouragement. And her quick response was a mere friendly vote of confidence to a fellow human, who had been down and was now on the way up. But each was aware — and intuitively conscious that the other was aware — of a compact; a curiously indefinable sense of belonging. . . . She released her hand, a moment later, and instantly realized it was the wrong thing to have done. . . . The withdrawal only seemed to be a retreat after an avowal. . . . More than that, it hadn't come about nearly so casually as it should. Her fingers had slipped slowly out of his hand, detained ever so slightly by his lingering pressure. . . . So, she had turned the glass, had she? . . .

"Oh, I see a light!" she cried. "In a window!"

With droll predictions of the manner of welcome they might receive, they quickened their steps, and presently knocked at the door. A farmer opened it and stood framed in the glow of an acetylene lamp suspended from the ceiling. Two small children hugged a leg apiece, registering curiosity.

After a brief parley, the man retreated for his cap, joined the pair outside, told them he would be along soon, and went for his tractor.

Bobby made no attempt to resume the conversation interrupted by the sighting of the cottage. He took his new friend's small hand, however, as they turned to retrace their steps, and tucked it under his arm. She gave it without shyness.

"You'll be going back to college, I expect," he hazarded.

"No, not this year. . . . And you?"

"Oh, I'm through," said Bobby maturely. "Beginning my professional course in a few days."

"Law — maybe?"

"Is that what you would pick for me?"

She laughed.

"I think I should know a bit more about you before I selected your profession."

"Well . . . if you were a man . . ."

"I should go in for surgery."

"Any special kind?"

"Yes," she replied, with quick decision, "I would be a brain surgeon."

"That's odd!"

"Why?"

Her question went unanswered. The noisy tractor was overtaking them. They were near the highway, and conversation gave way to the business at hand.

After much maneuvering into position, the farmer was ready. Bobby took the wheel of the coupé, its owner waiting at a discreet distance until the car should be tugged back upon the road. It was simply done, but the emergency driver of the coupé stammered something about the possibility that the steering apparatus might be in need of inspection. Sometimes a strain like this affected the steering gear, he said. He was not pressed for specific explanations. Perhaps, he suggested, it would be best to run down to the village and make sure everything was safe. He would gladly go with her if she wished. . . . It was quite agreeable to her, if he would be so good, and would he mind driving? . . . Under the circumstances, perhaps that would be better.

She asked the farmer for his charges and paid him more than he asked. He thanked her, awkwardly, feigning reluctance to accept so much. As she entered the car where Bobby sat at the wheel in proprietorial pose, his heart beating rapidly, the farmer, eager to be friendly, said, "That sure is one peach of a car! It looks just like the Packard that Doctor Hudson used to drive around up here."

"It is," said the girl quietly. "Good-night; and thank you again."

Mechanically, Bobby Merrick put the late Doctor Hudson's big coupé in gear, and they were off toward the village.

"It seems all right, doesn't it?" happily remarked the young woman in black who owned the big coupé that Doctor Hudson used to drive around up here.

Apparently, her new friend was not yet quite sure enough to reply. His eyes were intent upon the road ahead, and he grasped the wheel so tightly his knuckles were white.

Bobby was stirringly conscious of her on the seat beside him, more conscious of her than he had ever been of any woman he had known. There was no actual, physical contact; but she was most overpoweringly *there*.

"It's all right," he muttered thickly.

"I was on my way to the village, anyhow," she continued. "I do hope the little drug store will still be open."

Apparently her driver was not posted on the nocturnal habits of the druggist, for he did not venture an opinion. The accelerator received an extra pressure at that moment, and the powerful car suddenly bounded forward.

"I can't tell you how grateful I am," said the girl, a bit perplexed by his silence. "I'm sure I shouldn't have known what to do, if you hadn't happened along."

Bobby was occupied with the adjustment of the ignition lever.

"But I'm afraid I'm putting you to a great deal of inconvenience," she added anxiously.

He spoke, at length, as from a considerable distance.

" The car is in perfect condition," he said. " I'll get out here. You need not go to the garage." The brakes were applied with determination, and the car came to an abrupt stop. Bobby opened the door on the left and stepped out.

" Oh, but you're miles from where you found me! " she exclaimed. " Do let me put you down where you'd rather be. Please! "

He could not meet her eyes.

" I was just sauntering," he said absently. " It's no matter."

She slipped over behind the wheel and held out her hand. It trembled a little as he wrapped his fingers around it. She was bewildered. Whatever had she said to hurt him?

" Good-night, then; and thank you so much! " Her voice was unsteady.

He retained her hand for an instant, said " Good-night " in a tone that might mean weariness, dejection, or disappointment, turned, and stepped away into the darkness. She engaged the gears. The car moved slowly, tentatively, hesitatingly forward.

Bobby watched the little red tail-light until it vanished at the next turn.

A half hour later, he sat down at his piano in the tomby drawing-room at Windymere, and, vastly occupied with his reflections, toyed with an experimental ending to Schubert's " Unfinished Symphony."

V

IT WAS LATE AFTERNOON OF THE LAST SUNDAY IN SEPTEMBER. Nancy Ashford's snug retreat, immediately adjacent to the general administrative offices in Brightwood Hospital, had proved too small to house the radiant spirits of herself and her guest. She had gratefully accepted Bobby's suggestion that they take a drive. Sitting close to him in the big, gaudy, rakish roadster, her elbow touching his, it pleased Nancy to indulge the fancy that passers-by might think him her son. Her life had been filled and emptied twice. It was brimming again.

Nothing could have been more clear to the white-haired hospital superintendent, as she greeted her expected visitor, at the door of her little office, that afternoon, than that he was hopeful of stating his errand in a manner to insure against its reception with surprise or emotion. He had a very business-like air, and she determined to match it.

He had blurted out his story immediately upon arrival. Tossing his hat upon her desk, and seating himself by her on the little divan, he had said brusquely, " Well, I'm resolved to do it. It will be no surprise to you; for it was really your idea in the first place, even if you didn't specify the details. It's all arranged now. I am entering the Medical School at the University, a week from Thursday. . . . Are you glad? "

Nancy had reached out a hand for his, winked back the sudden tears and bit her lip in an effort at control. Her eyes shone. But she did not speak.

" Of course," continued Bobby hurriedly, as if reciting lines, " I have no illusions in this matter. It means a long, hard grind of drudgery, and I am not naturally industrious. It will be five years, at least, before I can even guess whether I am likely to succeed, or have only been making myself ridiculous. I take chances of becoming an obscure second-rater. In that case, I shall have become merely absurd at the cost of a very great deal of time and trouble. People would grin. They would say — I can hear them — 'Yeah; he's the fellow that thought he'd be another Doctor Hudson.' But maybe the threat of that will put a little more fight into me. It's foolish, I suppose, to hope that I might sometime be even a halfway substitute for him; but — I can move in that direction, anyway."

"I felt confident you would come to some such decision as this, Bobby," commented Nancy quietly, "and I feel even more sure — now you have decided — that you will succeed."

"Your hope will help — a lot!"

"Now you will be wanting to learn all you can find out about Doctor Hudson, won't you?"

At that juncture, the tiny office had seemed stifling. They would ride. Bobby would drive and listen; Nancy would do the talking. For fully twenty miles they had been weaving swiftly in and out of the Sunday traffic on crowded boulevards; and now, with speed reduced, were traversing a more quiet suburban street. Nancy had been recalling some of the more singular facts in the life of her hero, especially relating to his wide diversity of philanthropic interests and his odd whim of keeping them a secret.

"Did his family know?"

"I doubt it. Joyce was a mere baby when he began doing these queer things for people, and it is unlikely that he ever told her. And Mrs. Hudson, during a call she made at the hospital only last Thursday, asked some questions indicating he had not confided that feature of his life to her. Many of his wards and beneficiaries have been coming to see her with expressions of sympathy, and some with proffers of assistance if she needed it. She was naturally curious."

"Yes; I know just a little about that. Learned it only today. Tom Masterson dropped in, as I was preparing to leave Windymere, at noon. He had driven Joyce up to the Hudson cottage, where Mrs. Hudson is spending a few days. He came over to inquire if I would join them there for the afternoon. I told him of my engagement in town."

"Perhaps you should have gone. You could have telephoned to me. Have you seen Joyce, at all?"

"Not since I'm back from France."

"And I presume you never met Mrs. Hudson."

Bobby wished that question had not been raised. Perhaps it would be near enough the truth to reply in the negative. On second thought, absolute sincerity with Nancy Ashford was but her rightful due. He decided to be honest.

"Yes," he answered, reluctantly, "I spent a whole hour with her last night, on a country road" — adding, after a considerable pause, "But she doesn't know it."

"Meaning what?" demanded Nancy, in amazement.

Briefly he narrated the whole circumstance of their meeting. Nancy Ashford's blue eyes widened. Underneath the boyish recital ran a strong current of unmistakable personal interest which Bobby's attempted tone of casualness failed to conceal.

" I think you liked her, Bobby. Didn't you? "

He essayed a smile of indifference. He might even have been able to delude himself into the belief that Nancy accepted the smile as a sufficient answer to her query, had he not been so audacious with his little deceit as to look her full in the face. What he saw there of incredulity and disappointment instantly sobered him. There was no use trying to keep anything from this woman.

" My dear," he confessed, with an unsteady voice, " I like her so much I'd rather we didn't talk about it."

His big car had idled to a full stop alongside the curb flanking a little park. They were both silent for a while. At length, Nancy said mechanically, " Well, of all things! "

" Yes," agreed Bobby abstractedly, " something like that."

There was another protracted pause.

" And she did not know who you were? "

" I couldn't tell her."

" How long do you think you can maintain your — incognito? "

" Oh, that should be simple enough," Bobby declared, in a tone of self-deprecation. " I took pains to invent an alibi for the evening, when I talked to Masterson, in case some inquiries might be made. But Mrs. Hudson has probably forgotten all about the little episode by this time."

Nancy laughed.

" Bobby Merrick, do you really believe that a young woman of Helen Hudson's temperament could produce the impression she made on you without being fully aware of it? You confessed how acutely conscious you were of her — that was your phrase, wasn't it? — as you sat together in her car. Do you think you would have had that sensation had she not shared it? "

" Of course; why not? See here — you're taking altogether too much for granted in this case. Mrs. Hudson was no more than courteous, friendly, appreciative of a little favor. She had no reason to think me interested in her. In fact, I was almost rude to her when we parted." He did not feel it necessary to add that her car had crept along, in low gear, for fully two hundred yards, apparently reluctant to leave.

" Yes," said Nancy significantly, " she would notice that! "

" And she would know — by my abruptness — wouldn't she? . . . "

" Know what? " persisted Nancy ruthlessly.

" Why — that I was not interested."

" Dear boy, how very little you know about her! "

" Meaning that she has unusual gifts for interpreting other people's private thoughts? "

" No — Foolish! Meaning only that she is a woman! "

They strolled under the elms, stopping to watch some small boys sailing toy boats on the little lagoon, dappled with lily-pads. A bench was found unoccupied. By common consent, their discussion was resumed of Doctor Hudson's queer penchant for concerning himself with the private perplexities of nobody knew how many people, and the thick wall of secrecy with which these strange negotiations were surrounded.

" You may as well put it down as a fact, " Nancy was saying, with strong conviction, " that the curious manner of Wayne Hudson's costly investments in these cases, from which he never expected or accepted any reimbursement, was occasioned by no mere whim. He was not given to whims. He was not an eccentric. I never knew him to do anything without an adequate motive. Nobody could have said that he was reckless with his money or incompetent in business. He could drive a shrewd bargain. He knew when to buy and when to sell. Plenty of business men, with more commercial experience, asked his advice on probable trends in the real estate market and took his judgment about industrial stocks. I am convinced he did these strange things for certain people, in this furtive way, with a definite motive. In some fashion, which I don't pretend to understand, his professional success was involved in it. When you find out what that motive was, you'll know why Wayne Hudson was a great surgeon! "

" Do you know any more about it than you have told me? " regarding her searchingly.

" There is a little book — a sort of journal — I think you have a right to know about it. He kept it in the office safe, along with valuable records; some relating to professional matters, some to private business affairs. The book was there when I took over the management of Brightwood. Once — we were looking for some insurance papers — I asked Doctor Hudson whether the little book concerned hospital business. . . . "

" Couldn't you tell? " interrupted Bobby.

" It was not written in English, nor in any other language I ever saw."

" What did it look like — Spanish, German, Greek? "

She shook her head, and resumed her story.

" I asked him what the little book was. I vividly remember how earnestly thoughtful he grew, and how he stood, for many minutes, rubbing his temple with the tips of his fingers

— a trick of his when trying to arrive at an important decision — saying, after a long wait, 'It's just a personal record.' And then he added, smiling, 'You are at liberty to read it, if you can.' "

" Did you ever try? "

" *Did* I? " she echoed. " Hours and hours — lately."

" Get anything out of it? "

" Headache! "

" I wish I could see it! "

" I'll show it to you! Nobody has a better right to it. I told Mrs. Hudson there were many valuable documents of the doctor's in the hospital safe, and she insisted that we keep them until she was up to looking them over with me; so the book is still there."

" Let's go back," he said impetuously.

Darkness had fallen before they arrived at Brightwood. Nancy brought the book from the safe, and laid it on the desk before him. He sat down, and took it in his hands — a plain, black, leather-bound journal, eight inches by five, and more than an inch thick. On the fly-leaf was written, in Doctor Hudson's quite distinctive hand, the single sentence

TO WHOM THIS MAY CONCERN

" Nobody could be any more concerned than I am! " He glanced up at Nancy for approval. She nodded.

" Now, turn over to the next page, and see what you make of that! "

Bobby stared long and hard.

" It's in code! "

" You will find it difficult," said Nancy. " The way I have it figured is this: Doctor Hudson purposed not to have the matters which he kept secret divulged during his lifetime. The fact that so many of these odd wards of his are bobbing up now, ready to tell their stories of his strange dealings with them, convinces me that they were all virtually sworn to secrecy while he lived. Now that he is gone, they tell. I think the mystery is all contained in this book. Whoever reads it, knows the real story. Perhaps the doctor was willing it should be known after he was done with it; but made it inaccessible to anyone who might chance upon it while he lived."

"He's made it inaccessible enough — I'll say!" Bobby growled. "Did you ever see the like?"

"This first page," explained Nancy, "is unquestionably a sort of preface. You notice that all the other pages are completely filled. This one has only ten lines. It must be a foreword; an explanation; dedication, perhaps. . . . You take it along with you. . . . Know any Greek?"

Bobby shook his head.

"Oh, I know the alphabet," he qualified, smiling.

"That's enough. . . . What's the last letter?"

"Omega," recited Bobby glibly.

"And omega is a sort of stop-signal, isn't it? A sign for the end of something?"

He nodded.

"How many letters are there in the Greek alphabet?"

Bobby closed his eyes and counted on his fingers.

"Twenty-four."

"Omega being the twenty-fourth — and signifiying the end!"

"Right!"

"Now, what is the twelfth letter?"

"Mu," answered Bobby, after another calculation.

"Well, if omega means 'finished,' what do you suppose mu means?"

"'Half finished' — I suppose."

Bobby soberly returned to the preface of the little book and found, at almost regular intervals, the letters μ (mu) and ω (omega).

"Is that a clue?"

"I think so," said Nancy, "but it did me no good. I just offer it to you for what it seems to be worth."

◇ ◇

Not at any given moment of his long drive home did Bobby Merrick realize exactly where he was, as he swiftly covered the familiar road to Windymere. At midnight, he put up his car; went to his room; sat down before his desk, with Doctor Hudson's private journal, a pencil, and a thick pad of paper; and at dawn was still experimenting without a glimmer of encouragement.

Meggs, opening the door to call him to breakfast, found him sitting fully dressed, with his head on his arms, asleep, and tip-toed down-stairs, his eyes shining.

A few minutes later he whispered to the cook, in a tone of victory, "You lost your bet!"

"Drunk again?"

"Quite!"

Facsimile of first page of the Hudson journal

Rae Losdrom Jin u edren
Leyuy red w Adom N Y u
preede u N C Medor Esvrns
w Honak E Etz blttu Aiz cird
Haii yo w Ratibo yua eloh u
edkso Kohva stz w R G Toossi
Mr Aos u iht PS est yron w
Front L icpew lb. u Odig hanihr
ilz w M D Pansop oed u Acliay
svrez w

VI

THE GLOWING ELLIPSE CAST BY THE HEAVILY SHADED lamp at the head of her bed shone upon the weapons with which young Mrs. Hudson had armed herself against drowsiness when, at midnight, she had retired with a novel, two magazines, and a leather writing-case embarrassingly stuffed with unanswered letters, resolved to stay awake until Joyce returned.

Shortly before two, she had lost the battle and now slept with the light shining into her troubled face. Not that the trifling incident of dropping off could have worried her; but it was all of a piece with the general failure.

Had the late Doctor Hudson been subpœnaed to the witness-box on the day of his death to report on the success of the marriage he had contracted on behalf of his daughter, he, being unusually fastidious about truth-telling, might have found it an awkward question.

The three of them had stood up, that crisp January morning at St. Andrew's, in the presence of Uncle Percival and Monty — and the Senator Byrnes, who had run over from Washington — not so much as a bride and groom, attended by a grown daughter, cordially consenting; rather as a pair of strikingly lovely young women, attended by an elderly, distinguished guardian, invoking Church and State to legalize and bless their comradeship and give them a deed to it.

That it was candidly a *mariage de convenance* (the French for it was more euphonious than the English equivalent) caused Doctor Hudson no serious misgivings. He nursed no illusions on that subject, aware that if all the world's weddings were limited to romantic attachments in which no material advantages were at issue on either side, the human race would long since have been exterminated; and that if it were unethical for a young woman to marry with the knowledge that she could not immediately give herself with unqualified devotion to her husband, the Holy Virgin herself was at fault.

Immediately upon the consummation of his wedding, however, Doctor Hudson had found himself falling sincerely in love with his girl-bride, and the comradeship he had sought to insure between Helen and Joyce was put in jeopardy.

Joyce was a poor sailor, and the first three days were rough.

" No, darling; not a thing. . . . Please run along. I'd much rather you did."

So when, on Sunday noon, she had been persuaded to come down to the blanketed chair they had prepared for her on B-Deck, she realized that she was being solicitously attended, on either side, not by an indulgent father and a devoted college chum, but by a man and his wife — good friends of hers, unquestionably, but, well — there you were!

All three of them tried to twist the contemplated relationship back into focus, but it wouldn't go. Perhaps their very efforts to do so made it impossible. Hudson, in Paris, had enthusiastically encouraged Joyce in her shopping extravagances; and Helen, eager to join in her husband's approval, may have overdone it.

" What an exquisite coat! So glad you found it, Joyce! How very becoming! "

It was the right attitude, without a doubt, but it hadn't the right inflection. It wasn't as one girl to another, but as an ingratiating step-mother over-anxious to be generous, affectionate.

There were no disagreements. Perhaps it might have cleared the air if there had been. Nor was there any constraint on the surface. It was too deep to come to the surface. That was the difficulty. Everything they said to each other was amplified — as through a loud speaker — intensifying their mutual assurances of devotion until it took on a tone of unreality. Each knew the other was trying hard to be natural. Each knew the other was playing a difficult part. Almost desperately, they scrambled for the old position; but they had lost the way to it.

Shortly after the death of Doctor Hudson, the distance between them increased markedly. For the first few days, they had clung to each other with a rededicated bond that promised to be, if not a restoration of their earlier comradeship, at least an earnest of future indispensability . . . possibly to become a more valuable relation than any they had heretofore sustained. But it was not for long.

Joyce's grief, inconsolable for a week, quickly exhausted itself. It was only common honesty in her when she declared one day that she wasn't going to sit moping any longer, for, volatile as she was, any protracted mourning would have been mere affectation, even it she were capable of it, which was doubtful.

Presently there came a disquieting furtiveness in her explanation of late hours. Helen's gently tactful queries, implying an uneasiness about her social program, were either dismissed lightly with a chaffing reply, or met with a brief — albeit friendly — hint that one was quite old enough now to know where one wanted to go, and with whom, and until when. She was not to trouble her pretty head about her flighty Joyce. She was to live her own life and stop worrying about trifles.

" Don't sit up, darling! " Joyce would protest, at nine. " I'm going out with Ned." (Or Tom, or Pat, or Phil.) " We may be late, you know. Where? Oh — I'm not sure . . . to dance, some place, I suppose . . . and a bite of supper, later . . . Crystal Palace, maybe . . . Gordon's, perhaps."

" I don't like your going out to Gordon's, Joyce. Really — that's not a nice place. Tell me you won't . . . please! "

" Oh, very well! Only one can't do all the deciding. One's escort has something to say about that too."

◇ ◇

On the rose counterpane lay several letters; one of them from Montgomery Brent, brief, brotherly, suggesting that his counsel would be at his " little sister's " disposal should she be troubled about business matters, now that her responsibilities were increased.

" Only too glad, you know, to straighten out the kinks for you when it comes to income tax, investments, and the safeguarding of your estate. That sort of thing is my daily work."

" The dear boy! " she murmured half-aloud, as she reread it, "How decent of him; and not a bit bad idea, either. I wonder does he really know anything about business. He ought to by this time."

Montgomery, whom it pleased her to think of as her brother Monty (never more affectionately than now that she felt so desolated), was five years her senior. College not agreeing with him after his sophomore year, Monty had brought his saxophone to the jazz-market. Not quite satisfied to make a permanent profession of bouncing and writhing and puffing himself purple every night from eight until two in the front row of a dance orchestra, he had made some friends among the chalky-fingered youngsters who posted the board at a down town brokerage office. In a few months he had a desk and a small-salaried position in the organization.

"I'm a broker!" he would reply maturely, when some young thing coyly inquired, while they danced, what college he attended.

Doubtless he was doing well enough now. He had not borrowed from Helen for more than a year; had given her an expensive silver vase for a wedding present, appearing on that occasion in a morning coat, striped trousers, and spats, the only man present who had given no quarter to the request for informal dress. . . . It wasn't a half-bad idea. There was one friend left, anyhow — good old Monty!

Another letter was a brief note, written to Joyce, by the young Merrick person, dated from Ann Arbor; evidently composed with much care. It left many things unsaid which its author assumed would be read into it. He had entered the Medical School, hopeful of becoming of some use, eventually, to the profession which her father had so conspicuously adorned.

"I never would have picked him for the part," Joyce had interpolated, as she read that much of the letter to Helen. "Rather quixotic, don't you think?"

"Did it on impulse, likely," Helen had remarked.

"Rather fine of him, though — at that! Wouldn't you say?" championed Joyce.

"I'll tell you a year from now," Helen had replied, half-audibly.

Joyce had continued reading to herself. With a gesture of

impatience, upon finishing the letter, she tossed it across the table, and savagely dug into her grapefruit.

"I think you had better answer it, Helen. The only human, personal line in it is for you. Write and tell him you hope he gets on well with his teachers, and makes A in everything," she snapped, with frank asperity.

The only human, personal line read, "Please convey my sympathy and regards to Mrs. Hudson, whom I hope I may soon have a chance to know."

Helen had made no further comment. Her opinion of the Merrick person was based solely upon Joyce's disquieting references to him — a spoiled youngster with loose habits and too much money. It was clear enough that the girl entertained an infatuation for him which he had made no effort to capitalize. Helen was glad of it. She had no wish to meet him — had dreaded the day when he might turn up. It was enough that he had been the cause of her husband's tragedy. . . . Not his fault, of course; but she hoped he would not make it necessary for her to try to be nice to him. It was a closed incident. She was relieved.

The letter had remained in her pile of morning mail, beside her plate. Later, it had been tucked into her portfolio. She had read it again, in bed. Well, it was no concern of hers, whether he made good or not. At least, he was out of Joyce's calculations. . . . One questionable friend less to worry about.

Helen was awakened with a start, as the door of her room was cautiously opened far enough to admit the flushed face of Joyce.

" You, Joyce? "

The door was closing, slowly, cautiously.

" Sorry, darling. . . . Good-night! " came in muffled tones from beyond the door.

" Come in, dear! " called Helen.

There was a considerable delay before the door opened again. Joyce came in, jerkily, all but asleep on her feet, dazedly rubbing her forehead with the back of the hand in which she clutched her crumpled hat; the other groping, uncertainly, for something to support her. She leaned heavily against the foot of the bed, swaying dizzily.

" Oh! — but, my dear! " cried Helen, in consternation, propping herself up suddenly on her elbows. " What in the world — ! Where have you been? "

" Gordon's! "

Joyce ground out the gutteral between tensely locked jaws, and smiled fatuously.

Helen sat up and peered incredulously, silently, at her disheveled step-daughter, who grew restive under the inspection.

" Been — been writin' letters? " Joyce surveyed the litter on the bed with a pitiable attempt at casualness.

Helen nodded briefly, and pressed both hands tightly against her forehead in a gesture of despair, which Joyce decided to ignore.

" And if there isn't ickle Bobby? " She leaned far forward over the foot of the bed and with elaborate precision flicked the letter contemptuously with her finger. " That! — for you! — Doctor Merrick! "

" Why — Joyce Hudson! — you're drunk! "

Helen stepped out into her slippers, caught up a kimono, and put her arm about the girl's sagging shoulders.

"Who? Me?" giggled Joyce amiably. "Me — drunk? You should shee Tommy!"

"Let me help you to bed," pleaded Helen brokenly. "No — here! You may sleep in my room."

Joyce fumbled helplessly at her buttons with one hand, the other clumsily mopping her dripping brow with her little hat. Presently she crumpled on the bed, and Helen tugged off her dress and laid a cold towel across her eyes.

"Thanks, darling!" mumbled Joyce, between heavy sighs. "Much bother . . . too bad . . . all my fault. . . . Don't blame Tommy. Tommy nice boy! Goin' — goin' to marry Tommy. . . . Well — can't you congrat — can't you felic — I'm afraid I can't say it very distinc'ly — but aren't you glad — about Tommy and me?"

"Let's wait and talk it over in the morning, dear," soothed Helen, turning the towel and patting it about the flushed temples.

"No — sir!" babbled Joyce, with an expansive gesture. "We're goin' talk about it —" she brought a slim, lovely hand down with a clumsy slap on the pillow — "ri' now!" The towel was brushed aside, and she gazed up militantly with swollen eyes. "Tha's just like you! You cry! I come home — all happy — to announce my engagesh to Tommy — and you cry! What's the big idea? Do you want him?"

Bridling her impatience, Helen urged the drunken girl to leave off and go to sleep. Maudlin tears of self-pity bathed Joyce's face.

"Nobody loves me!" she wailed. "Nobody but good old Tommy! . . . But I won't marry him! . . . I won't!"

Presently she relaxed, licked her stiff lips, sighed deeply, and slept. Helen knelt by the bed, her face buried in the covers to escape the heavy fumes, and wept piteously.

Wayne Hudson had left her with a responsibility quite too serious to be met. Only one thing had he expected of her. She had failed him.

◇ ◇

At length, rousing stiffly from the cramped position in which she had fallen asleep through sheer fatigue and nervous exhaustion, she mechanically collected the scattered letters from the floor, turned out the light, and went dejectedly to Joyce's bed-room. She put down the letters on the little vanity table and bathed her face with cologne.

Bobby Merrick's rather stilted note lay open before her as if inviting attention. Between the lines it announced that he considered himself under a moral obligation to Doctor Hudson. . . . She had been disposed to wave that implication aside as a mere pose . . . a bit of ephemeral martyrdom to be toyed with until he tired of it . . . a pretense of gallantry. She averted her eyes from the letter, perplexed, accused by it. Was she too under a certain moral obligation to Doctor Hudson? Young Merrick was trying to discharge his! How about hers?

She carefully folded the letter, and stood for a long time preoccupiedly deepening its creases with nervous fingers. It occurred to her that she would like to have a long, confidential talk with Bobby Merrick. Perhaps he might have something to suggest. . . . She stared at her haggard reflection in the mirror and shook her head. No — the way out did not lie in that direction. She tucked the letter into her writing-case, and tumbled wearily into bed.

VII

AT ONE O'CLOCK ON THE MORNING OF THANKSGIVING DAY, young Merrick solved the riddle to which he had devoted much of his spare time for nearly two months.

After only a week's sporadic work on it, he had written to Nancy Ashford:

"When the light breaks on this it will not come like a valley dawn. The book is going to be pitch dark up to a certain moment, and after that it will be clear and bright as a June morning. There's no halfway business about a job like this. Either you can read it all, with ease and understanding; or you can't read a syllable!"

The Thanksgiving recess having begun at noon on Wednesday, Bobby determined to spend the brief vacation on the cryptic journal. It would be a good time. Distractions and interruptions would be reduced to a minimum, for no sooner had the noon whistles blown than the student quarter was as deserted as if warned of an impending epidemic of the Black Plague. He had made a tentative promise to have evening dinner on Thanksgiving Day with old Nicholas "provided I finish a problem it is important to complete at once."

All Wednesday afternoon, he turned from one futile experiment to another, most of them being variants of schemes already tried. It annoyed him that he seemed unable to bring his attention to a sharp focus. Now he would sit at his desk for an hour, sharpening pencils and gazing glassily at the mocking script. Now he would fling himself across his bed and, supporting himself on an aching elbow, set down columns of letters in every manner of eccentric sequence. Oblivious of the passing time, his own discomfort, his need of exercise, he continued to lay out diagrams and tear up paper. Night came down and he turned on the lights. Midnight found him very weary, his brain operating mechanically, sluggishly. He tapped his teeth with his pencil, and went wool-gathering in spite of himself. He even made a brief mental excursion on foot along the highway to the north of Windymere and assisted a motorist in distress. Recovering himself, impatiently, he pursued his endless diagrams.

Then a fresh idea occurred to him. Here was something he had not yet tried. He wrote the first few words of the unintelligible script in a running line, utterly disregarding the spaces between them. (It had long been his practice to reproduce the letters in capitals, thinking this might help to simplify the words.)

Now he broke in two what was obviously the first sentence, at the point where the Greek letter " μ " indicated a half-stop, and set down the remainder of that obvious division immediately below it:

R A E I O S D R O M F I N
E D R C N I E Y U Y R E D

Moved by sheer caprice, he wrote the lines again, the second division lacking one space of meeting the left margin:

R A E I O S D R O M F I N
 E D R C N I E Y U Y R E D

For full five minutes he stared at this combination until the lines blurred and blended. Of a sudden, his heart speeded up. His pencil shook as he rapidly re-wrote the letters, mortising the lines:

READERICONSIDERYOUMYFRIEND

"*I have it!*"

He shouted, aloud; laughed, ecstatically, half hysterically. How ridiculously simple it was — now that he had cracked it open. Within five minutes of feverish copying and mortising, he had decoded the brief message of the first page:

READER I CONSIDER YOU MY FRIEND AND COMMEND YOUR PERSEVERANCE HAVING ACHIEVED THE ABILITY TO READ THIS BOOK YOU HAVE ALSO THE RIGHT TO POSSESS IT MY REASONS FOR DOING THIS IN CIPHER WILL BE MADE PLAIN AS YOU PROCEED

With the long strain relaxed, Bobby awoke to the fact that he was wolfishly hungry. He dressed for the street, a broad grin of self-satisfaction on his face. It was good to have conquered something! As he stood before the glass, knotting his scarf, he glanced at the little black book on the table as a gladiator might have regarded a recumbent antagonist.

Stepping out into a stinging sleet-storm, invigorated by its tonic thrust, he squared his shoulders, lengthened his stride, took deep inhalations, laughed joyously, sang the Marseillaise, and marched to it, swinging his long arms with a triumphant swagger.

There was a little chop-house only a block south of the Michigan Central station where one Tony held forth all night. Tony was typical of the occasional small shopkeeper, erudite barber, philosophical cobbler, or picturesque restaurateur to be found in every college town, by whose eccentricities, combined with a sincere interest in varsity athletics and the institution at large, they contrive to achieve local fame.

Many a full professor at the State University would have been happy and lucky had he been able to call as many undergraduates by their names as Tony. The turn-over in population in a college town being bewilderingly rapid, Tony's eleven years residence in Ann Arbor had made him a fixture, an institution. It was as if he had been there since the sixth day of creation.

He was reputed to be quite well to do, in spite of the fact that he extended credit and made unsecured loans to students with a naïve faith that would have closed a bank in forty-eight hours.

On the cigar-case lay open a cheap day-book. Attached to it, by a cotton string, was a pencil. If a student came into Tony's place without funds, he ordered what he liked and upon leaving wrote his name and the amount of his indebtedness in the book. It was not necessary to establish one's credit. One wrote in the book. When one got around to it, one paid off the score, leafed back through the book, located and personally deleted the item. Tony unemotionally accepted the payment. His failure to smile his thanks over the liquidation of the debt was in itself a pretty compliment. Having known it would be paid, there was no occasion for breaking out into rapture.

Tony himself came on duty at six in the evening and stayed the night. Nobody ever saw him at his place of business in the daytime, capable assistants being in charge through the breakfast and luncheon hours.

"Tony, how come you work only at night?" he was frequently asked by his clients, as he plunked platters of ham and eggs on a bare wooden table.

"You rather I not be here at night — eh?" Tony would inquire, grinning, quite aware that in the noisy protest which this rejoinder would evoke, their original inquiry would be forgotten.

Periodically young reporters on *The Michigan Daily*, hopeful of developing what they suspected was an unusual flair for feature writing, would engage Tony in conversation about his business; how much did he lose annually through bad loans and loose credit; why did he work only at night when business was unimportant; and sundry queries phrased in the best conventional manner of journalistic impertinence. But no story had ever appeared on this subject, Tony invariably taking refuge, when hard pressed, behind his inadequate knowledge of English.

"I couldn't get anything out of him. He's too damned dumb."

"Yeah?" the sophisticated Sunday editor would reply. "My boy, you have made the customary blunder of mistaking Tony's depth for thickness!"

Bobby Merrick knew from experience that Tony would be on hand tonight, to attend to his pressing wants. He would be served with amazing rapidity a steak well able to hold its own alongside many a more snobbish cut of select beef with a Parisian name, all buttoned up the back with mushrooms and presented with stiff salaams on a silver-mounted plank at a cost ten times the tariff Tony levied. There would be freshly-made coffee and a salad worthy of an exacting palate. Tony knew exactly when to stop rubbing the bowl with garlic.

Bursting into the little café, Bobby found himself the sole patron. Tony, drowsy but amiable, made haste to draw out a chair for him. With the grace of a courtier, he took his guest's heavy fur coat and deftly shook the snow from its shoulders.

His client enumerated his desires with the eloquent conviction of one who knows exactly what he wants, and Tony made off with his instructions.

"Needn't bother about the potatoes, Tony," called Bobby, as his host began to rattle his pans.

"Out dam' late, doc!" shouted Tony, above the hiss of the hot grill. He had an unerring instinct for identifying medics; probably because they were older than the rah-rahs, and had a pungent smell. Medics were always highly aromatic of their future trade.

"Baby case, mebbe?"

He liked to make the young medics think they looked old and wise enough to be internes, at least, or out on call, understrapping for their snug-in-bed betters. Eventually the more industrious and persistent would be "doctored" officially, some fine June morning at Hill Auditorium, in the sonorous tones of the President; but every one of them had long since received his degree from Tony. They chaffed one another about it; but never chided him, or suggested that he discontinue the practice.

"No, Tony," drawled Bobby, "nothing like that. Not for a long time yet. And no babies — ever!"

Tony plopped the thick stone dishes down with a comforting clatter on the bare table, adorned only by deep-carved initials — some of them to be pointed to with pride; many of them reminiscent of excellent stories without which the university traditions would have been seriously impoverished.

The steak was a masterpiece. The potatoes had arrived, magnanimously unmindful of the guest's feeling of indifference toward them. There was a head of chilled lettuce, half the size of a small cabbage, dripping with a creamy Roquefort dressing not to be had in that exact degree of all-rightness in more than six other places in the North Temperate zone.

" Coffee, doc? "

" You bet, Tony! Strong as brandy and hot as hell! I'm in great need of nourishment! "

Tony put down the steaming mug, thrust his big thumbs under his apron-string, in the vicinity of his waistcoat pockets, and considered his voracious customer with deep satisfaction. The next best thing to broiling a choice steak was watching a healthy client making proper use of it.

" No babies — eh? "

Bobby shrugged a shoulder and shook his head.

" Eye-ear-nose — mebbe? Lots of dem fellers."

" Heads! " declared Bobby, stoutly abjuring ophthalmology, otology, and all their works.

" Ah — so? " Tony grew excited. " I show you a head! You like for to see heads? Look, doc! " He bent down and offered for minute inspection a four-inch strip of bare white scalp. Straightening, he lightly tapped the scar and nodded several times very solemnly, " I dam' near die. . . . Very bad! "

" Accident? " inquired Bobby.

" Railroad! "

" Wreck, maybe? "

Tony chuckled.

" Nah! Work on da railroad. Jus' — what you call — wop! Not ride."

" So, after you were hurt, you thought you had enough of working on the railroad, eh? "

" I'll say da world! " concurred Tony, whose amazing use of the prevailing slang was by no means the least of his conversational charms. " Doc Hudson — he set me up here."

" You don't tell me! " Bobby put down his fork and gave attention.

Tony nodded vigorously.

" Doc Hudson — Detroit — he fix me. Patch da head. Put me in da business. Great feller! Too bad he die! "

When it was evident that his patron wanted to know all about it, Tony was eager to furnish information. The sanguinary account of his accident was recited dramatically with much stress upon the grisly details, not omitting a quite voluminous report of the minor incidents leading up to the event, many of which were less essential to the pathology of the case than to the histrionic technique of the narrator.

All but dead, he had been; yes. The company surgeon had called in Doctor Hudson. Hudson had done " da eempossible! " But never again must Tony be working under the hot sun — never!

" ' But what I do? ' I cry. ' I starve; mebbe? ' . . . ' Can you cook, Tony? ' he say."

It developed into a long story. Doctor Hudson had spent a whole day helping Tony locate a suitable place for his little restaurant; had guaranteed the rent of the building; had been present at the purchase of the range; had deposited to Tony's account in the leading bank a sum sufficient to carry him until his income was assured.

" I never heard about this before, Tony," said Bobby.

" No! Nobody know! Doc say, ' Tony! Tell nobody. Not while I leeve.' He dead now. I can tell! "

Bobby's glassy look of abstraction was mistaken for waning interest in the story, and Tony had no wish to bore his guest. He would return to the medic's pet interest. It was reasonably sure he would be attentive to an inquiry about his own aspirations.

" So! — You do heads, too, mebbe — like Doc Hudson? "

" I hope to, Tony. Some day," said Bobby, rising.

" Great feller — Doc Hudson! . . . Nobody know! "

◇ ◇

Young Merrick paid his bill, donned his coat, said good-night, lingered with his hand on the latch. Tony had begun clearing the table.

" I say — Tony! "

Tony put down a double handful of dishes.

" Did Doctor Hudson ever tell you why he wanted you to keep it a secret about his setting you up here? "

Tony inserted his thumbs under his apron-string and strolled forward, meditatively shaking his head.

" Dam' funny feller! He say, jus' like I tell you, ' Tony, I fix you so you no more work in da hot sun. While I leeve, you tell nobody.' I say, ' Doc, you one dam' fine feller. I pay you back some day.' He say, ' Nah — but, Tony,' he say, ' some dam' cold night, eef a feller come een, hongry and broke — ' "

" Yeah? " prodded Bobby; for Tony had apparently changed his mind about the advisibility of this confidence and had dismissed the rest of the sentence with a gesture. His red face crinkled with perplexity, and he rubbed the side of his bulbous nose with a corner of his apron. Nodding, jerkily, after the manner of an old man, he turned away, and was resuming his interest in the dishes.

"What then?" pursued Bobby — at his elbow.

"Doc say never tell nobody while I leeve."

"You mean — you never tell about these fellows who come in here hungry and broke? . . . Listen! I'll bet you a new fur-lined overcoat against a package of fags that that little account book, over there, on the case — and all these fellows who come in here hungry and broke — "

Tony interrupted. His face was very serious. He picked up his tray, and, as he straightened dignifiedly, he replied, in a thickening dialect significant that he was about to submerge and become incommunicable, "Ees eet dat you would make old Tony onhappy? Da leetla book! Eet ees for me to know! Doc Hudson — he say, 'Tony — you tell nobody! For why he say that, I do not know; but — I tell nobody!"

"I'm sorry, Tony!" said Bobby contritely. "I had no right to intrude in your personal affairs. I beg your pardon."

Tony smiled absently.

"Oh — eet ees all right," he said reassuringly. "Gooda night, doc. Come again!"

VIII

HAGGARD FROM A SLEEPLESS NIGHT AND THE EXPERIENCE of more mental agony than he had suspected himself capable of, young Merrick sank dejectedly into a club chair on an early train for Detroit.

In response to the long and excited telegram he had sent her from the railroad station while en route to Tony's, the night before (he heartily wished, two hours afterward, he had not sent it), Nancy Ashford had wired she would be waiting for him at the Michigan Central depot.

It was the picture of her, radiant with anticipation and bubbling with questions, that he dreaded most. Nancy must not be hurt.

As for himself, he would get over it. Somehow he would be able to accommodate himself to the utter abandonment of his cherished illusions about Doctor Hudson, and the hero-worship that had held him up in his dull, monotonous grind at the Medical School; though, now that the bottom had fallen out of everything, he wondered how he could go back and tread the mill again.

But, however difficult that might be, it was simple enough compared to the pending job of sitting down beside Nancy Ashford and hunting for pleasant words with which to tell her that her sainted Wayne Hudson, to whom she had unrequitedly given her full devotion, was crazy.

He was not even an interesting lunatic. A lunatic, often as not, was a brilliant mind that had blown up under compression — blown up splendidly, with a loud report, the neighbors hurrying with straps and stretchers to collect the débris and lug it off to the mad-house.

No, this man Hudson had not been good enough to himself to explode so that everybody could hear it and know what the big bang meant. He was just a plain nut! . . . Can you feature it? . . . Grown-up man . . . of good standing professionally, respected and admired . . . toiling interminably over the detailed report of what some wild-eyed crank had told him of impossible experiences, and then going to the enormous bother of concealing that hodge-podge of delusions in a code — a performance worthy the mind of a seventh grade schoolboy playing sleuth with a toy pistol.

Returned from Tony's, wide awake and exultant, he had resolved, late as it was, to decode a few pages of the journal. He had read patiently at first, with a broad smile of anticipation. Presently he found himself wishing the eccentric author would soon have done with his commonplace preliminaries and settle to business in the disclosure of his big secret — for it would have to be a big one to justify all this elaborate hocus-pocus of the code.

Surely nothing was discoverable, so far as he had gone, that required any thick wall of secrecy. It might be difficult to induce the general public to read it, were it printed in English for free circulation; but to pretend it was a deep mystery was idiotic.

After awhile he had come upon a paragraph that drew down the corners of his mouth and dragged a bitter " What t'ell! " from an oversmoked throat. He pushed the little book aside contemptuously; rose, paced the floor, lighted his pipe, tossed it clatteringly upon the table; undressed and went to bed — but not to sleep.

His disappointment was the most serious jolt of his life. Never until three months ago had he ever taken any stock in "big moments," "crucial decisions," "great renunciations," "consecrations," and the like. If people suddenly left off doing one thing and went galloping away in another direction, it was because they had sighted something more to their advantage. As for the legends of Saul and Saint Francis and Joan — well, if there was any substratum of truth in them, the psychiatrists could explain it.

Nor had he ever had any patience with that sticky confectionery of sentimentalism, that daintily perfumed moonshine, which effeminate visionaries referred to as "ideals." He had always been willing that all such blather should be left to the exploitation of preachers, poets, and the sob sisters.

Lately he had changed his mind about that. The coincidence of his having been saved from the lake at the same hour a valuable life had been lost in it, and at the price of that life, had stampeded him into a grand orgy of sentiment. He could understand Saul and Joan. . . . Hudson had become his ideal, his star, his sun, his totem-pole! . . . Now it was all over! . . .

There had been an old story about an idol that had fallen down because it had clay feet. His had tumbled over with vertigo . . . sick in the head! To have grown to manhood without an "ideal" of any kind; to have espoused one, belatedly, with crusading zeal; to have discovered, after burning all his bridges behind him, that his hero was a sap! . . . It was a nasty wallop!

He had gouged his hot face into his pillow and decanted his wrath to its bitter lees. . . . It wasn't that he had any fault to find with Hudson's penchant for poking a prehensile snout into other people's affairs with a passionate urge to do his one good deed per day, like the Boy Scout his silly little journal proclaimed him . . . but . . . My God! . . . Hudson wasn't the first man in all human history who had titillated his ego and busted the buttons off his weskit by doing alms! . . . What a pother about nothing!

At long last he had drifted off into an uneasy sleep, growling that he had a damned good notion to go on to New York in the morning and hop the first boat for Cherbourg. . . . His passport was still alive. . . . Grandpère would gladly send it to him. . . . Then he wouldn't have to stop and face Nancy. . . . What a rotten trick that would be! . . . And Grandpère? . . . The dear old boy had taken a lot of pride in him lately. . . .

He would be in Detroit now in five minutes. He must be careful not to offend Nancy. Why not hand her the journal and the code-key and make off hurriedly to keep some urgent engagement? He could say his grandfather needed him badly. It would be true enough if he said he himself was sick.

She was waiting for him at the gates, wide-eyed and smiling when he first sighted her from the tunnel; a bit perplexed as he drew nearer. . . . So it was plastered all over his mug, then! . . . He tried to pull a smile — a sickly smirk he knew it was; slipped an arm through hers; inquired, without meeting her eyes, if she'd had anything to eat, which she hadn't; told the porter to check his bags; and propelled Nancy to a quiet corner of the station restaurant where he made much ado about helping her with her coat — nervous as a caged fox.

"But I thought you had succeeded, dear." She followed him with inquiring eyes as he multiplied his little attentions and made no end of trouble for himself trying to find a place for her umbrella. "You don't resemble a conquering hero.

You look more like the man who had set out after a beautiful butterfly, under the impression it was some kind of a bird; and found, after battering its wings to bits, that he had captured a worm."

Bobby put down the menu, which he had begun to pore over assiduously, and emphasized his rejoinder by planting a long index finger close to her plate.

"Now you've said it! I went after a butterfly and came back with a worm!"

"And whose fault was that — the butterfly's?"

"Take your base, Nancy," he conceded with a chuckle.

"Take my base — indeed! . . . What about? . . . Your wild pitching? . . . I tell you it was a safe hit and a home run! . . . But — no matter about the butterfly. Wake up, stupid; and let me into the secret!"

At that he attempted to rally, cleared his throat, made pretense of rolling up his sleeves. He wasn't going to let Nancy down. Maybe he himself could carry on without the guidance of the Hudson specter; but Nancy couldn't. He would save the honor of her precious ghost if he had to profess faith in voodooism, necromancy, and witchcraft!

"I'm tired; that's all. . . . Up nearly all night. Let's talk to the waiter first."

She was not reassured, but willing to be patient.

"It's simple as addition!" he declared, when the waiter had trotted off. "That is —" pleating the tablecloth with restless fingers, "the mere mechanics of converting the script into readable sentences is easy enough. But — to understand what it's about, once you've done that . . ."

He broke off suddenly and smiled. . . . By the Lord Harry — he'd been handed his cue — at last! Now he could make his speech! He'd tell her the stuff was too deep for him! That would be infinitely better than to say it was childish piffle!

"Why — how very exciting!" exclaimed Nancy. "Out of one mystery into another!"

Bobby took the book from his pocket and opened it on the table before her, their heads close together. He was smiling now, quite pleased with his decision to let her explain it to him.

"Look! I'll read you the first page . . . . Easy enough, isn't it?"

Nancy was ecstatic. She spread her hand over Bobby's and gripped it hard. Almost too good to be true, wasn't it? He nodded, adding mentally, "or even entertaining."

"How far have you gone?" she inquired, leafing the unintelligible pages. "Aren't you just thrilled to death?"

Bobby had no enthusiasm to match hers, try as he would.

"Over to here . . . about twenty pages. Thrilled? Well — no; not that, exactly. . . . Just stupified. . . . It's over my head, you see. . . . I suppose I'm like your clumsy naturalist chasing the butterfly. I've been expecting so deuced much, and have worked so long to pry the lid off this thing that, now it's off, maybe I've damaged it somehow, or perhaps I haven't the mentality to — "

Nancy clutched his hand again — savagely.

"Look me straight in the eyes, Bobby Merrick! You've not been yourself for one instant since you arrived. You can't put anything over on me! I've been all through you with a lantern! You're trying to keep something back! I won't have it! Come clean, now — and tell me all about it! What's the trouble, boy?"

Bobby flushed and hung his head like a naughty child caught in the jam-pot.

" Aw — the stuff's no good! . . . Bunk — if you ask me. . . . If anybody else but Doctor Hudson had — I say, Nancy, are you quite sure he really did write this? It isn't signed, you know."

" Don't talk nonsense! . . . What's it about? "

" Well — it isn't exactly religion, I guess; but it reads like those goofy tracts that shabby chaps with dirty whiskers toss into the open window of your car . . . slush you can have by the ton for a whole lot less than the asking! And why he should have gone to the pains of jiggling the words all out of shape, as if they spelled some precious secret, the good God only knows! If anybody else had written it, I'd say he was all unhooked! "

Nancy had been tapping the table with her finger-tips, thoughtfully, impatiently, indignantly, and now explosively.

" How old are you, Bobby? " she snapped.

" Twenty-five-goin'-on-twenty-six," he recited, in the tone of one six-goin'-on-seven — a pleasantry she failed to acknowledge.

" Well — when Doctor Hudson was just coming into national renown for having performed the first head operation of its kind in the history of surgery, you still had some of your milk teeth to cut and were galloping about the nursery on a stick-horse! When he wrote this ' bunk,' you hadn't learned to wash your own ears! I don't mean to be too rough with you, sonny; but you need a drubbing, and you're jolly well going to get it from your Nancy Ashford this day! "

" Go ahead! . . . I'd rather you were sore at me than — than — "

" Hadn't nerve enough to finish it, had you? You were trying to say you hoped I wouldn't discover that

Doctor Hudson was a fool. . . . Don't give yourself any concern about that. I won't! . . . I presume you never had your attention called," she went on, biting her words into bits, " to the psychology of the genius. Why should you, indeed? Freshman medics aren't troubled much, I presume, with excursions into the rarer altitudes of psychiatry which deal with obsessions. They're kept too busy peeling the pelts off cadavers; trying to remember which is incas and which is stapes; trying to distinguish carpal from tarsus! . . . Oh, *I* know! You needn't hoity-toity *me* with your wisdom! "

She suddenly sighted the open-mouthed waiter.

" Here! . . . If you're looking for something to amuse you, take this cold coffee away and bring a fresh pot . . . some that was made this morning — preferably."

Bobby burst out with a peal of laughter as the fellow paddled away.

" Nancy — you're a scream! . . . Do go on! "

" I mean to! . . . I'm going to give you your first information about the genius-type. . . . The genius won't pigeon-hole! He won't card-index! He won't file. . . . And because he won't, the dull-eyed dolts who hadn't needed any trimming to fit whatever pack they properly belonged to, think him crazy. They can't understand him, so — he's unhooked! He romps away where they can't follow, so — he's gone wild! . . . He bestrides an idea and rides it furiously across country, over ditches and fences, through people's houses, trampling down fields and gardens, knocking even his best friends down, and never knowing it . . . never looking back . . . or caring a tinker's dam . . . so long as he can retain his seat on that one tremendous idea!

" Now — our Doctor Hudson was that sort of a person, and he became obsessed with an idea. He conceived a notion . . . I'm sure I don't know how he came by it; maybe this book tells; I have hoped it would . . . that his professional success depended upon certain eccentric philanthropies which had to be kept secret to be effective. That much I managed to guess, long ago. . . . Then the thought occurred to him, apparently, that he would put his theory into such shape that his heirs or successors or admirers might have a go at it. But he wanted to be insured against the ridicule of some pinhead who, pouncing upon it by accident — "

Bobby raised a hand.

" You're getting rather excited, aren't you? "

" You find it ridiculous that he employed this silly cipher," she continued, lowering her voice. " Well — suppose he'd written it in Latin, which he easily could have done without a lexicon; would that have caused you any less bother? . . . Or Greek! He could have done it in Greek! How much Greek do you know — beyond the letters on your fraternity badge? . . . He wanted to make somebody dig for it — I tell you — and that was all of a piece with his obsession! It was part of it! "

" You win, Nancy," admitted Bobby quietly. " You and I think the same thing about Doctor Hudson. We just say it differently; that is all. . . . I said he must be mentally unhooked, and you say he was a genius and that all geniuses are unhooked. . . . Very good. . . . Now we can read the little book together and understand each other — even if we can't understand the book."

◇ ◇

" I'll give you a brief digest of what I've read so far. . . . Nancy — it isn't that I begrudge him the time I've spent untangling this involved cipher. It's only that there's really nothing in it that calls for such mysterious handling. You'll see! "

" I won't be sure about that until we've read the book — all through."

Bobby fingered his notes.

" The story begins about a year after the death of Joyce, his first wife. Her long illness had slowed him up; absorbed all the neural energy that should have gone into his professional training. On the edge of failure and in deep depression, he was half-minded to give up surgery and go into business. . . . It occurred to him, one day, that Joyce's grave should be marked. . . . "

" Ah — there you are! " ejaculated Nancy, with suppressed excitement.

Bobby glanced up, inquiringly.

" That tombstone was a milestone! " she explained, with emotion. " How often, when he wanted to date some event in his experience, it would be 'shortly after I had erected the little marker for Joyce.' . . . Do go on! "

" He went to a concern dealing in memorial stones and selected an inexpensive monument. On the blank form he wrote his wife's name and the vital dates. The manager asked if he wished a brief epitaph. It seems to have been customary, at that time. Unable, on the spur of the moment, to think of an appropriate sentiment, and eager to close the business at once, he was advised to stroll out into the production department and look about. Perhaps he might see something there that appealed to him.

"So — he went through the factory, where monuments were under construction, and there he accidentally came upon this man Randolph."

"You speak of this man Randolph as if he figured somewhat in the tale. I never heard of him."

"Yes, Randolph is by way of being the hero of the piece, as far as I have gone. I leave it to you to say, after you've made his acquaintance, whether Randolph is an apostle of light or as mad as the Hatter. Personally, I haven't any use for him. He makes his début in the story as an exceptionally gifted hypnotist. . . . Turns out to be a sort of — miracle-man."

"Are you trying to tell me," demanded Nancy, "that Wayne Hudson took an interest in a person of that sort?"

"Well — you shall see. . . . This Randolph fellow was in a studio partitioned off from the main production room. He was not a mere stone-cutter, but a sculptor — an uncommonly good one. . . . Artist type. The piece he was doing, according to the journal, was a triumphant angelic figure, heroic size, gracefully poised on a marble pedestal, altar-shaped; an exquisitely modeled hand shading the eyes which gazed toward the far horizon, entranced by some distant radiance. . . . It had all the combined delicacy and strength of a Canova —"

"Are you quoting?"

"Yes; it's in the book — just that way."

"But Doctor Hudson knew practically nothing about art!"

"He may have known more about it than you thought. He was heavily influenced by this crazy Randolph, as you shall see; and Randolph was a consummate artist."

"Oh, I wonder — do you suppose it could have been

Clive Randolph? You know — the sculptor who did that group of children in the Metropolitan. He has been dead for years. Why, Bobby, I do believe he used to live here in Detroit! "

" Likely as not." He put his penciled notes down on the table and sat for some time with half-closed eyes, absorbed. " Another genius," he mumbled. " Nancy, geniuses do have a right to be batty, don't they? "

" Certainly! " Nancy glowed. Bobby was seeing the light.

He took up his memorandum.

" Well, on the face of this altar-shaped pedestal was engraved, in high relief, in ecclesiastical letters, these words: ' Thanks Be to God Who Giveth Us the Victory.' "

Nancy murmured that she thought it odd.

" How do you mean ' odd '? It's in the Bible somewhere, isn't it? "

" Doubtless," she conceded, with a nervous laugh. " It could be in the Bible, almost anywhere, and still be odd, couldn't it? But what I mean is that it seems queer to find Doctor Hudson reciting a quotation from the Bible. He wasn't the tiniest mite religious! "

" Don't you be too sure about that! " he warned.

" Why, Bobby, he was not only unconcerned; he was almost contemptuous of religious organizations; hadn't been inside a church, except at weddings, for twenty years. He was soured on churches as a small boy; told me once — it was when some quite dreadful evangelist was here and the papers were full of his cheap vulgarities — that the churches in his village were forever haranguing people to ' come apart from the world,' when they had nothing to offer in exchange for such renunciation but the vestigial remains of medieval superstitions! "

"But, couldn't he have been interested in — in the supernatural without being a church adherent?"

"Well, would he? . . . It isn't customary."

"Oh, well! if you propose to analyze this thing in the light of what's customary, let's go to the football game and quit torturing ourselves. . . . I ask you! . . . Is it customary for a man to conduct his ordinary charities by stealth; scampering, squirrel-fashion, into his hole and pulling the hole in after him, at the approach of anyone who might discover he had done somebody a good turn? Is it customary for a man to write the story of his madness in a kiddish cipher? I'll tell you what he was! . . . one of these old-time mystics! . . . believed in fairies . . . had visions . . . played with the angels!"

"Bobby Merrick — you're c-r-a-z-y!"

"No — not yet; but I've a queer feeling I'm going to be."

Nancy pushed back her plate and impatiently waved the waiter away when he asked if everything wasn't all right.

"No —" Bobby slowly shook his head, judicially. "It wasn't really religion that he had; not what I think of as religion, anyway. I don't pretend to know much about it, but isn't religion just a more or less perfunctory acceptance of a lot of old myths abstracted from the folk-lore of the Jews; tries to make people say they believe this and that about God; imagines it knows what God wants humanity to do — sometimes waiting sadly for mankind to do it, and at other times pushing people about so that they've got to do it, willy-nilly; takes up subscriptions to send barkers to the so-called heathen, warning them they'll seethe in hell if they don't leave off calling their God whatever-it-is and call Him something else?"

Nancy laughed.

"It isn't that bad, Bobby. It couldn't possibly be that silly. People do get a lot of comfort out of their religion, or they wouldn't stick to it."

"Comfort!" he echoed. "I'm glad you used that word. I believe I can tell you now what I think was the difference between this stuff that Doctor Hudson had — and the conventional sort of religion. Ordinary religion is intended to bring comfort. Believe such-and-such, and have comfort, peace, assurance that all is well and a Great Somebody is looking after things. Well — this religion that Hudson had certainly brought him no comfort! . . . Rode him like the Old Man o' the Sea . . . lashed him on . . . hounded him by day and haunted him by night . . . worked him like a slave . . . obsessed him!"

"He could have given it up, couldn't he, if it annoyed him?"

"Ah — there you are! Now you've touched the vital spot! No! He couldn't give it up because it furnished his motive power! It was what kept him going! . . . Says it made him — professionally!"

"I'm afraid you've let this book get horribly on your nerves, Bobby." Nancy drew on her gloves. "Let us go out to Brightwood, where we'll not be interrupted, and see what it's all about."

Bobby was slow to rise.

"Nancy, my whole attitude toward this matter is changing, since talking it over with you. I don't mind telling you I was never so disgusted or disappointed in my life as last night when I tried to read this stuff. But that was because I expected it to be a normal account of a normal man's experiences. And when I found it wasn't normal, well — I committed the usual blunder of pronouncing it silly!"

Nancy was radiant.

" Exactly! . . . So long as he was saying the customary thing, the normal thing, the thing you understood, he was sane! When he got to the unusual, the thing you did not understand, he was crazy! . . . That's the way the average mind operates; but you daren't make snap judgment like that, for you're to be dealing with queer heads all your life! "

◇ ◇

Throughout the long taxi drive to the hospital, their conversation studiously avoided the mystery they had confronted. They talked of his medical course. What did he like best? She shuddered when he spoke of his delight in anatomy.

" One gets used to that," he assured her. " And old Huber's a prince! He handles those poor cadavers as if they were our relatives. I'll bet if some of them had been given as much tender consideration while alive as Huber gives them in the lab, they might have lived longer. . . . Buries their ashes, Huber does, at the end of the semester . . . conventional interment — bell, book and clergy. . . . Contends that these paupers and idiots and criminals, however much they may have burdened their communities while they lived, have so completely discharged their obligation to society by their service in the lab, that they deserve honorable burial. . . . A fine old boy is Huber, believe me!"

The talk shifted to Nancy's affairs. She admitted she was worried. Rumor had it that Joyce Hudson was quite out of bounds; that Mrs. Hudson, apparently, could do nothing with her any more. She was being seen at the wrong places, with the wrong people.

"Do you suppose there is anything you could do about it, Bobby? Joyce is still your friend, isn't she?"

"I presume." His tone lacked interest. "I haven't seen her for nearly a year, you know."

"It may be just a notion of mine, but I always thought Joyce was a little in love with you, Bobby."

His gesture denied it.

"She isn't; but — suppose she was! . . . Would that be a good reason for my mixing in, over there? I'm not in love with her. No — I don't believe my obligation to Doctor Hudson involves my serving *in loco parentis* to his daughter."

"I'm not so sure it doesn't," reflected Nancy. "You've had an ambition to finish out his life for him, and part of his job was Joyce. There were times when all of his job was Joyce! You've no idea how much he gave up for her! Why, he even married — to keep her straight!"

"That shouldn't have been much of a sacrifice." Bobby grinned.

"Have you ever seen her — since?"

"Never tried to."

"Still think about her, sometimes?"

"Why do you want to know?" His tone hinted that he would like to close a door between them — not rudely, but — to close it, nevertheless; and, prompt to feel it, Nancy disclaimed her right to inquire.

"Forgive me, won't you? I haven't anything to do, you know, but amuse myself wondering about things like that."

"Then I mustn't do you out of your occupation."

◇ ◇

Nancy hung their coats in her closet, drew up a chair beside him, and together they faced the book again, agreeing that she should read the script, letter by letter, while Bobby arranged it into words.

" First, let me finish telling you the part I have already deciphered," he said, putting down his pencil. " Randolph pointed to the epitaph and inquired, ' How do you like this one? '

" ' Means nothing to me! ' replied Doctor Hudson. ' If there is a God, He probably has no more interest in any man's so-called victory, which can always be circumstantially explained, than in the victory of a cabbage that does well in a favorable soil.'

" ' Then you're related to God same as a cabbage! ' chuckled Randolph. ' That's good! '

" He resumed his work, deftly tapping his chisel. ' I used to think that,' he went on, talking half to himself. ' Made a little experiment, and changed my mind about it.' He put down his mallet, leaned far forward, and, cupping his mouth with both hands, confided, in a mysterious tone, ' *I've been on the line!* ' "

" He must have been crazy! " Nancy muttered.

" Tut, tut! . . . What's come of your genius theory? You're willing Doctor Hudson should be one — why not Randolph? "

" Quite right! Go on! . . . But he does sound a little off, doesn't he? "

" Decidedly! . . . And dangerously, I should say! . . . The most cold-blooded, calculating, sacrilegious lunatic you ever met! . . . I'll show you. Here is the exact copy of my translation! Listen to this:

He did not have the tone or stance of a fanatic; spoke quietly; had none of the usual tricks by which aberrations are readily identified; talked well, with absolute self-containment. " Victory? Well — rather! I now have everything I want and can do anything I wish! . . . So can you! . . . So can anybody! All you have to do is follow the rules! There's a formula, you know! I came upon it by accident! " He took up his chisel again.

He was a queer one. I felt shy and embarrassed. Clearly, he was cracked, but his manner denied it. I tried to remember he was an artist, with permission to be eccentric; but this was more than an eccentricity. He made me shivery. I wanted away. So — I was backing through his doorway when he called, " Doctor — do you have victory? "

" Victory over what? " I demanded, impatiently. . . . I had not told him I was discouraged; hadn't mentioned I was a doctor. . . . I never did find out how he guessed that — the question being eclipsed by more important mysteries.

" Oh — over anything — everything! Listen! " He climbed swiftly down from his scaffolding, and gliding stealthily toward me as if he had some great secret to impart he whispered into my ear — his hand firmly gripping my coat-lapel, somewhat to my own anxiety — " Would you like to be the best doctor in this town? "

So — then I knew he was crazy, and I began tugging myself loose.

" Come to my house, tonight, about nine o'clock," he said, handing me his card, " and I'll tell you what you want to know! "

I must have looked dazed, for he laughed hilariously, as he climbed up again. I laughed too as I reached the street — the epitaph matter having completely left my mind for the time. I had never heard so much nonsense in my life. " Like hell," I growled, as I started my car, " will I waste an evening with that fool! "

"This writing is authentic, Bobby."

At nine o'clock, I was at Randolph's door. . . . When these words are read I shall be unable to answer any queries as to my motive in going there that night. And that will be fortunate; for I have no explanation further than to say (and this will unquestionably be regarded with distrust and disappointment) that I was propelled there against my wishes. I had no thought of going; went in response to some urge over which I had no control. . . . I was down town to dinner, that evening; returned home at eight; went immediately to bed — quite contrary to my custom, for I never retired before midnight — and began reading a book, unable to concentrate on a line of it. I could not keep my eyes off the clock. It ticked louder and louder and my heart beat faster and faster until the two of them seemed synchronized. At length, becoming so nervous I could no longer contain myself, I rose, dressed hastily, dashed out for my car, and drove to Randolph's address without regard to boulevard stops or angry traffic officers. My mouth was dry, my heart thumping.

◇ ◇

"How do you like it — far as we've gone?" he asked.

Nancy's elbows rested heavily on the desk, her clenched fists digging deeply into her cheeks.

"Why, Bobby — isn't this just *awful?*" she whispered. "*It's tragic!*"

"You'll think so — presently. It hasn't begun to get awful yet!"

His eyes traveled back to his copy.

"You had not intended to come, had you?" inquired Randolph, taking my hat.

"No!" I replied, sourly.

"That's what I feared," he said, gently, "but I felt so sure you needed to have a talk with me that I —"

"That is what I want to know!" I demanded. "*What did you do?*"

He grinned slyly, rubbed his hands together softly, satisfiedly, and said, "Well — I earnestly wanted you here; and, as I told you, this morning, whatever I earnestly want — *it comes! I wanted you here! You came!*"

He motioned me to a seat — I was glad enough to accept it for my knees were wobbly — in a living-room furnished in exquisite taste. His daughter, whom he had gracefully presented, promptly excused herself, and left us alone. Offering me a cigar, he leisurely filled a long-stemmed churchwarden pipe for himself, and drew his chair closer. In his velvet jacket, at his ease, he was all artist; quite grizzled, wore a short Van Dyke beard; had a clear, clean, gray eye that came at you a bit shyly and tentatively, but left you no way of escape.

He lost no time in preliminary maneuvers. Reaching to a small book-table, at his elbow, he took up a limp-leather Bible. I knew then that I was in for it. Impetuously, I resolved upon an immediate, if inglorious, exit. Savagely, I put up a protesting hand and said firmly, "Now — if it's that, I don't care to hear about it!"

"See?" shouted Nancy. "What did I tell you?"

To my surprise, he put the book back on the table, and calmly puffed at his pipe, thoughtfully, for a while; then replied, "Well — neither am I — except as it's really an important history of a great religious system. Quite useful, I presume; but I'm not specially interested in it — except one page —" He blew a few smoke rings, his head tilted far back against his tall chair. "— and I have cut that page out. . . . I just wanted you to see this particular copy of the Bible. I was about to say — when you plunged in with your impatient remark — that this copy of the Bible lacks the secret formula for power. I keep that one page elsewhere! "

" What's on it? " I inquired, annoyed at my own confession of interest.

" Oh — " he replied casually, " it's just the rules for getting whatever you want, and doing whatever you wish to do, and being whatever you would like to be. But — you're not interested in that; so we'll talk about something else."

" What is on that page? " I demanded — my voice sounding rather shrill.

" Do you really want to know? " he challenged, leaning forward and fixing me intently with his gaze.

" Yes! " I barked.

His next words came slowly, incisively, single-file.

" *More — than — you — have — ever — wanted — to — know — anything — before?* "

" Yes! " I admitted — and meant it.

" Say it! " he commanded.

I repeated it: " *More — than — I — have — ever — wanted — to — know — anything — before!* "

His manner changed instantly.

" Good! Now we can talk! "

He went down into an inside pocket and produced a morocco wallet. From the wallet, he extracted a folded page. I read it, and he carefully interpreted its meaning.

Nancy's eyes were a study, when Bobby stopped reading to search her face.

" Are you prepared now for a complete knock-out? " he inquired. " If so — I'll give you the next paragraph.

I did not leave Randolph's house until four o'clock, and when I finally went out into the dark, considerably shaken, I was aware that my life would never be the same again. Whatever of success has come to me in my profession dates from that hour

and can be explained in terms of the mysterious potentiality which Randolph communicated to me that night.

There was a long silence between them.

" That's almost as far as I've gone," said Bobby.

" Far enough — I should say! " Nancy's deep sigh was ominous of dejection.

" Then let's call it a day." He rose, and glanced at his watch. " You and I can't help knowing that this is something Doctor Hudson must have written when he was under very heavy pressure of work; half dead on his feet; seeing things; hearing voices. Perhaps we shouldn't be reading it at all. Maybe it isn't fair to his memory. How about giving it up — and forgetting we ever went this far into it? "

Nancy tapped the table, thoughtfully, with her finger-tips.

" I wonder what was on that page! "

He laughed.

" That sounds like Doctor Hudson! That was what he wanted to know. Now it's your question! I'm bound to confess I'd like to know too." He gripped her arm in strong fingers. " And — no matter how stiffly we revolt against this thing, we're sure to be sneaking back to it, one at a time, to investigate; so — perhaps we should be honest with each other, and look into it *now!* Are you willing? "

She nodded, without looking up.

" Take warning! It's likely to make us as nutty as he was! "

Lighting a cigarette, Bobby strolled to the window, hands in pockets. He turned, and leaning on the window-sill, faced her studiously.

" Not me! I'm not going to do it. I can't afford to

dabble in such stuff. It isn't good for me. I had no idea I could be so impressionable toward this sort of thing. You can go into it, if you want to. . . . I'm out!" He dismissed it peremptorily, with widespread fingers.

Nancy's voice was husky.

"You'll not be able to get away from it! You're too far in! . . . And you know it! . . . It's got you! . . . I know it's got *me!* I understand now why he went to the Randolph house, that night! There's something — something sort of inevitable about it! . . . A form of insanity, maybe; but — once it beckons to you, it's got you! You may as well come along — first as last! . . . It has curious, invisible tentacles that reach out and wrap their feelers about you . . . and draw you up . . . and into . . . and drag you along . . ."

"Stop it, Nancy! . . . That's ridiculous!"

◇ ◇

Young Watson could hardly have chosen a less opportune moment to put his head in. Mrs. Ashford had a caller, and it was clear that both hostess and guest were laboring under an unusual mental tension . . . having something of a storm, indeed! Realizing he was *de trop*, he was for making a hasty retreat, when Nancy recalled him.

"Come on in! You remember Mr. Merrick."

"Quite!" extending his hand. "I shall always remember you as putting up the gamest fight with pneumonia that I ever watched! And now, I hear, you're having a battle with old man Gray."

Turning to Mrs. Ashford, he stated his errand:

"Your Mr. Folsom is rapidly slipping out. In an hour or

two he will be quite unconscious. He inquired for you a few minutes ago. Perhaps you will want to run in and see him. There seems to be none of his people in town."

Murmuring regret, Nancy rose to go.

"Will you wait for me?"

Merrick nodded.

"I'll go on with this. Take your time. You'll find me here when you come back."

The door closed softly behind them.

◇ ◇

I reached out my hand greedily for the page Randolph had unfolded, but he shook his head.

"Not just yet," he said, smiling at my eagerness. "I mean to let you see it; but I must tell you something about it, first. This page contains the rules for generating that mysterious power I mentioned. By following these instructions to the letter, you can have anything you want, do anything you wish to do, be whatever you would like to be. I have tried it. It works. It worked for me. It will work for you!"

Combined impatience and incredulity brought a chuckle from me which he did not resent.

"You saw that piece I was working on when you came in, this morning?"

"Beautiful!" I exclaimed — sincerely.

"You liked it that much?" He was pleased with my enthusiasm.

"Nothing short of a masterpiece!"

"Perhaps I should be more grateful for that compliment, doctor; but I really have had very little to do with it. . . . You may be interested to learn that I was an ordinary stone-cutter until about three years ago, hacking out stamped letters with a compression chisel. From my youth, I had cherished an ambition to do something important in stone. But there was never any money for training; never any time for experiment. Such crude and hasty attempts as I had made, from time to time, had netted nothing but discouragement.

"One day, I went to the church my little girl attended, and heard a preacher read what is on this page. It evidently meant nothing to him, for he read it in a dull, monotonous chant. And the congregation sat glassy-eyed, the words apparently making no impression. As for me, I was profoundly stirred. The remainder of the hour was torture, for I wanted out where I could think.

"Hurrying home to our bare little house, I found — with considerable difficulty, for I was not familiar with the Bible — that page from which the minister had read. There it was — in black and white — the exact process for achieving power to do, be, and have what you want! I experimented."

Nancy's face, sober and troubled, appeared at the door.

"Bobby," she said softly, "I don't like to leave you alone so long, but my patient seems to want a hand to hold. I'm afraid I must stay with him a little while."

"Quite proper," he agreed, without more than a glance at her. "Stay with him and don't worry about me. I may have something very important to tell you when you come back. It looks as if the big mystery may be cleared up now at any minute."

She hesitated, and was about to ask a question; but, seeing how complete was his absorption, withdrew and quietly closed the door.

With that, Randolph handed me the magic page. Some twenty lines of it were heavily underscored in red ink. In silence he puffed his pipe while my eye traversed the cryptic paragraphs, and when I looked up, inquiringly, he said:

"Of course, you will not realize the full importance of all this, instantly. It seems simple because it was spoken dispassionately, with no oratorical bombast or prefatory warning that the formula he was about to state was the key to power!"

Edging his chair closer to mine, he laid a long hand on my knee and looked me squarely in the eyes.

"Doctor Hudson — if you had a small, inadequate brick house, and decided to give yourself more room, what would you need for your building? . . . More brick. . . . If you had a small, inadequate steam-engine, you would want more steel to construct larger cylinders — not a different kind of steel to house a different kind of steam, but merely more room for expansion. . . . Now — if you had a small, inadequate personality, and wanted to give it a chance to be something more important, where would you find the building materials?"

He seemed waiting for a reply, so I humored him.

"Well — according to the drift of your argument, I presume I would have to build it out of other personalities. Is that what you're driving at?"

"Pre—cisely!" he shouted. "But — not 'out of!' . . . *Into!* . . . Glad you said that, though; for it gives me a chance to show you the exact difference between the right and wrong methods of making use of other people's personalities in improving one's own. . . . Everybody is aware, instinctively, that his personality is modified by others. Most people go about imitating various scraps and phases of the personalities that have attracted them — copying one man's walk, another's accent, another's laugh, another's trick of gesture — making mere monkeys of themselves. . . . This theory I am talking about doesn't ask you to build your personality *out of* other personalities, but *into* them!"

"I'm afraid all that's too deep for me," I admitted befuddledly.

He rose and stamped back and forth in front of the grate, shaking his shaggy mop of grizzled hair, and waving his long-stemmed pipe as if trying to conjure a better explanation.

" See here! You know all about blood transfusion. That's in your line. Superb! . . . One man puts his life into another man. . . . Doctor — how do you accomplish a blood transfusion? Tell me in detail! "

◇ ◇

Merrick glanced up as the door opened.

" Is he gone? "

Nancy nodded, soberly.

" What has been happening since I left? " she asked, drawing up a chair beside him.

He pushed his notes toward her and watched her face as she read.

" Just what *is* the best process of blood transfusion? Let's see how much you know! "

" Well — it's simple enough, except for one obstacle. The blood must be kept from coagulation as it passes from the donor to the recipient. Even when the artery and the vein are attached by a little cannula, the blood soon clogs the glass; so, to avoid that stoppage, the vein of the recipient is passed through the cannula and cuffed back over the end of it. Then the cannula, carrying the vein, is inserted into the artery of the donor. The point is, you see, to insure against any outside contact."

" Bobby — what was on that page? "

" I haven't learned yet."

" Do you think he is ever going to tell us? "

" He's got to, sooner or later. Let's read on. I imagine we're close to it now."

Nancy took the pencil and began to copy from his rapid dictation.

I explained the principles of transfusion, briefly, and Randolph seemed mightily pleased, especially with that feature of it which concerned the problem of coagulation.

"Bright boy — Bobby!" cried Nancy. "You did know, didn't you?"

He acknowledged her sally with a grimace and continued dictating.

"You will notice there," pointing to the page in my hand, "that this first step toward the achievement of power is an expansion — a projection of one's self into other personalities. You will see that it has to be done with such absolute secrecy that if, by any chance, the contact is not immediate and direct — if, by any chance, there is a leak along the line of transfer — the whole effect of it is wasted! You have to do it so stealthily that even your own left hand — "

Nancy tossed her pencil down on the desk, and relaxed in her chair.

"Bobby! I've got it! *I can find the page!*"

"Is there a Bible handy?"

"I'm afraid I haven't one, dear."

"Well — that can come later, then. Continue!

Randolph returned to his chair, and went on, in a lowered voice:

"Hudson — the first time I tried it — I can tell you the incident freely because nothing ever came of it, although it had cost me more than I could afford, at the time, to do it — the chap was so grateful he told a neighbor of mine, in spite of my swearing him in. He had been out of work and there had been a long run of sickness in the family, and he was too shabby and down at heel to make a presentable appearance in asking for a job. I outfitted him. He told it. A neighbor felicitated me, next day. So there was more than Sixty Dollars of my hard-earned cash squandered! "

" Squandered! " I shouted, in amazement. " How squandered? Didn't he get the job? "

Randolph sighed.

" Oh, yes," he said. " He found a job. I was glad enough for that, of course. But — that didn't do *me* any good! You'd better believe — the next time I made an outlay I informed the fellow that if I ever heard of his telling anybody, I would break his neck."

" Did you ever hear of anything more diabolical? " broke in Nancy, indignantly. " Can you imagine such fiendish selfishness? . . . Just doing it to benefit himself! . . . Not even willing the other fellow should be grateful! . . . And yet he thought he was getting himself connected with God, that way! . . . It gives you the creeps! "

" Well — keep it in mind he's obsessed with a delusion."

" Possessed of a devil — I'd rather believe! "

" Maybe Doctor Hudson will explain it. . . . Let's proceed."

He laughed merrily at the remembrance of the incident.

" The man thought I was crazy! " he added, wiping his eyes.

" And you weren't? " I inquired, in a tone that sobered him.

" Really — it does sound foolish, doesn't it? I mean — when you first hear of it. I don't wonder you're perplexed."

" I am worse than perplexed," I admitted, bluntly. " I'm disgusted! "

" You and me — both! " interpolated Bobby, under his breath.

" You might well be," admitted Randolph, " if I were trying to get power, that way, to stack up a lot of money for my own pleasure. All I wanted was the effective release of my latent ability to do something fine! . . . And, as for being disgusted because I requested the man not to tell anybody what I had done for him, if that offends you, you wouldn't like the Lord himself! . . . For he often said that to people he had helped."

" I'm sure I don't know," I said. . . . " Not very well acquainted with what he said. . . . Go ahead with your story."

" Thanks. . . . But, first let me lead you just a little farther into the general philosophy of this. . . . On the night of the day I made my first successful projection of my personality — I cannot tell you what that was — I dare not — I went literally into a closet in my house, and shut the door. That's the next step in the program, as you have read there on that page. You see — I was very much in earnest about this matter; and, having already bungled one attempt, I was resolved to obey the rules to the letter. . . . Later, I discovered that the principle will work elsewhere than in a closet. Just so you're insulated."

" Oh — Randolph — for God's sake! " I exploded. " What manner of wild talk is this? "

" Good! " interrupted Nancy. " It was high time he called him! "

" I confess I can't understand," said Randolph, impatiently, " why you find this so hard to accept! Why — it's in line with our experience of every other energy we use! Either we meet its terms, or we don't get the power. What did Volta's battery or Faraday's dynamo amount to, practically, until Du Fay discovered an insulation that would protect the current from being dissipated through contacts with other things than the object to be energized? . . . Most personalities are just grounded! That's all that ails them!

" So, I went into a closet; shut the door; closed my eyes; quietly put myself into a spiritually receptive mood; and said, confidently, addressing the Major Personality, — *I have fulfilled all the conditions required of me for receiving power! I am ready to have it! I want it! I want the capacity to do just one creditable work of statuary!*

" Now — you may be inclined to believe that I experienced only a queer delusion, at that moment. As a scientific man, you may think that my mental state can easily be accounted for by principles well known to psychology. If you think that, I have no objection. The fact that a process of achieving power by the expansion of the human personality admits of an explanation, in scientific terms, does not damage its value at all, in my opinion. I dare say the time will come when this matter is made a subject of scientific inquiry.

" But — whether it is explicable or not, I can truthfully assure you that upon finishing my experiment in that closet, I received — as definitely as one receives a shock from an electrode, or a sudden glare of light by opening a tightly-shuttered room — a strange inner illumination!

" It was late in the night. I came out of that dark, stifling little closet with a curious sense of mastery. It put me erect, flexed the muscles of my jaw, made my step resilient. I wanted to laugh! I tried to sleep; and, failing of it, walked the streets until dawn. At eight-thirty, I approached the manager of the factory and asked for six months' leave. When he inquired my reason, I told him I had it in mind to attempt a piece of statuary.

" Something we might use, perhaps? " he asked.

" I am confident of it," I said, surprised at my own audacity. It was enough that I had determined to survive somehow, without wages, for six months; but now I had made an extravagant promise to the manager. He was thoughtful for a while and then said:

" 'I'll give you a chance to try it. For the present, you are to have your usual pay, and a studio to yourself. If you produce something we can place, you will share in the sale. Your hours will be your own business. I should be glad if you succeeded.'

" I began work at once in a flutter of excitement. The clay seemed alive in my hands! That first day was a revelation. It was as if I had never really lived before! All colors were more vivid. I want you to remember that, Hudson. See if you have the same reaction. Grass is greener; the sky is bluer; you hear the birds more distinctly. It sharpens the senses — like cocaine.

" That night, I went into my closet again, and was immediately conscious of a peculiar intimacy between myself and That Other; but it was not so dynamic as on the previous night. I decided that if I was to get any more power that way, I would have to make some further adjustments of my own spiritual equipment.

" That was on a Friday, the tenth of June. On the first day of September, I invited the manager in to see the cast I had made. He looked at it for a long time without any remark. Then he said, quietly, 'I have some people who may be interested in this.'

" It was the figure of a child, a chubby little fellow about four years old. The boy was posed on one knee. He had just raised up from his play with a little dog that stood tensely alert, in front of him, with a ball in his mouth, waiting for the child to notice him. The boy's shirt was open at the throat. His tight little knickers were buttoned to broad suspenders. The legs were bare to the knee. He was looking straight aloft, his little face all squinted up with baffled amazement, wonderment, curiosity. His small square hand shaded his eyes against a light almost too bright for him, the head tilted at an angle indicating that he had heard something he could not quite understand and was listening for it to be repeated.

"The next afternoon, the manager's clients came in — a man and his wife. She was in black. They had recently lost their little boy. She cried at first, heart-breakingly. But, after a while, she smiled. It made me very happy when she smiled. I knew then that I had been able to express my thought.

"I was told to go on with my project and put it into white marble. . . . Quite incidentally, the people adopted the boy I had used for a model."

It was about four o'clock when I left Randolph's house that night. I was in a grand state of mystification. I went home resolved that I would make an experiment similar to his. Before I went to bed, I tried to project my thoughts to some remote spiritual source, but was conscious of no reaction whatsoever. In the morning I decided that I had been most outrageously imposed upon by an eccentric and scowled at my own reflection in my shaving-mirror. Nobody but a visionary could do these things with any hope of success, and I was, by training and temperament, a materialist and a very cold-blooded one, at that. All that day, however, I was aware of being on a quiet, unrelenting search for some suitable clinical material to be used for an experiment in the dynamics of personality-projection. . . . The strangest feature of my mood, however, was the fact that the power I had begun, rather vaguely, to grope for — under Randolph's urging — was not the mere satisfaction of an ambition to make myself important or minister to my own vanity. . . . For the first time, my profession seemed to me not as a weapon of self-defense but a means of releasing myself!

The last thing Randolph said to me, at the door, was this caution: "Be careful how you go into this, my friend! I do not know the penalties this energy exacts when misused. . . . I've no notion what dreadful thing might have happened to the Galilean if he had turned those stones into bread! . . . But, I warn you! . . . If you're thinking of going into this to feather your own nest, you'd better never give it another thought. . . . I'm not sure — but I think it's terribly dangerous stuff to fool with! "

My own experiences are hereinafter set forth as possible aids to whomever has had the curiosity to translate this journal. I trust I have made it quite clear why I have chosen this peculiar method of passing it along. Had I ventured to report my experiments, it would have been at the expense of my reputation for sanity. I do not know of a single friend to whom I could have told these things without putting an unpleasant constraint between us. It has been a hard secret to keep. It is equally hard, I am discovering, to confide — even with the realization that these words are unlikely to be read during my lifetime. I dislike the idea of being thought a fool — dead or alive.

You — whoever you are — may be inclined to read on; — perhaps personally interested in making an experiment; perhaps just curious. I wonder — would it be asking an unreasonable favor — if you would not consent to stop, at this point, if you are smiling? . . . You see, some of these experiences of mine have meant a great deal to me, emotionally. I don't believe I should want them laughed at. . . . If the thing hasn't gripped you a little by now, put it down, please, and think no more about it. . . . If however you seriously wish to proceed, let me counsel you, as Randolph counselled me, that you are taking hold of high tension! Once you have touched it, you will never be able to let go. . . . If you are of the temperament that demands self-indulgence to keep you happy and confident enough to do your work — and many inestimably valuable people are so built and cannot help it any more than tall men can help being tall — leave all this alone, and go your way! . . . For if you make an excursion into this, you're bound! It will plaster a mortgage on everything you think you own, and commandeer your time when you might prefer to be using it for yourself. . . . It is very expensive. . . . It took the man who discovered it to a cross at the age of thirty-three!

◇ ◇

Young Merrick pushed back the papers and turned slowly to face Nancy but their eyes did not meet. They felt strangely embarrassed in each other's presence, and sat for many minutes in silence. . . . Bobby spoke.

" ' Bound,' he said. ' Once you go into it, you're bound.' Hudson has had me bound ever since he died! . . . He should have been content with that."

Nancy rose and rested her capable hands on his shoulders.

" It's a good place to stop, wouldn't you say? "

He agreed. Perhaps they might have an hour or two together tomorrow. He had half promised his grandfather he would be out for dinner. Tom Masterson had talked of going, too.

" Are you meaning to take the book along? "

" I'll match you for it! "

" Heads! "

He slapped a coin on his wrist.

" Sorry, Nancy. . . . I'll bring it back tomorrow."

IX

"GRANDPÈRE," SAID BOBBY, SLOWLY TWIRLING THE STEM OF his glass, "I wish you would tell Tom about the time you and Mr. Anderson butchered the pigs at the Country Club."

The talk had been growing too serious. Masterson had an annoying tendency, when exhilarated, to become didactic. It was all clever enough, informative, interesting — but more dogmatic than suited the temper of a Thanksgiving dinner.

By a circuitous route they had arrived at the problem of caste in America, Masterson conducting the excursion and pointing out the essential facts of interest to be noted along the way. Bobby was for a change of topic. Old Nicholas had some convictions on this subject. He would probably not express them to the same degree with which he believed them; but Masterson must not be encouraged to deliver himself of too many sentiments unshared by his genial host.

Why shouldn't there be a leisure class? Loafers — if you like that word better? This was about the only sign America had exhibited that she was maturing, ever so little, in a few restricted zones. Wasn't our brand of democracy dangerous? Referendum — huh! What did the average voter know? Every nation that had become great had achieved its distinction through the leadership of small social and intellectual minorities!

Masterson was still talking — Hyde Parking, almost — a bit flushed about the temples. Bobby determined upon a change of subject.

Old Nicholas was not in accord with many of young Masterson's views, but he liked his views better than the manner in which he delivered them, and liked both the views and the delivery better than the way he drank his wine.

Meggs had been told to bring up a long-neglected bottle of choice Burgundy. In the opinion of the elder Merrick, wine like this deserved to be caressed, its color admired, its fragrance inhaled, its story reconstructed. It was to be sipped, drop by drop. It pleased him that Bobby seemed to know how. Liquid sunshine, it was; sunshine that had warmed the pleasant banks of the Rhone, in tranquil days before the war. One did not toss it off at a draught. Masterson gulped it. It was good to see Bobby close his eyes as his lips touched the rim of the glass, as if he saw merry groups of bare-legged little girls tramping it out in the shade at the corner of some Provencal vineyard. The boy was maturing rapidly, reflected old Nicholas. He had the posture and gesture of a man.

" Bobby occasionally insists upon this story," said Nicholas obediently, " I have repeated it, at his request, many times."

" And each time it is better," commented Bobby, appreciatively.

" Let's have it then, by all means! " shouted Masterson, much more boisterously than he had intended, an error he instantly endeavored to correct by bowing very formally and dignifiedly in an affirmative to Meggs' unspoken query as the bottle was again tilted, tentatively, inquiringly, over his glass. Meggs had tried to put into the gesture just the right degree of reserve, but the finesse was a bit too subtle for his customer.

◇ ◇

" Well," said Nicholas, clearing his throat, " it was this way. You see, where Axion now stands, there used to be nothing but pasture fields. Joe Anderson and I, when we were kids, had a contract with most of the village folks to drive their cows out to pasture, every morning, in the summer, and bring them home in the evening to be milked. Each cow was worth a dollar a month to us.

" Out there, in those fields, where we freckle-faced youngsters, with stone bruises on our calloused feet, sat all day, whittling kite sticks, playing mumble-peg, and bragging about the teams we captained at school — three-old-cat; you never played it, either of you —Joe and I later built a couple of big factories which quite changed the look of the landscape.

" These factories also brought changes in most people's mode of living. Many men, who might have spent all their lives in ordinary financial circumstances, came to have quite a little money. They built big houses, and their children took on airs. It was hard to recognize the place, after a while, and even harder to recognize some of the people.

" Well, no matter how much absorbed we became in our business, Joe and I remained, through the years, just kids — to each other. I suppose it was a subject for many little jokes with other people. We kept up our boyish relations — always bragging about our speed, strength, and endurance, whenever we met, and invariably in the language we had used in the old days. Like ' Gemunee Crickets! ' and ' Gosh darn ut! ' and ' Fer the love o' Mike! ' It was rather silly, I'll admit; but we enjoyed it.

" Joe and I used to help our fathers with the hog butchering in November. Every family, in those days, had a few hogs in a pen. The time came, when we were in our late 'teens, that the annual slaughter was left pretty much to our management, and we usually combined forces — pulling it off at the Anderson place, where they had better facilities for such work. We became quite expert butchers, and were very proud of our accomplishment. I dare say our fathers flattered us in the hope of making us too vain to see how glad they were to dodge the job.

" Well, one day, after Joe and I had retired from our business concerns, we were having lunch together at the Country Club. It was brand splinter new; had been open only a week. The only natural hazard, on the golf course, was a little stream where Joe and I used to fish for crawdads and minneys. Nobody ever said 'minnows.' On the knoll where the new club house stood, there had been quite a nice little grove. Joe and I used to sit among those trees, on a log, slapping mosquitoes, and watching for gray squirrels. He owned an old muzzle-loading shotgun. Mighty dangerous toy, too. Wonder we weren't killed a dozen times.

" We were having a good time reminiscing. It seemed queer to be sitting there, on that spot, lunching at a solid mahogany table sprinkled with Venetian doilies that slid about under crested silver. Everybody belonging to that club had plenty of money, and the club house had been built and equipped without regard for expense. There was a lot of swank too. The servants seemed to have been let into the secret that this was one of our better clubs. The institution was by way of becoming a bit snobbish, we feared. Practically all the natives who belonged to it had been derived from quite humble origins, like Joe's and mine; and we worried a bit about the decline of the old democracy. It struck us that the mere fact of our having accidentally made a little money didn't require us to pretend we were of the British peerage.

" At adjoining tables sat some of the second-growth crop of Axionites — male and female — talking about polo and derbies and regattas and Biarritz and grouse in Scotland;

and we thought the general tone of the place should be improved. So we fell to discussing some of the good old times the Axion boys and girls used to have before the automobiles came along and scared the horses off the roads, and drove the cows out of the pastures to make room for the golfers. Then, one of us remembered about the butchering.

"Joe recalled that one time we put on a contest to see which of us could dress a hog in the shortest time. I recalled the incident perfectly, but was sure I had won the small stake we had put up. Joe disputed me so strongly that the neighboring tables became interested and, presently, alarmed. When we observed that we had collected quite a sizable audience, we obligingly continued our debate chiefly for their benefit. The upshot of the argument was that Joe and I bet a thousand dollars a side that each of us could dress a hog in less time than the other. The old chaps, when they heard of it, insisted that the contest be held in the grill-room, and a book was made which, I learned afterward, involved bets running into scandalous sums.

"The engagement was put on the club calendar. I'm not sure it was pointed to with much pride by the younger set; but the old fellows seemed to want it there, and, seeing their wishes really had to be consulted, more or less, the polo crowd waived their objections. On the next Tuesday, after luncheon, no man went back to his office — if he had one. Two live pigs — pretty good sized ones, too — were fetched in crated. A tarpaulin was spread on the grill-room floor, and Joe and I stripped to the skin and put on butchers' togs. We went through it, from squeal to sausage. I was told, afterward, that the club house had to be gone over, from crypt to spire. They had grease on the stairsteps and bristles in the soup and cracklings in the rugs for days thereafter."

"Did it improve the democratic tone of the club?" asked Masterson, laughing.

Old Nicholas shook his head and smiled.

"No. I don't think so. Once you outgrow the simplicities, you can't recover them or even remember them with any satisfaction. It's not far, you know, from corn pone to plum pudding, but it's a long way back!"

"What do you make of our new second generation, Mr. Merrick?" inquired Masterson.

"You mean — yours and Bobby's, perhaps? Yours is the third, you know — counting from where I am. Well — I presume there's more to be hoped for from yours than from the one that immediately preceded you."

Nicholas' eyes strayed in Bobby's direction, and he continued, "There's a youngster, for example, preparing to be a doctor. His father, at his age, was an amateur deer slayer. When Cliff heard about the hog-dressing episode, he was considerably excited. I said, 'But, Clif, I heard you bragging about skinning and curing a buck.' 'Oh, well,' he said, 'that was quite a different matter.' . . . And — I 'spect it was," he added generously, after a pause.

"Our family" — there was a trace of cynicism in Masterson's tone — "has been curiously undisturbed by the problems incident to the accumulation of large fortune. My father is the editor of a small town paper in Indiana. His father was a country doctor, his grandfather a Methodist circuit rider. All the trouble that money has ever given us has been how to get enough of it to pay our bills. . . . But, so far as Bobby is concerned, he isn't running true to type, at all. . . . He's a biological — or, should one say — a fiscal sport?"

Nicholas was meditative.

" Well, yes — Bobby's case is, as you say, somewhat unusual."

Masterson's corrugated brow signed that he was tuning his kettledrums to this key and would presently be holding forth again unless promptly checked.

" Let's not bother to diagnose my case," protested Bobby, with an amicable growl. " Besides, I haven't done anything yet. And this is no time for serious talk. . . . Grandpère — how about telling Tommy the story of the time you and Mr. Anderson bet on which one of you could mow the most hay in an hour."

Masterson furtively glanced at his watch and was caught at it by old Nicholas who immediately pushed back his chair, ignoring Bobby's suggestion, and led the way toward the big drawing-room where he paused to toy with the music on the piano desk.

" What's this ' Unfinished Symphony,' Bobby? . . . Mind playing it for us? "

" Not much in a mood for that one, Grandpère. . . . Too stuffed. We need something a bit livelier."

" How about this one — ' Neapolitan Nights '? "

" Pretty good; but it's rather soft and sticky too for a holiday celebration."

" Something with a lot of bang to it then," said Nicholas, sinking with a satified sigh into a deep chair.

Masterson edged up to Bobby and muttered, under his breath, " I say, do you think your grandfather would take it nicely if I ran along? I've promised to look in, later, at Gordon's. There's a special little party on there tonight . . . a Revue. . . . Wouldn't care to come along, would you? "

" Who all will be there? "

" Oh — everybody! The old gang . . . that you've snooted so damnably for months! "

Bobby was thoughtful for a moment; then, quite on impulse and greatly to Masterson's surprise, he said, " I believe I will, Tommy. I'd rather like to see the bright lights again, myself. It's been a good while."

Masterson drummed nervously on the top of the piano. Recalling himself suddenly, he said with enthusiasm, " Attaboy, old mole! Let's tell Grandpère and hop. . . . Just make the eight-twenty-five. . . . In at midnight. Right time to be there."

" You weren't taking anybody, were you? "

" Well — yes," Tom admitted hesitantly. " That is, I had a tentative arrangement to pick up Joyce Hudson, around midnight, and drive her out — provided it was quite agreeable I should return from here. But there's no reason why you can't come with us, is there? "

" Not so good! . . . Don't care to horn in. . . . But — I'll run down with you and spend the night at Grandpère's club. . . . Have to be there in the morning, anyway. . . . Perhaps I'll drop in for a look at Gordon's. . . . We'll see."

Old Nicholas was glad enough to have done with both of them. So long as they stayed, he must be mindful of his sacred obligation as host. Late that afternoon he had arrived at a most perplexing situation in *The Tragedy in Stateroom 33*, and was feverish to discover whether the pilot, whom the count had tied up in the closet, would contrive to release himself and warn the American girl before the motor-launch returned with the conspirators.

" Willing you should go? " rumbled Nicholas, as they scampered upstairs, " Great Snakes! "

X

GORDON'S! . . . GORDON'S — THE COLORFUL! . . . Gordon's — the exotic! . . . Gordon's at two-thirty in the morning! . . . Brilliantly lighted, packed to suffocation, strangling in the smoke, sticky with sweat; shrill with gin, begotten of dirty messes in moldy cellars and proudly carried in monogrammed silver flasks; clamorous with the new music but lately imported, duty free, from the head waters of the Congo and brought to triumphant perfection by the highest paid orchestra in the States — fresh from New York where its engagement had been abruptly terminated by a padlock. . . . Gordon's Gardens!

Fiddles squeaked, saxophones squealed, oboes giggled, clarionets wailed, tubas yawped, triangles clanged. . . . " Lament of the Damned," perhaps? . . . Not at all! . . . " I'm Lonesome and Blue for You."

Bobby Merrick, waiting in the rococo lobby for his coat check, listened with the ear of a man from Mars and drew a crooked smile.

His coming had been quite on impulse. Long before the train had reached Detroit, he had made up his mind not to go out to Gordon's. The announcement of his decision had, he observed, eased the constraint that had fallen upon their talk. Tom had brightened, visibly, though making gallant pretense of disappointment.

" I've a book that interests me," explained Bobby. " I'd rather go to the club and read it than mill around with a lot of high school sheiks."

" And then there's your rheumatism, Uncle Dudley! "

sniffed Masterson. " You ought to be careful at your age. . . . Aw — why don't you snap out of it? "

" No — I've graduated from all that stuff. It's the bunk! It's too depressing, Tommy. . . . Everybody pretending! . . . Little chap at the next table poking his fork occasionally into a cold dinner that costs him seventeen dollars for the two of them — half his week's wages. . . . Hopping up with his mouth full to push Mazie around again through the wriggling pack, wishing he had the courage to ask her to marry him, and wondering where he'd dig up three hundred for a sparkler. . . . Mazie wouldn't wear one that cost a nickel less. . . . And that sad wail they dance to; though — God knows — one can't blame Clarence for liking sad music. He's a sad young man. His credit's bad with his papa, and he's been drinking too much Dago mash."

" Had you ever thought of joining the W.C.T.U.? "

" Don't get peevish, Tommy. You run out to Gordon's and give 'em what you got for your last story, and I'll go read my book."

" That must be a damned fine book. What's its name? "

" Oh — it's a treatise by a medical man. You couldn't read it."

" Taking yourself rather seriously, aren't you? "

" Æsculapius is as jealous as Jehovah, my son."

By consent, they had stopped ragging each other, and Bobby was asking interestedly about various members of the set from which his attention had lately been deflected. On mention of Joyce's name, he inquired casually, " Seeing much of her, these days, Tommy? "

Masterson nodded.

" Serious? "

"I wish it might be thought so."

"Upstage with you, is she?"

"Quite! . . . And you damned well know why!"

"Nonsense! I haven't seen her for a whole year!"

"Well, it isn't nonsense . . . not with her. You're very much on her mind, doc."

Bobby repudiated the idea with a gesture.

"Fine girl! . . . Wish you luck, Tommy!"

"Thanks! Go bump yourself off, and maybe I'll have it."

"By the way, Tommy, do you see something of the young Mrs. Hudson occasionally?"

"Of course. . . . Gorgeous. . . . Irreproachable and unapproachable! . . . Goes nowhere. . . . In mourning, you know. . . . Southern old school notions about weeds — and all that. . . . She'll come out of it one of these days and stir up a sensation! . . . Lovely? . . . Gad! . . . Don't know her, do you? Well, then you've never been anywhere and hain't seen nothin'!"

"Bad as that? I'll call sometime and give myself a treat."

"You'd better not. . . . You've hard work to do, and shouldn't be distracted."

The train groaned and ground into the ugliest station between Bombay and the Aurora Borealis, and they parted to hail taxis, promising each other an early meeting.

◇ ◇

Cordially welcomed and comfortably established at the Columbia Club, Bobby slipped out of his clothes and into a dressing-gown to resume his work on the Hudson journal.

It was the beginning of a new chapter which took the reader into the author's confidence more intimately than before, as if, having met the latter halfway by the very act of proceeding with the translation, the legatee of the book was now on new terms of comradeship.

It is important that you should know how serious are the conditions to be met by any man who hopes to increase his own power by way of the technique I pursued under instructions from Randolph.

I must mention them, at this juncture, because it is quite possible these words may be read by some impulsive enthusiast who, eager to avail himself of the large rewards promised, may attempt experiments from which he will receive neither pleasure nor benefit; and, dismayed by failure, find himself worse off in mind than he was before.

Indeed, this was my own experience at first, Randolph having neglected to warn me that certain conditions were imperative to success. I learned them by trial and error.

It must be borne in mind, at the outset, that no amount of altruistic endeavor — no matter how costly — can possibly benefit the donor, if he has in any manner neglected the natural and normal obligations to which he is expected to be sensitive. Not only must he be just before attempting to be generous; he must figure this particular investment of himself as a *higher altruism*, quite other than mere generosity.

Every conceivable responsibility must have had full attention before one goes in search of opportunity to perform secret services to be used for the express purpose of expanding one's personality that it may become receptive of that inexplicable energy which guarantees personal power.

My own life had been set in narrow ways. I had had but small chance to injure or defraud, even had I been of a scheming disposition. There had been a minimum of buying and selling in my program. I had lived mostly under strict supervision — in school, in college and as an interne — with no chance to make many grave or irretrievable blunders.

Once I began to discharge my obligations, however, it was startling to note how considerably I was in the red. For example: I found that there were a good many men, scattered here and there, who had been scratched off my books. Either actually, or to all practical intents, they had been told to go to hell. In some cases, there had been enough provocation to justify my pitching them out of my life, I thought. But, more often than otherwise, they were to be remembered as persons with whom I had sustained some manner of close contact — close enough to make a disruption possible. I discovered that almost without exception the people I had pushed away from me — consigned to hell, if you like — were once intimately associated with me. . . . So far as I was concerned they had gone to hell taking along with them a very considerable part of me!

To lose a friend in whom one had invested something of one's personality was, I discovered, to have lost a certain amount of one's self.

The successful pursuit of the philosophy now before you demands that you restore whatever of your personality has been dissipated, carted off by other people. If any of its essential energy has been scattered, it must be recovered.

The original proposer of this theory, aware of the importance of insuring against such losses, advised that all misunderstandings should be settled on the spot. When an estrangement takes a friend out of your normal contacts with him, he leaves with part of you in his hand. You must gather up these fragments of yourself, by some hook or crook, so that you have at least all of the personality that rightfully belongs to you, before you attempt its larger projection.

In the next place: you may make the mistake of seeking far and wide for opportunities to build yourself into other personalities through their rehabilitation. A happy circumstance kept me from doing that. Strangely enough, the first really important service I was permitted to do, prefatory to experimenting with this mysterious dynamic, was for the daughter of the man who had shown me the way to it. . . . I risked what small repute I had, and put a mortgage on whatever I might hope to acquire, by the performance of an operation that saved her life, and, quite incidentally, brought me three pages of comment in the next edition of the *Medical Encyclopedia.*

Bobby left his papers as they were, dressed carefully, called a taxi, and proceeded to Gordon's. He had no one definite answer to give to himself for his sudden decision. If queried, he would have had to say that there came a moment when he felt he was needed at Gordon's. Certainly he was not going in quest of pleasure.

His arrival at the famous cabaret could not have been better timed. An hour earlier he would have found a noisy, chaffing welcome at a table of silly and excited friends hopeful of seeing him as drunk as themselves; half resentful of his appearance sober.

Because it was a festival night, the cabaret's bill of amusements was more elaborate than usual.

The girl chorus, obviously much the worse for the holiday hospitality — during intermissions they were accorded many courtesies at the tables of diners — were softly caterwauling the refrain of a popular opera song, while a huge fellow, open-shirted, velvet-trousered and bandanna-ed in a bandit rôle, held the spot-light with a solo dance.

Aleppo was the headliner on the bill. Primarily an acrobat and strong man, with fancy dancing and a bit of florid song to supplement his feats of agility and strength, Aleppo's versatility was acknowledged with tumultuous applause. Smug satisfaction and self-assurance were spelled in every line of his swarthy face as he executed his intricate dance steps.

Bobby waited, just inside the entrance, until the number should be finished. He was too far from the stage to hear Aleppo's announcement. Some time afterward, he learned that the cad had called for a volunteer dancing partner from the audience. A tall blonde, in blue chiffon, was unsteadily mounting the steps to the stage. She lurched into the big dancer's arms, and he swung her into rhythm with him in a fast and furious fox-trot. The girl was Joyce Hudson.

The crowd cheered them lustily. The orchestra took fresh interest. The chorus receded to give them room.

Eager to offer a final thrill to his audience, the huge Aleppo lifted his amateur team-mate to his shoulder. No one but an experienced acrobat could have met the situation gracefully. Aleppo continued to spin about the stage with light steps. His burden meant nothing to him. Dizzily drunk, Joyce swayed, clutched at Aleppo's shaggy head for support, and sank back limply over his shoulder, while he, with big, muscled arms encircling her knees, revolved like a top, quite as if the act had been rehearsed, and he need have no concern about his partner's safety. Joyce's hair stood straight from her head and her arms wildly groped as the rapid revolutions of the dancer whirled her through the air.

Bobby could not remember later how he arrived at the stage. There was some ruthless elbowing through the crowd, chairs upset, tables pushed aside, as he made his way. He ran up the steps and confronting the dancer with an outstretched arm commanded him to stop. His face was grim and pale. With an ironical smile, Aleppo eluded the intruder, and Bobby rushed him. Pandemonium broke loose among the tables, and the diners jostled about the foot of the stage.

Tom Masterson forced his way through the crowd, climbed the steps, and clutched at Bobby's sleeve.

" What the hell's the matter with you? " he screamed. " If Joyce wants to have a bit of fun with this fellow, what business is it of yours? "

The orchestra had stopped now. Aleppo put Joyce down, and she crumpled on the floor. Several girls from the chorus bent over her, and one ran for water.

With a pugilistic swagger, Aleppo strode forward. His beady little eyes flashed dangerously. His pugnacious jaw seemed coming along somewhat in advance of him. His big fists were clenched. Baring his teeth in a crooked grin, he snarled: " Now! — You're so damned anxious to get into trouble — "

" Look out! " shouted Masterson, " Don't do that! "

" Sock him! " yelled some youngster from the crowd.

Aleppo advanced belligerently until he was within reach of a surprise.

There were three quick, crunching blows in his face, a right to his left eye, a left to his right eye, and a right to the point of his chin. The big fellow's knees buckled under him, and he collapsed without a sigh.

It was very quiet at Gordon's for a moment. Everybody was stunned by the sudden turn of events.

Roughly pushing Masterson aside, Bobby turned to Joyce, stooped and gathered her up in his arms, and started down the steps of the stage, the crowd falling back to make way for him.

"Just a minute!" shouted Masterson, pursuing him. "I'll take care of her. You needn't be so officious!"

Bobby turned toward him, and said in a low voice, "You should have taken care of her a little sooner!"

Masterson was in a drunken rage over his humiliation.

"Well — if you think you can get away with that — "

He clutched Bobby's throat, ripping off his collar; clawed at his hair; his cuff-link dug deeply into his friend's cheek, and the blood flowed freely, dripping from his jaw to his shirt bosom.

Supporting his limp charge with his left arm, Bobby let loose a short-arm jab at the pit of Masterson's none too able stomach, which demoted him to the ranks of the noncombatants, and, taking Joyce again in his arms, marched forward, pushing chairs and tables out of his way with their bodies.

At the door, the burly head waiter barred his progress.

"Did you bring this young lady here?"

"No! But I am taking her away!"

"Well — not so fast! Let's look into this!"

Again Bobby lowered Joyce's feet to the floor, steadied her with his left arm, and growled, "Open that door! I have no intention of mixing it with anybody else here to-night, but if you try to stop me I'll put you to sleep along-side your little friend up there."

The bruiser hesitated. Someone shouted, "Let him go, before the joint gets pinched! He'll see her home! Here — take her coat!"

◇ ◇

The crisp blast of cold air swept Joyce back to partial consciousness.

A waiting taxi drove up under the porte-cochère. Bobby

lifted her in, told the grinning driver to head east on the boulevard and he'd let him know presently where they wanted to go, and seated himself beside her.

Confusedly she recognized him, looked up dully into his face and mumbled thickly, " Oh, Bobby, you came at last, didn't you? I've waited so long! I've wanted you so! "

She nestled her head against his shoulder, and he put his arm around her, spared the necessity of replying, for her revival was brief. In a moment she slumped and slept.

Now he'd got her, what should he do with her? It occurred to him he might take her some place and sober her up before presenting her at home, an idea he instantly rejected. She wouldn't be even approximately normal for hours. Joyce was drunk, and no mistake! . . . Had he really done her a good turn with his swashbuckling excursion into her affairs? Perhaps it would result in more damaging notoriety for her than had she been left to go her own gait. . . . Could he and Tom Masterson ever be friends again? . . . Doubtful.

The driver turned his head for definite instructions, and Bobby gave Joyce's address. He'd have to take her home. Maybe he could put her into the house without stirring it up. He shook her awake as they neared her corner.

" Joyce! Where is your house-key? "

She began to fumble with her coat, and, acting on the clue, he discovered it in an inside pocket. The taxi drew up at the curb and the driver obeyed his fare's order to shut off the engine and wait.

Rousing, as the cold air rushed in through the opened door, Joyce twined her arms about Bobby's neck and kissed him on the cheek. He was bleeding, but she was too far gone to notice.

It was easier to carry than drag her. The front door was quickly reached, opened and closed quietly. He remembered the appointments of the house. Depositing her on the davenport in the living-room, he drew off her slippers and covered her with a heavy steamer rug. Her face was bloody. That would undoubtedly call for explanations which would drag out the whole story, adding even more discredit to her plight and more chagrin to someone else whose dignity better deserved protection.

Presuming there must be a lavatory on the main floor, he looked about for it, and having made experimental forays into two coat closets, finally discovered the little wash room off the library; dampened a towel, and was on his way back with it when he heard a throaty voice that had never quite left his consciousness. It so completely bridged the weeks that it seemed to take on exactly where it had left off, "Good-night, then — and thank you so much!" —— "Joyce, you've been hurt!"

There was no reply . . . and a moment's silence. Doubtless she was noticing the light in the library. Perhaps she had observed his coat, tossed across a chair. He decided not to be caught in ambush. . . . They met at the door.

She seemed not quite so tall as he had remembered her, possibly because the little red and black slippers had lower heels. The disarray of her bobbed head, her tousled bangs, made her look like a child suddenly roused from sleep, to which juvenile effect her suit of Japanese pajamas contributed — black with red poppies, buttoned high about her throat. Bobby was aware of the exquisiteness of her ensemble, but all that he saw distinctly was her bewildered blue eyes searching his with mystification.

On sight of him, she gasped with surprise; put the back

of her hand to her lips as if warding off a blow; stared inquiringly at his blood-smeared cheek.

"Why — it's *you!*" she whispered. "Whatever are you doing here?"

"I brought Joyce home. . . . I'm sorry I startled you. . . . I'd rather hoped we might not have to disturb you."

"But I thought she was going away with Mr. Masterson. Was he hurt? You've been, I see! Was there an accident?"

"Something like that. . . . Nothing serious at all. . . . And Joyce isn't hurt. She's just — just pretty tired and sleepy."

"Her face is bloody. . . . You were going to do something about it, I notice."

He handed her the towel.

"You'll find she's not hurt. That blood she rubbed off of me when I brought her in. I thought I would wash it off so you wouldn't be alarmed when you saw her."

For a long moment they stood gazing, appraisingly, into each other's eyes — hers wide with curiosity, hurt with disappointment, but half sympathetic; his, eloquent with appeal for suspended judgment; both of them at a loss for words to meet their predicament; unable to release themselves from this speechless recognition of their brief comradeship's claims.

"So — you knew you were coming to my house, then . . . Perhaps you'll tell me who you are. . . . You didn' say — that other time."

Into Helen's eyes, and, an instant afterward, upon her lips, there came the suggestion of a smile. Bobby hesitated: then blurted out, "Merrick."

"So you're Bobby Merrick!" Her eyes narrowed. She dug her little fists into her ribs with a defiance that would have seemed deliciously absurd had the occasion been less serious; for she had not been naturally cast for tragic rôles and her costume was everything but militant. "You hadn't brought us enough trouble, had you? What we'd been through wasn't quite sufficient! You must add a little humiliation to it! You've brought Joyce home to me drunk! You look as if you had been drinking, too! . . . Fighting, weren't you? . . . If you could only see yourself! . . . Oh!"

"Yes — I know. I'm not very pretty to look at — and the evidence isn't good. Joyce will tell you all about it in the morning. . . . Meant it all right. . . . Sorry."

"You'd better go now."

He caught up his top-coat.

"It's too bad!" he muttered, half to himself, as he passed her.

As if he were already out of the house, Helen sank down on the davenport at Joyce's feet, put both hands over her face and cried like a little child threatened with punishment. It was a devastating scene. She seemed so pitiably alone, so desperately in need of a friendly word.

With arrested step, Bobby regarded her with a deeper compassion than he had ever experienced, swept again with that strange sense of their belonging. He turned and took a hesitating step toward her. Suddenly aware of him and divining his thought, she slowly shook her head.

"No. . . . There's nothing you can do for us . . . but go!"

His voice was torn with pity.

"I can't leave you this way. . . . Am I to remember you — always — sitting in a crumpled little heap — crying because I had hurt you?" He bent over her with extended hand. "Say good-night to me, won't you?"

Her eyes traveled up to his face.

"You're still bleeding," she said dully. "Better do something. . . . Go in there and wash it off."

Tossing aside his coat, Bobby returned to the little lavatory, disinterestedly mopped at his stains and flung down the towel, bitterly. . . . She was waiting in the open doorway when he turned; leaning limply back against the door-post, face upturned, eyes closed, with a roll of surgical bandage, adhesive tape, and scissors in her hands.

"You're mighty thoughtful." He reached for the dressings.

"Not at all," she said evenly, ignoring his gesture. "I'd do as much for a hurt dog. . . . I was too upset to notice that you really needed attention. . . . Come over here to the light. I'll try to fix you."

He followed her to the table. With deft fingers she shaped a gauze pad, sheared off some strips of tape, and gave her attention to his torn cheek with all the impersonal interest of a veteran nurse in a charity clinic. . . . The sleeves of her jacket slipped back as she reached up. . . . The touch of her hands on his face, the warm nearness of her, the little tremulous catch in her throat when she breathed, set his heart racing furiously.

"There!" she said at length, lifting the longest lashes he had ever seen, and looking inquiringly into his eyes, "Does that feel better?"

Hours afterward, when her tempest of indignation had subsided through sheer fatigue, her self-reproaches began to eclipse the scorn she felt for him.

Exquisitely tortured, she had lived it over and over again,

each second of it — for it had all happened swiftly — as one who follows the minutia of motion on a slow film.

Perhaps, had she turned away at once, he might have stammered his appreciation and left. . . . How indiscreet of her to have looked up, at close range, to inquire, with honest solicitude, " Does that feel better? "

It felt so much better, apparently, that he must express his thanks by taking her hand, as it was withdrawn from his face, lifting it quickly to his lips. She jerked it away from him angrily. . . . Later, as she thought it over in her chaos of angry shame, she reflected it would have been better had she submitted dignifiedly to his impulsive gesture of gratitude . . . and signed him to be off.

He stood humiliated, abased, as if she had struck him a blow. Then, huskily, measuring his words, he said, " I wonder if you would have done *that* to a hurt dog, grateful for a little unexpected kindness."

What a slyly mean advantage to have taken of her sympathy — of her instinctive courtesy!

" That was awfully rude of me. . . . I've been through a lot, tonight. . . . I'm not quite myself. . . . Please go — now."

She should have commanded; not entreated.

" I know you have been cruelly troubled . . . and it nearly breaks my heart! " he had said.

As she milled it over, with her flushed face buried deep in her pillow, she tried to explain how it all happened. For an instant, when he had put his arms gently about her, she forgot that he was Bobby Merrick. Bobby Merrick was just some mythical person she didn't want to know. She remembered only that this was the quiet, pensive, lovable chap who had led her like a little child along a dark country lane. . . . And she was so desolately lonely and in need of tenderness.

He softly touched her wet eyes with his handkerchief. . . . How could she have stood there, calmly submitting to his impudent attentions? . . . What had she been thinking of to allow herself to be placed in such an impossible predicament? What a beast he had been to make capital of her yearning for a bit of human kindness . . . at a moment when, he knew, her whole world was breaking up under her feet! . . . Well, he surely was made aware, before he left, what she thought of his despicable treatment of her! . . . Hadn't she told him, so bitterly, so scathingly, that he had cringed under it? . . . But — that was small balm for her injured pride. . . . She had actually stood with her forehead pressed against his arm, while his slim fingers caressed her hair, utterly unable to exert her will . . . dreamily visioning a thin trickle of fine sand pouring into a small red-brown heap at the bottom of an hour-glass . . . and wondering how to shut it off. . . . Why — she must have been hypnotized!

"Won't you forgive me — now?" he whispered.

Why couldn't she have freed herself, smiled; agreed — in a matter-of-fact tone, "I'll not hold anything against you. Good-night." . . . She repeated into her pillow several variants of that commonplace, devoutly wishing she could remember having said it; trying to persuade herself she really had.

But he had pleaded so wistfully! . . . She had lifted her eyes, and her lips were parted to speak a single word of friendly assurance when — it happened. . . . And she had offered no resistance! . . . Oh — how cheap he must think her! How little respect he had had for her — widowed because of him — and, worst of all, he would probably be cad enough to imagine that she had responded to his kiss. . . . It was the haunting fear he might think she had shared it that tortured her most.

Of course — she had done what she could, quickly, savagely, to reinstate herself in his regard. Breaking free, she had pushed him from her; forbade him ever to speak to her again; left the room in a grand state of emotional tumult without so much as pausing to glance at the stupified Joyce, heavily sleeping through a scene that could not have failed to interest her, had she been aware of it.

Seated before her mirror at nine, gazing remorsefully at her haggard reflection, she straightened, stiffly, and said aloud, "Well, whatever he may care to think, I'm certain I didn't."

◇ ◇

Sleepy servants at the Columbia Club grinned and exchanged winks when Bobby arrived at a quarter of four, sullen and disheveled.

"Teddy," he growled to the elevator boy, "bring me a bottle of Scotch and a siphon of soda."

He disrobed, mixed a stiff drink, and another, and a third, in swift succession, scowled hatefully at himself in the bathroom mirror and muttered "Piker!" . . . He had forfeited the thing he most wanted — the only thing he wanted in this world! . . . Now she would never consent to see him again. . . . She had said it, and she meant it. He had imposed upon her kindness; had stampeded her into an impetuous response to his sympathy which she would regret with self-loathing. . . . What was the good of anything — now?

The Hudson journal lay on the desk where he had left it; a sheaf of club stationery beside it, scrawled with rows of letters.

He gave the book a contemptuous push with the back of his hand and it fell into the wastebasket.

"Damned silly nonsense!" he muttered. "To hell with all that kind of blah!"

XI

"PLEASE BE SEATED, MR. MERRICK," THE SECRETARY HAD said, stiffly, twenty minutes ago. "Dean Whitley is busy now."

A qualitative analysis of Mr. Merrick's scowl as he sat fidgeting would have resolved it into two parts curiosity, three parts anxiety and the remainder annoyance. . . . Of chagrin — a trace.

The note had said eleven, and he had entered while the clock was striking. It had not specified what the dean wished to see him about. That would have been too much to expect. Courtesy and consideration were against the rules governing the official action of deans.

Big universities, like monopolistic public utilities and internal revenue offices, enjoyed high-hatting their constituencies; liked to make an impressive swank with their authority; liked to keep people waiting, guessing, worrying; liked to put 'em to all the bother possible.

Mr. Merrick glowered. He glowered first at the large photograph of an autopsy suspended above the secretary's desk in the corner. . . . Seven doctors owling it over a corpse. All of the doctors were paunchy, their pendulous chins giving them the appearance of a covey of white pelicans. They were baggy under the eyes . . . a lot of fat ghosts swathed in shrouds. The corpse too was fat. Why conduct a post over this bird? Any layman could see at a glance what had ailed him — he was a glutton. Let these wiseacres take warning in the presence of this plump cadaver, and go on a diet of curds and spinach before some committee put them on a stone slab and rummaged in their cold capacious bellies to enhance the glory of *materia medica*. . . . They were the bunk — the whole greasy lot of them!

Having temporarily finished with the autopsy, Dean Whitley's impatient customer glowered over the titles of the big books in the case hard by. . . . Simpson's *Nervous Diseases* . . . the old sap. You had to read his blather in front of a dictionary; weren't ten words in the whole fourteen pounds of wood-pulp with less than seven syllables. . . . Mount's *Obsessions*. . . . Why was it that these bozos thought it unscholarly to be intelligible and undignified to be interesting? And as for obsessions, old Mount was a nut himself — one of these cuckoos that tapped every third telegraph pole with his cane and spat on fireplugs. . . . If he missed one, he had to go back, it was said. . . . About the same mentality as Fido's. Well, Mount ought to be an authority on obsessions!

A tall, rangy medic came out of the dean's sanctum, very red but with a jaunty stride, crossed the room in four steps and banged the door. . . . Bet it was no new experience for that door!

Distracted from his invoice of the book shelf, Mr. Merrick glowered at the bony maiden who rattled the typewriter. Smug and surly she was; mouth all screwed up into an ugly little rosette, lashless eyes snapping, sharp nose sniffing. . . . Easy to see what she was doing — writing a letter to some poor boob inviting him to come in at nine and see the dean. . . . She ought to add a postscript that he would be expected to spend half of a fine June morning in this dismal hole waiting for his nibs to finish the *Free Press* and his nails, take his legs off the table, and push a buzzer to let the beggar in.

"Dean Whitley will see you now, Mr. Merrick."

◇ ◇

"Mr. Merrick," said Dean Whitley, after Bobby had taken the chair recommended to him, "I must have a friendly chat with you. During the first few weeks of last semester, you gave promise, I am informed, of an exceptionally interesting career in the medical profession. Shortly after the mid-semester examinations, which I see you passed with the highest marks of your class, you began to slip. You quickly used up all your cuts. You became disinterested and disgruntled. What's the trouble?"

"I think you'll find I've been doing average work, sir."

Dean Whitley shook a long, bony finger.

"Exactly! Average work! Do you hanker to be an average doctor?"

"Well — when you put it that way — of course not."

The dean tilted back in his swivel-chair and clasped his hands behind his head.

"Your case is somewhat unusual, Merrick. You are the heir apparent to a large fortune. You did not have to seek a vocation. It was a surprise to all your friends that you came here. Your line of least resistance was polo. But you plunged into your work with an enthusiasm that put the whole first-year class on its toes and challenged the instructional corps to offer the best it had. Now — precisely what has happened to your spirit? Is there anything we can do to put you in the running again?"

Bobby twisted the links of a platinum watch-chain, head hanging.

"You're quite right, Dean Whitley. I suppose it was the novelty kept me alive at first."

"Yes — but see here!" The dean reversed a sheaf of

tabulations and pushed it across the table. "Just follow that line from opening day to the Thanksgiving recess, and there isn't a cut! You didn't flick a class! . . . Pursue it the rest of the way and see what you did to your scholastic credit! . . . What happened to you on or about Thanksgiving? . . . Perhaps you should be treated for it — whatever it was. You're too promising to lose if we can save you!"

"I just got tired of it. Too much drudgery."

"It wasn't drudgery before!"

"Well — I think I began to notice that it was, about that time."

"Ever think of giving it up?"

"Oh — no, sir! I can't do that!"

"Why not? You don't aspire to be a mere second-rater, do you?"

"I suppose I'll have to content myself with that. I'll have plenty of company, won't I?"

The dean fiddled with a paper-knife and looked down his nose glumly.

"This is very disappointing! . . . Sure you don't want to give me your full confidence and let me try to help you?"

Bobby moved to the edge of his chair, and took up his hat.

"There's nothing you can do, sir. Thank you for your interest. I'll try to do better."

◇ ◇

On the front steps he met Dawson, a first-year medic with whom he had a mere nodding acquaintance. Dawson was a lean-faced, hollow-eyed, shabby chap, who had a desperate time of it trying to keep up. Slightly older than the average, more was expected of him than he was able to deliver. Not infrequently he was scornfully panned by his instructors who seemed to enjoy watching him wince under their satirical jabs.

A question, having been muffed by three or four, would be tossed at him in some such fashion as, "And of course *you* wouldn't know, would you, Mr. Dawson?" Seven times out of nine, he wouldn't. Bobby's sympathy had been excited, occasionally. . . . What were they trying to do to the poor devil? . . . Drive him into the river?

"Hello, Merrick! . . . Been deaning?"

"Oh yes," said Bobby brightly. "But not in the way you probably suspect. You see, the dean and I meet frequently for a game of cribbage. He's good too. I presume you're having tea with him presently?"

Dawson was grim.

"Naw — I'm going in to tell him I'm through and that they can all go to hell!"

"That would be a great blunder, Dawson." Bobby became owlishly didactic. "They might go — and where would that leave you? You see, my son, every time you send a man to hell, with whom you have had close personal contacts, he takes part of you along with him. And then, some fine day, when things are ever so much better with you, and you need to collect all there is of your scattered personality for some noble purpose, a considerable chunk of you is missing — and — and you have to go to hell after it."

"What's the big idea? Trying to kid me? If so, don't! I'm in no mood for it. . . . Up to the last ditch — if you don't mind my weepin' on your neck!"

"How about a bite of lunch together?" suggested Bobby, amazed at his own proposal of hospitality to this morose, threadbare fellow. "All you're seeing him for is to tell him to go to hell. Put it off till tomorrow. He won't object to the delay."

Yielding with a crooked smile to Bobby's persuasion, Dawson fell into step.

"Anything you'd like to get off your chest?" inquired his host, after their order had been given. "Perhaps you'd enjoy singing a few verses of your hymn of hate. If so, go to it — and I'll join you in the chorus where the fancy damning comes in."

"Thanks, Merrick. You're a good sort. Perhaps it wouldn't be bad for me to let off steam. I'll tell you a little about it. . . . I always wanted to be a surgeon . . . prattled about it as a child . . . never thought of anything else . . . thought of it as a novitiate in holy orders thinks of his vocation! . . . After college, I was out for three years trying to scrape up enough to bring me back. . . . Got discouraged; gave it up; fell in love; married. The girl revived the old hope in me. . . . Worked like dogs — both of us; she in an office, I selling bonds. . . . So we came, last September. . . . She found a job. . . . Then the baby came . . . lot of expenses. Living was higher than we figured. . . . I began to work down town nights in a bowling-alley . . . setting pins for freshmen to knock down one at a time. . . . How's that for your inferiority complex?"

"Well, it certainly wouldn't drive a man into a state of hallucinatory omnipotence; that's sure!"

"A woolly caterpillar! . . . That's what it made of me! . . . No wonder I was a dunce! . . . And now — as if I hadn't already enough to . . . But — hell — what's the good of talking about it?"

"Drive on!" commanded Bobby. "It's no farther through to the other side than to back out. Let's have the rest of it. You were a caterpillar and a dunce — and now you're something else again? . . . What's happened lately?"

"My wife is sick. No — nothing acute. Just fagged and undernourished and neurotic; says she's a dead weight on me and wishes she were dead. She's brooding over it. I'm half afraid to go home for fear I'll find that she has destroyed herself!"

"She should be out in the country for the summer," advised Bobby. "Fresh air, good milk, sunshine."

"Might as well suggest a trip to Europe," muttered Dawson. "We've nothing."

"Hasn't she people she could go to for the summer?"

"Nobody. . . . There's a tight old step-father who threw her out when she married me. He'd picked a yokel for her who lived in the neighborhood. . . . My mother is a widow, living with my sister, up state. They're poor too and crowded."

"How about a little loan? You're not always going to be on your uppers. Almost anybody would consider that a safe investment, I should think."

"I don't know any one I could approach with a proposition like that."

Bobby's guest ate hungrily. His hand trembled when he cut his meat.

"I have a little money that isn't in use just now."

Dawson shook his head.

"No! — By God, I didn't tell you my story with the hope of panhandling some money out of you. You're probably like all the rest of the medics — just scraping along. . . .

Thanks all the same, old man. . . . It's mighty generous of you. . . . No — I'm going to give it up and get a job!"

"You didn't understand me, Dawson. I didn't mean to propose handing you the price of next week's groceries. I'd like to lend you, say, five thousand dollars."

Here was one chap that had accepted him as a pal in poverty. . . . Natural enough, though. Dawson had had his nose to the grindstone; kept aloof from the others. He needn't have heard that there was a wealthy student in the class. . . . And this interview had not been of his seeking.

"You mean that?"

"Of course! . . . You didn't think I'd joke with you about a business matter involving five thousand dollars, did you?"

Bobby would never have suspected the fellow of so much sparkle and spontaneous wit. He expanded as if some miracle had been performed on him.

"Merrick," he said solemnly, as they reached the street. "You've come near saving a couple of lives today! . . . Mind if I run home now? . . . I've got to tell her! . . . I say — wouldn't you like to come along?"

◇ ◇

They were a shabby pair of rooms on the third floor of a third-rate apartment house over north of the big hospital, disorderly with the clutter incident to an attempt to make a bed-room, dining-room, nursery and kitchen of such cramped quarters.

Marion Dawson had no apologies to offer for the appearance of her house. Bobby liked her for that. He was instantly delighted with this pale, tawny-haired, hazel-eyed young woman who gave him a man's hand-grip and unloaded a chair for him without a flurry of embarrassment. The baby was dug up for inspection and greeted the visitor with big, blinking eyes, amusingly like his father's. Having had no experience with babies, Bobby regarded this one with something of the same solemn interest it bestowed on him. Marion laughed.

" You can't get acquainted with him that way," she exclaimed. " You've got to boo at him, or something! He expects it, you know. He wouldn't think of making a little ass of himself by booing at you; but he'll be dreadfully disappointed if you don't make some idiotic noises at him."

Bobby knew he was going to like this girl.

" Marion," said Dawson, with an unsteady voice, " Mr. Merrick is going to lend us some money. He says we're a good risk. I'm not sure about me; but I know you are."

She dropped her air of banter and stared at their guest for a long moment, trying to realize the significance of her husband's announcement; then said, with deep feeling, " So — after all we've been through — Jack is to have his chance, at last! " She put a hand on his shoulder. " Dear boy! . . . It has been so long — so hard for you! "

She reached out her left hand to Bobby and clasped his with grateful fingers. " What a lovely thing for you to do! " she said.

" Oh — everybody has his troubles," stammered Bobby, hoping the situation would be spared a debauch of sentimentality. " The least trouble in the world is a shortage of money."

" Unless one hasn't any," chuckled Dawson.

◇ ◇

Bobby arrived late in the little amphitheatre of the surgical clinic, that afternoon. The operation proved of exceptional interest. He found himself leaning far forward. That night, he almost enjoyed his Brill. Before he went to bed at one, he wrote to Nancy Ashford, to whom he had owed a letter for weeks.

"I had a very interesting visit today with a young medic and his wife — the Dawsons —" his second page began; but, after looking at the words critically for a moment, he crumpled the page and started a fresh one with no mention of the Dawsons.

"Have you ever deciphered the rest of the journal?"

He had sent it back to her with the brief statement that he didn't care to bother any farther with it. . . . He wasn't the right type to pursue any such philosophy with hope of pleasure or profit, he said, and it really wasn't sporting to read it for curiosity's sake — especially after Doctor Hudson's request that one stop when one's personal interest had flagged.

"Perhaps you will tell me, at least in a general way, how it all came out if you completed it. . . . I learn, in reading about unusual obsessions, that a marked mystical tendency occasionally shows up in the minds of very materialistic people who deal practically, otherwise, with all their interests. I dare say Doctor Hudson was a typical case."

Two days later he had her reply.

"Mrs. Hudson has the journal now, along with all the other things we kept for her in the office safe. I doubt if she has made any effort to discover what it's about. Perhaps she hasn't opened the box in which she received them. At all events, she has not queried me, as she might have done if she had been mystified by the code. . . . I feel confident she would let you have the book, now that your interest in it is revived.

"Yes, I deciphered the rest of it. . . . An amazing record! . . . If it were done into a book, it would sell a hundred thousand! People would pronounce it utterly incredible, of course; but they would read it — and heartily wish it were true. And I have a notion they would be sneaking off to make experiments, no matter how they might have giggled when discussing the theory with their friends.

"I wish I dared tell you . . . you know why I cannot . . . about the quite startling experiences I myself have had lately. . . . It's all true, Bobby. You do get what you want that way, if what you want contributes to the larger expression of yourself in constructive service. . . . You even get letters that had been so long delayed you wondered if you'd been forgotten. . . . Does that sound foolish?"

It sounded foolish.

"I'm sorry," mused Bobby, folding the letter. "Nancy had such an interesting mind. Now she'll be goofy for the rest of her life. . . . Glad I stopped the bally nonsense before it got me."

He smiled bitterly over Nancy's suggestion that he ask Mrs. Hudson for the journal. . . . His contrite note of apology, dated December first, had not been answered. For the first two weeks, he had shadowed the postman.

◇

On the Sunday morning that young Mrs. Dawson and the baby were taken to the country, Bobby, on pressing invitation, joined the party.

The place they had chosen was a quiet cottage owned

by a middle-aged widow, a few hundred yards from the shady shore of Pleasant Lake — an hour's railroad trip to the north.

Relieved of his long anxiety, Jack Dawson had lost his pallor. His step was elastic; his shoulders were squared. As for Marion, she was radiant.

They made a picnic of it, and ate their lunch on the lake shore — Jack, junior, left in the custody of Mrs. Plimpton who, immediately on being alone with him, decided he would be all the better for a bit of old-fashioned rocking and a few Gospel songs.

" Now — none o' that! " declared Marion, setting out the contents of their basket. " You two old doctors have plenty of chances to talk wisely about disabled gizzards, all through the week. It makes me sick to eat my meals off the operating-table, anyway."

Apparently they had known nothing of Bobby's wealth before he had interested himself in them. Doubtless they knew now. But the Dawsons' attitude toward him was unchanged. There was not a trace of shyness or sycophancy. Thoroughbreds — they were. He wished he had a sister exactly like Marion Dawson.

The men took a late afternoon train back to town, separating at the station.

" So long, Bobby," said Dawson. " Thanks much for coming along. See you soon. Glad the stuff's going better for you. You've certainly given me a shot in the arm! "

" It's been good for both of us," said Bobby.

◇ ◇

That night he carried out a decision he had resolved upon the day before. Randolph had seemed able to get all the information he wanted from a certain important page of the Galilean report on the one man who apparently knew the principles imperative to an expanded personality. Bobby considered himself entirely capable of pursuing such research as Randolph had made.

He had never owned a copy of the Bible. Yesterday he had bought a testament. The salesman had laid out quite an assortment. Bobby had chosen a copy that looked more like an ordinary secular book than the black ones with limp leather covers. His choice was based upon his expectation of treating it as he would any other book.

He leafed in it, back and forth, for a long time before he came upon the particular thesis which the sculptor had considered important to a man's quest of a dynamic personality. He read it with as much intensity of concentration as he might have studied the map of a strange country through which he expected to travel.

There was a certain quaintness of phrase that intrigued him and commanded his interest. On and on he read, far into the night, without weariness. The little book amazed him. When and if he had thought about it at all, he had considered this ancient document a jumble of soporific platitudes, floating about in a solution of Jewish superstitions, and accepted by simple-minded people as a general cure-all for their petty anxieties and a numbing narcotic to dull their sense of wanting what they couldn't have.

It was rapidly becoming apparent to him that here was one of the most fascinatingly interesting things he had ever read. Not only was it free of the dullness he had ascribed to it; it kept hinting of secrets — secrets of a tremendous energy to be tapped by any man with sense enough to accept the fact of it as he would any other scientific hypothesis, and accord it the same dignity, the same practical tests he might pursue in a chemical or physical laboratory.

It was astounding to feel that he had in his hand the actual textbook of a science relating to the expansion and development of the human personality. How queer that people seemed bent upon setting it to music, and drawing long faces while they piously intoned it! How ridiculous! And how unfortunate! This wasn't the libretto for grand opera, or epic stuff to meter into maudlin little hymns! This was a profound, scientific thesis! The very act of chanting it would be proof you didn't know what it was about!

One of Merrick's most important discoveries, that night, was the fact that unlike the usual scientific dissertation, which would be accessible only to the trained mind, there was enough of simple counsel in the book to be of high advantage to the least sophisticated. It was not a treatise intended for highbrows. But it was plain to see that the potential constituency of the book was sharply classified into groups. With the utmost candor, the Galilean had postulated three types of general capacity related to one another as 5:2:1. He had been entirely frank about saying to his intimates, in an intensive seminar session, that there were certain mysteries he could and would confide to them which he had no intention of discussing before the general public for the reason that the majority of people would be unable to understand.

He noted, also, with keen interest, the numerous occasions when the Galilean, having performed a service for someone, would ask him, as a special favor, not to tell anybody about it.

" Practicing his own theories, all right! "

It was clear, from the record, that men became interested in this strange, uncanny power by various processes of introduction to it. One man would see the remarkable power and beauty of it in the hands of another, and would resolve to have it for himself if it cost him his last dime. The matter was stated pictorially in a fable concerning a man who saw a pearl in another man's hands and sold everything he had to buy it. It was further stated that occasionally a man came upon this almost incredible thing by sheer accident. There was a story of a traveler who, while taking a short cut across a field, stumbled upon a treasure chest. The book did not say what was in the chest. It just reported that the traveler gave up his journey, went home, converted everything he had into funds, came back, and bought that field.

But nothing struck Bobby more forcibly than the constantly reiterated advice to approach life audaciously. Anything a man really wanted, he could have if he hammered long enough at the doors behind which it was guarded. If he didn't get it, it was because he hadn't wanted it badly enough! No matter how patently futile it was to continue battering the door, any man who wanted anything earnestly enough could open any kind of a door!

" Got to have bloody knuckles," reflected Bobby, " before you can say you tried it and it wouldn't work! "

The fable accompanying this proposition told of a poor widow, with no influence at all, who wanted justice from a rich man. The judge was an utter rascal. The woman had no attorney, no friends, and no case; but she kept coming until she wore the judge out.

He found himself entering more and more confidently into the mood of the man who had proposed these principles of what he called a more abundant life, particularly struck by his poise and audacity.

◇ ◇

At length, he closed the book and closed his eyes. He was not conscious of formulating a definite request. Had anybody told him he was praying, he would have been greatly surprised. He was endeavoring to construct a mental image of the kind of a man who might be likely to have proposed such a philosophy.

The thing that happened to him came quite without further invitation than that.

As he attempted to analyse it, later, the sensation he experienced — the most vivid and vital experience he had ever had — was as if a pair of great double-doors, somewhere at the far end of a dark corridor in his mind — in his heart — in his soul — somewhere inside of him — had quietly parted, shedding a soft, shimmering radiance upon the roof, walls and pavement of the long hall. The walls were covered with maps, charts, diagrams, weapons, and glittering instruments and apparatus in glass cases.

It was only a fleeting glimpse. The doors parted but a very little way. They quickly closed, and left the corridor so dark he could no longer tell where it was.

Rousing, bewilderedly, he became conscious of a curious sense of exultation. Had he been asleep? He did not think so.

He rose and walked unsteadily about the room, trying to recover as much as possible of his momentary illusion.

"Doors! . . . Light behind doors! . . . Light shining through! . . . I wonder if the corridor was always there —

waiting my discovery! . . . Perhaps I can do something to open those doors wider. . . . I must! . . . Well, one thing is sure: I've seen it! It's there! It's real! . . . Maybe I'll never get very far with it — but — it can be done! . . . Randolph wasn't as crazy as I thought!"

◇ ◇

Next morning, as he was starting to the dean's office to arrange for his summer course in the face of old Nicholas' urgent request that he knock off until September and return to Windymere, he received a note from Nancy Ashford.

"Perhaps you've read it in the papers, but I'll make sure, for I know you will be interested. Friday night, Joyce Hudson and Tom Masterson slipped over to Toledo and were married. Mrs. Hudson expects to sail, on Saturday the tenth, for Europe. She just called up to inform me of her plans. . . . Leviathan. . . . I thought you'd want to know."

At intervals, all day, he debated the advisibility of sending flowers to the ship, and decided against it. She would probably consider it an impertinence. No — he had irretrievably cut himself off. . . . All that he had left now was his mounting interest in his work, into which he plunged with renewed enthusiasm.

XII

IT WAS NINE O'CLOCK IN THE MORNING — EARLY September.

The last of the summer trippers had gone, reluctant to leave all this beauty behind them and pledged to a prompt return. . . . With their hands filled with bulky bouquets of garden flowers, graciously bestowed by long-time servants who seemed sincerely regretful over their departure, they had edged along the slippery seats of the station bus to make room for the tardy, scurrying back from one last look at the blue bay from the terrace wall. They would go down the hill to Bellagio, cross the bay to Menaggio, and take a funny little funicular over the mountain en route west — and home.

The Villa Serbelloni was very quiet, this morning. . . . Not that it was at any time a rackety place, even when filled to its small capacity. There was something about the ineffable tranquillity of the old mansion that slowed one down to its leisurely tempo; that mellowed the voice and blurred the vision.

Its atmosphere seemed strangely sedative, giving a curious unreality to the whole region. One felt one's self walking about through a Corot. The changing cloud-shadows on the mountains and the bay, synchronized with warming wisps of autumn breeze, played unaccountable tricks with one's estimates of distances and hours. One never knew certainly whether it was Tuesday or Thursday — or cared.

Somebody had declared it was as if the picture were blurry . . . out of focus. There were no sharp, angular outlines, either to the purple hills or the turquoise lake below. The very pebbles on the carriage drive were unreal, each wrapped with a tiny, shimmering aureole of pale opal. . . . Each grape, in the shapely clusters dependent from the trellis sheltering the breakfast nook, was encircled by an amber nimbus as if glowing with some inner radiance. . . . An excellent place for day-dreaming.

To appreciate it properly however the guest must bring to the little arbor a quiet, unworried mind, else the timeless calm of the place would only accentuate the internal tumult. . . . Unless one were at peace with himself, here, he could be more desperately lonely and depressed than in a desert.

The arbor was all but deserted. Except for the elderly English couple at the last table in the row against the low terraced wall, absorbed in their letters, groping occasionally for the handles of their coffee cups, Helen Hudson had the place to herself. She was so lonesome she watched with comradely concern the antics of an ambitious bee that disputed her right to the little jar of honey.

It might never be determined where was the next to the loveliest spot in the world. . . . La Jolla? . . . Lake Louise? . . . The Columbia River Highway? . . . Royal Gorge? . . . Grand Canyon?

During her three years abroad, Helen had successively shifted her allegiance from the Grand Canal under a full moon to the Upper Corniche Road, the Amalfi Drive, the Neckar glimpsed through the tree-tops from the crumbling balconies of Heidelberg Castle.

But there never could be any doubt about the *loveliest* scene in the world. She faced it — Lake Como — from the little arbor flanking on the east the Villa Serbelloni, on the hillcrest overlooking Bellagio . . . looked at it without seeing it today; for her eyes were preoccupied.

◇ ◇

Her morning mail had practically confirmed certain harassing suspicions. It was reasonably sure now that Monty had been manipulating her estate to her serious disadvantage. How to protect herself against grave misfortune — if indeed that misfortune had not been already guaranteed — without plunging her family into disgraceful publicity, was too intricate a problem to be solved.

Not at any time since her commitment of all her affairs to Monty, upon his renewed persuasion, a year ago, had his remittances been in full of her expectations.

When, in January, he had written that Northwestern Copper was in the midst of a " reorganization " which was temporarily depressing its value and reducing its dividends, she had been disposed — albeit puzzled — to accept his statement as correct. She made no pretense of understanding the explanation he offered with an infinitude of befuddling detail phrased in a jargon utterly incomprehensible. The situation troubled and inconvenienced her, but she had tried to believe what Monty said. There was nobody at hand to query; no one she cared or dared to consult by correspondence. She had made Monty her business agent with full power of attorney. She was in his hands to do with as he pleased. It was most disturbing.

In mid-July, he had written lengthily his deep regret and disappointment that Northwestern Copper was making so slow a recovery; still in a tangle over " reorganization " difficulties, " refinancing " problems, and " the tiresome delays of senseless litigation " — Monty was gifted with an extraordinary capacity for redundant ambiguities. In short, Northwestern Copper had passed its semi-annual period of accounting to its stockholders without declaring any dividend at all. . . . He was sorrier than he could say — but, of course, it wasn't his fault.

Stunned to the realization that she was alone in a foreign country without income or any assurance that it might be restored, she had spent whole days fretting about her next move in this awkward predicament.

It had occurred to her that something might be liquidated of her holdings at Brightwood. She was aware that her inherited stock in the hospital had no market value. It was not at all like ordinary commercial or industrial securities. The income was small and uncertain; the stock itself being worth just what some philanthropic purchaser might be willing to pay for it.

Moreover, there was a sentimental value attached to it in her mind. Under no circumstances, short of actual pressing need, would she have consented to part with it. But, sentiment or no sentiment, she would have to live. Her funds were very low.

After a month of worry, she had written to Nancy Ashford. Rejecting, after some debate, the thought of confiding the exact state of her affairs, she limited her inquiry to the possibility of converting her Brightwood stock into cash at the earliest moment a purchaser could be found. Mrs. Ashford would be surprised and disappointed, doubtless, but she would have to think what she liked about it. The real reason could not be divulged.

" Now — I wonder exactly why she wants to do that? " Nancy had said to Doctor Merrick, upon receipt of it.

"Surely she has enough to live on. . . . The income on her Northwestern Copper can't be a penny less than six thousand a year. . . . Preferred stock . . . sound as Gibraltar. . . . Do you suppose somebody has been defrauding her? She knows so little about business."

"Who's handling her affairs while she is gone?"

"Nobody — so far as I know. . . . There's nothing very complicated about her business. . . . I think she said her brother — her cousin, rather — would assist her in making out her income tax report."

"D'you know anything about him?"

"Not a thing. . . . Might he be handling her money?"

"Unlikely. . . . Why should he? . . . Unless she gave him carte blanche to buy and sell; and she wouldn't do that."

"What shall I say to her, Bobby?"

"How much is her Brightwood stock worth?"

"Conservatively?" Nancy grinned.

"No — optimistically! — a Micawber appraisal!"

"About twenty thousand, I should think. . . . Want it?"

"Yes. . . . You tell her you have contracted to dispose of her Brightwood stuff for — for twenty-five thousand dollars. . . . Tell her the man wishes to pay for it in twenty-five monthly installments. . . . That will insure her against being broke, over there; and meantime . . ."

"Yes? . . . Meantime?"

Doctor Merrick moved toward the door.

"Oh — I don't know — I'm sure. . . . It's her affair."

◇ ◇

Again Helen took up the long letter she had just received from Mrs. Ashford with its life-saving enclosure and the definite promise of more to come. The possession of it filled her with misgivings. She had snapped an important tie connecting her with Doctor Hudson's most cherished interest. It was like closing a door on something he had lived for.

There was no reproach in the letter, either direct or implied. . . . Easy to detect a note of anxiety, however.

"I hope this disposal of your Brightwood stock does not mean that your income from other sources is in any way depleted. . . . Is there anything you would like to have us look after for you?"

Following the briefly clear statement of the deal she had made, and the terms of the sale, Nancy Ashford had served up a potpourri of local news. . . . You wouldn't know Detroit! . . . New clubs, new theatres, swagger hotels, metropolitan shops! . . . Even the hospital was adding a new unit. Plans already drawn.

"Young Doctor Merrick is with us now. Or perhaps you knew that. Of course it is a delight to me to see the rapid progress he is making, for I've always been interested in him. . . . Naturally he has a great advantage over the typical interne because, having known from the first day of his medical course that he was going in for brain surgery, he comes here with more specialized knowledge and experience than any other young doctor who ever joined our organization. . . . Already Doctor Pyle is treating him with a deference that amuses me. (Doctor Pyle is *so* short with the cubs.) . . . Bobby got permission to fit up a little laboratory of his own. There was a small alcove — perhaps you recall — just off the main solarium on the top floor. We had it partitioned. You should see the apparatus he has installed. It's more of a physical than a chemical laboratory,

I think. . . . Glass-blowing! . . . A forge! . . . A blast-furnace! . . . All manner of electrical things! . . . You can't get any information out of him. . . . I was in there yesterday, and asked him if he was making a new radio set, and he said, 'Something like that.' . . . But that doesn't mean much when he says it, except that he wishes you wouldn't bother him.

"Oh — I never had a bigger thrill in my life than at his graduation! I had hoped so much for him, all along. . . . And when it came to the big day . . . with his name starred on the Commencement program (he hadn't said a word to me about his taking second honors!) well, I just sat there and wept silly tears. . . . His mother couldn't come, so I pretended I was his mother. . . . And you should have seen his grandfather! Proud? When the class marched across the platform for their diplomas, dear old Mr. Merrick stood in his seat, trying to wave his handkerchief and blow with it at the same time, until somebody pulled him down by the coattails."

The sheets trembled in Helen's hands as she read.

The last line on that page — it was numbered eight — had been scratched out, but was still legible:

"The young doctor who received — "

The next page had been originally numbered twelve. That had also been ineffectually deleted in favor of nine.

On second thought, Nancy Ashford had omitted a considerable part of her letter.

◇ ◇

"Here's that draft for a thousand," Bobby Merrick had said, as he stood by Nancy's desk.

"Thanks. I've just finished writing to her. I'll get it off today."

"That's good! . . . By the way — you said nothing about the Dawsons, did you?"

"Why — yes. . . . Rather I'd not?"

"Leave it out. . . . I don't think she'd be interested much . . . and — well, I have a reason."

"As you like," said Nancy, hastily extracting the pages on which she had written:

"— first honors is Doctor Merrick's closest friend. . . . Damon and Pythias . . . the kind of a friendship you read about! They worked together throughout their medical course — same specialty. First honors now carry a prize offered by Mr. Owen Simmons (Simmons Turbine Co.) — a year in Vienna, all expenses, scholarship, liberal allowance, etc. . . . The Dawsons were here last Thursday — the day your letter came. She was going to New York to see her husband off.

"Actually, the three of them were like brothers and sister. I couldn't help being jealous. They were closeted here in my office for a whole hour, and when they came out, and I met them in the hall, Mrs. Dawson was all excited. She seemed so happy that I said, 'You look like Christmas morning!' 'Why shouldn't I?' she replied laughing. 'I'm going along!' . . . 'To Europe?' . . . 'Absolutely!'

"They have a dear little boy — going on four. I never saw a child so beautifully trained. Doctor Merrick went along with them to New York and brought little Jack back with him to stay at Windymere until Mrs. Dawson returns. I dare say old Mr. Merrick can be found, at this minute, leading the pony he has bought for him." . . .

◇ ◇

There was a letter from Joyce:

"No, darling, I'm sure you will take no pleasure in thinking or saying 'I told you so.' For that wouldn't be you. . . . Never a day passes that I do not scourge myself for the abominable way I used you that winter when you were trying so hard to step in between me and myself.

"I wasn't fair to anybody through those days. Not even to poor Bobby. I never told you the straight of that. I meant to; but, you see, I telephoned to him the next morning and asked him to come and see me. I'd a hazy notion that he was — well — kind to me the night before, and I thought he might renew our friendship. He made some excuse. I was hurt and humiliated. I knew something had happened to cause an estrangement between you and Bobby, for — can you forgive me, darling? — I noticed a letter you had from him shortly afterward, and peeked into it. He wanted to be forgiven for causing you a lot of suffering. I knew that meant he hadn't told you all the truth. You thought he was in that souse party at Gordon's, and I just let you think so — after he refused to see me again. The honest fact was that he went there sober and fought everybody in the place to get me out when I was so blind drunk I didn't really learn what it was all about for three days. I know Bobby means nothing to you and that you despise him, but it's only fair to him that you should know how he happened to bring me home, that Thanksgiving night.

"No, darling, it's not any better. It's never going to be any better. I know that now. Tommy can't help it. One night he comes home drunk, surly and obstinate; the next night drunk, silly and sentimental; the next night drunk, argumentative and critical; the next night drunk, savage and abusive — but always drunk. I can definitely count on that! I never know what mood he will be in — whether I am to be upbraided for imagined indifference to him and his work (little enough he does of it!) or pestered with pretenses of an affection neither of us feels — but I can always be sure of one thing: he will be drunk!

"At first, he claimed he wrote better when stimulated, and I believed him; drank with him — all times of the day, in all sorts of places, with all kinds of people. He said it helped him to the local color necessary to his story writing. I took his word for it. Then I saw that it was rapidly doing him up. He was losing his magazine market. His things began to come back with curt little notes. I hated to nag him, but the time came when I had to rebel against being dragged about with his greasy crowd of drunken pretenders to some sort of literary or artistic talent — would-be's and has-beens!

"Now he is out on his own, doing little or nothing. Thank God, we don't have to worry about the rent or where the next meal is coming from. Dear old dad saw to that. So long as they continue to mine copper in the Upper Peninsula, Tommy and I can go through the motions of living, but it's dull business and life has gone flat. I would leave him tomorrow if it were not that I feel under a sort of obligation. I'm as much responsible for his habits as anyone. What would you do in my place?"

◇ ◇

So — nothing whatever ailed Northwestern Copper or Joyce would be having trouble with her dividends. She would write to Monty and press some serious questions. Had Monty volunteered to look after her business with the purpose of appropriating her income? Why had she not sought counsel before putting herself at his mercy? There were plenty of reliable trust companies. . . . Perhaps there was an explanation. . . . Well, he should have his chance to offer it . . . very soon, too! She would write today! . . . No — tomorrow. She wasn't up to it today. . . . So he was taking Brightwood by storm, was he? . . . Glass-blowing! . . . Whatever for? . . . What had surgery to do with glass-blowing? . . . Why hadn't he told the truth about that episode at Gordon's? . . . She was glad his letter of apology had been too vague for Joyce to understand. . . . Poor Joyce!

Gathering up her mail, she arose from the table, smiled at old Martino as he drew back her chair, and strolled slowly down the winding carriage-drive. The gay little parasol refused to share her trouble, and brightened her face. She descended the narrow flight of steps to the next level of the mountain road that spiraled up from the village; followed a graceful arc of it to the second long flight which widened to a street flanked by picturesque little shops.

Yesterday she had promised herself that this morning she would make an excursion to the Villa Carlotta. Diagonally across the bay, on a heavily wooded shore of indescribable beauty, the famous home of an absentee prince was open to tourists. . . . Some important Canovas, some rare orchids, a wide variety of exotics. . . . She must see them. Everyone did.

There was no lack of attentive service as she stepped down into the red-and-blue canopied motor-boat. . . . It required many assistants at the little wharf in front of the Villa

Carlotta to attend to her disembarkation. The diminutive parasol was handed up to the nearest member of the reception committee, the Baedeker in its leather cover was passed to another, the field-glasses on a strap were unslung from her shoulder; and, regretting with a gesture of dismay that there was nothing further to take off, she reached up both hands and permitted the envied pair who remained uncommissioned to help her over the gunwale.

Smilingly collecting her possessions, she ascended to the huge iron gates and into the coolness of the great hall — ceiled, walled, floored with white marble.

A young American woman, about her own age — possibly a little older — was seated on a graceful marble bench — the only place in the room where one might sit — intent upon the famous Cupid and Psyche. She was modish in a gray tailored suit with a close fitting gray hat fringed with tawny curls.

With a brief glance they took each other's measure, nodded, smiled. Helen sat down beside her.

" It's the best thing he did, don't you think? " ventured the girl in gray.

" Exquisite! "

Well — she ought to know what things were exquisite, reflected Marion. The word described herself. . . . Somewhere in this vicinity she expected to meet a young woman with blue eyes, long lashes, blue-black hair probably coiffed in what was known as a wind-blown bob, a smile as tantalizing as Mona Lisa's, and a voice that made you think of a 'cello. (" Bobby — for Heaven's sake! " she had protested. " Are you sure it isn't like a heavenly harp? " . . . " Well — something like that," he had agreed.)

"What else is there to see?" she inquired, after a long silence.

"I never was here before," Helen replied. "The gardens, I think, and some foreign trees and ferns. Shall we look? You're alone, aren't you?"

"Quite — alone and lonesome."

The patter of their heels echoed through the spacious corridor as they sought the autumn sunshine. On the terrace they hesitated, inquired of an attendant, and took the broad path northward through the artfully landscaped gardens.

"You came over from Bellagio?"

She had. Last night she had arrived from Lugano, and was stopping at a little hotel in the village. . . . Thought she'd stay a week, perhaps.

"Oh — then you must move up to the Villa Serbelloni. I'd be so happy if you did!"

Immediately they had disclosed their identities, the budding friendship developed with all the rapidity natural to a meeting of two lonely fellow-countrymen in a foreign land. Young Mrs. Dawson's story was quickly told.

"He'll be all the better for not having me to bother with until he settles into his routine," she explained. "And, anyway, it's my first experience of Europe. I want to ramble about and see things."

"Queer you should have come to Bellagio direct from Paris. I'm glad you did, of course; but there's nothing here but an amazingly fine view. . . . People don't, you know. They go to — oh, down into the chateau country, or along the Riviera; Rome, Naples, Florence. . . . How did you happen to come here?"

"I read about it in a book . . . long time ago. . . . Always wanted to come here!"

It was fun to search for mutual interests. Doctor Dawson had just finished the Medical School in June. His first honors had taken him to Vienna. Brain surgery — that was his specialty. . . . Helen had had a letter, just this morning, from a friend in Detroit who knew intimately the young doctor taking second honors in that class. Without doubt, Doctor Dawson knew him well.

"Merrick?" Marion's brows wrinkled in an attempt at remembrance. "Oh, yes — tall, serious chap, wasn't he? But, you never met him —"

"I've seen him . . . I think that describes him — pretty well."

"What a duck of a grotto! . . . Let's go down!"

They descended into the mossy, fern-fringed enclosure and rested on the circular stone seat, facing a stucco Pan on a graceful pedestal.

"What did he have to be so serious about?" queried Helen. "Surely things should have come easy enough for him!"

"Do you think he looks serious? . . . Why — he's the most roguish thing I ever saw! . . . Serious? . . . With that impish grin?"

"Oh — you mean Pan! . . . He's a little devil!"

"And you were still thinking about young Doctor Merrick." Marion pinioned her lower lip in an understanding smile and mysteriously half closed one eye. "Maybe he wasn't serious, at all. He wouldn't need to be. Awfully rich, isn't he?"

They wandered on, occasionally coming upon delicious surprises — a short flight of worn steps by a wall mantled with Banksian roses descending to a shady water-gate — a little classic pavilion, the flagging strewn with fugitive yellow leaves. Marion loosed her imagination, prattling of romances and intrigues sheltered by these sequestered nooks, through the years.

"He's at Brightwood now," observed Helen, at the first full stop in her new friend's rhapsody. "That was Doctor Hudson's hospital; so — naturally — I'm interested."

"Yes — you would be." Marion smiled, cryptically.

It was far past noon now. The little boat that had brought Helen over was moored at the wharf. They were helped into it. Neither spoke for full five minutes — Helen regarding their silver trail on the placid water, Marion's eyes held by the lovely terraces and gates of the Villa.

"I think," said Marion dreamily, "that is the most wonderfully beautiful place I ever saw!"

"What I can't understand —" Helen's face was a study in perplexity. "— is how they could have helped knowing each other — intimately. . . . Taking the honors together . . . and specializing in the same thing . . . a very restricted field, too!"

Marion turned and regarded her with a slow smile.

"If I'd known I was ever to find somebody who was so interested in him, I'd have made it my business to get acquainted. . . . Let's poke about in some of those funny little shops before we go up. . . . Want to?"

◇ ◇

Marion Dawson went to her room that night — she had moved up to the Villa — with many troublesome misgivings. So far as the success of her mission was concerned, it was assured. Bobby had sent her to find out the whole truth about Helen's financial misfortunes and to put him on the track of their possible remedy. He had confided that his interest was in the main philanthropic. Had Doctor Hudson lived, she would not have met this disaster; and Doctor Hudson's death was more or less chargeable to him. At least, he admitted a heavy responsibility. Her welfare was his concern.

" Sure there isn't any more to it than that, Bobby? " she had teased.

" I wish there was more to it," he had confessed, " but there can't be. . . . I've quite put that idea out of my mind. . . . Frankly — she hates the sight of me! "

It hadn't required much feminine intuition to discover that Bobby's estimate of Helen Hudson's attitude toward him was exactly wrong. . . . How she could delight him, if she wished, with an impressionistic report of today's conversation. . . . But that wouldn't be fair. . . . Precisely where was her allegiance in this matter? . . . It was traitorous enough to extract Helen's confidence about her money difficulties — but that would be ultimately to her advantage. When she learned — if she ever did — how her financial anxieties were relieved, she would not question the method. . . . But she would never forgive a breach of confidence about her interest in Bobby. . . . Really, it was most unpleasant — being a spy.

All afternoon they had been together, rambling in and out of the crooked little streets; at four, grinding laboriously up the hill in the ancient fiacre with the high, steel-tired wheels; at seven, tarrying over their dinner in the arbor — each conscious of a friendship destined, they felt, to become very valuable. Helen had insisted upon her having a room next her own, on the south side where the big balconied windows looked out upon the bay. . . . Tomorrow they were having an early breakfast so they could catch the little steamer on its first trip of the day to Como.

"I'd flick this job tonight," wrote Marion, "and come straight home, if it wasn't that I knew my detective work would benefit her. She's been terribly lonely, awfully troubled; and she's going to tell me all about it in the next few days. I won't have to ask her a single question. She's going to tell me of her own accord. But I do feel so mean, Bobby, with this deception. What an adorable creature she is! I never met anybody to whom I was so quickly drawn. Please don't ever let her find out about my part in this. I don't believe I could bear it if she learned I had cultivated her for a purpose!"

The shopkeepers in little Bellagio became quite accustomed to the sight of two remarkably attractive young American women on their streets, and the skippers of the pleasure craft, plying Lake Como, were proud to have them for frequent passengers. Every morning they breakfasted together in the arbor, every evening they strolled, arm in arm, through the lovingly tended gardens of the hotel.

There was very little about each other's story that they did not know now. Their confidences had been tender, girlish, unreserved. It was no ordinary friendship. From the first moment, they had been irresistibly attracted, and made no effort to sustain the reticence each would have felt, naturally, toward a stranger.

All forenoon of that tragic Tuesday, which they were to remember with agony, they had hiked along a torturous mountain road above Menaggio. Helen had laid bare her whole dilemma in the case of her business dealings with Monty, and was strongly counseled to wait a while and do nothing until her return to the States, seeing that her income was assured for the present. . . . With the bars all down, she talked freely about Bobby too, confessing by her tone all that she hesitated to put into words.

It began to rain, after luncheon. They agreed upon a siesta, and went to their rooms. . . . An hour later, Helen, having wakened, decided to write some letters. She remembered she had left her guide-book in Marion's room. Quietly turning the knob and finding the door unlocked, she tiptoed across the room, smiling at the sleeping face on the pillow, and took up her Baedeker from the writing-desk. Beside it, stamped and ready for mailing, was a bulky letter addressed to *Dr. Robert Merrick, Brightwood Hospital, Detroit, Michigan, U.S.A.*

She was stunned . . . as if someone had dealt her a blow over the heart. Scarcely able to breathe, she groped her way blindly out of the room, so fearful of rousing Marion that she left the door ajar rather than risk rattling the latch.

For a long time she sat on the edge of her bed, shoulders bowed, hands listless on her knees. The world had caved in. With hot cheeks, she recalled some of the things she had whispered to Marion Dawson — confidences no Inquisition machinery could have twisted out of her. . . . Doubtless all these impulsive confessions had been spread on paper to satisfy the curiosity of Bobby Merrick. It was clear enough now! . . . What an odd coincidence they had thought it — she and Marion — that they had been brought together in this accidental way, and found the dearest friendship either of them had ever known! . . . Coincidence — indeed!

◇ ◇

Marion slept heavily until five and roused with the uneasy sensation that something unpleasant had occurred. It was raining torrents. The room was dark. A strong draft was blowing through. The door was open. She distinctly remembered having closed it.

Suddenly she gasped and clutched at her throat with both hands. She walked with short, reluctant steps to the desk. Helen's Baedeker was gone! It would have been impossible for her to recover it without noticing the letter. She flung herself across the bed, swept with remorse.

A half hour later, frantically drumming on her temples with her fingers, she resolved to take the letter to Helen and beg her to read it. She would tell the whole story, and try to explain how she came to be involved in this benevolent treachery.

Heart pounding, face flushed, she tapped gently at Helen's door and received no response; tried the latch and found it locked.

Returning to her room, she nervously dressed for dinner, and went slowly down the winding stair-case; searched the lounge, glanced into the dining-room; finally summoned her courage to approach the desk of the concierge.

" Has Mrs. Hudson come down? " she asked, with a dry throat.

" She is gone, madame. . . . You did not know? "

" Gone? . . . You mean she has left the hotel? "

" About four o'clock, madame."

" But — where? "

" She left no address, madame. . . . She said she would send for her trunks, later."

Marion turned slowly away and retraced her steps spiritlessly to the foot of the stairs; then, after some hesitation, came again to the desk.

" Will you see if there is a message for me? "

Obediently he went through the motions of inspecting several pigeon-holes on the wall behind him and thumbed a pack of letters, looking for something neither of them expected he would find.

It poured hard all night, and the Villa Serbelloni — if not the loneliest place in the world — was a close runner-up to the Continental Hotel in Milan, for that distinction.

XIII

THE GIRL WITH THE PINK HAIR, LANGUOROUS LASHES gummy with an overdose of mascara, and ugly black muffins over her ears, was informing Mr. Brent that a Doctor Merrick was in the lobby and wished to see him. . . . No, he hadn't said.

" Mr. Brent is dressing for dinner and can't come down," she said coyly, with one hand over the mouthpiece. " He says can you tell him on the phone what you want. Just step into booth number two, please."

" Tell him I'll be right up."

She relayed the message, while the tall young man with the shoulders of a discus-thrower and the tapering waist of a fencer tapped the high counter in front of the switchboard with slender, impatient fingers.

" He says it won't be convenient," she reported, visibly reluctant to transmit the blunt discourtesy.

" What's his room number? " inquired Doctor Merrick, unruffled.

" Three hundred and seventy-eight; but — he said he couldn't see you, you know."

" Here, boy," to the bell-hop at his elbow, " put those bags in check, and then show me up to three hundred and seventy-eight."

Mr. Brent was not dressing for dinner. He was packing a trunk; and chairs, bed and table were littered with clothing, papers, books, toilet articles and mussy linen. The room was in great disorder. It was with a very surly scowl that he opened the door to inspect his visitor.

" Merrick — you say? Never heard of you. What's

wanted?" He planted his short, stocky bulk defiantly in the doorway, hands on hips.

"Ask me in and I'll tell you," said Merrick quietly.

Brent reluctantly stepped back.

"Oh, very well," he snapped, peevishly. "But make it peppy. I'm busy — as you see. . . . Thought I'd sent word down that I didn't care to be bothered."

The loud-checked coat that matched the trousers he had on was lifted from the back of a chair and tossed on the bed.

"Sit down — if you want to."

Young Merrick ignored the sour invitation and proceeded to state his errand.

"I live in Detroit where I am associated with Brightwood Hospital."

Brent's face, pallid, and bristly with two days' beard, went a shade paler.

"Yeah?"

"You may recall that Brightwood Hospital was brought into prominence by your cousin's late husband — Doctor Hudson."

"Well — and then what?" growled Brent, insolently.

"It came to our attention, about thirty days ago, that Mrs. Hudson — now in Italy, as you know — was obliged to dispose of her interest in the hospital."

"And how's that any of your damn business?" demanded Brent, stepping toward Merrick belligerently. "You're just a doctor, aren't you? Couldn't she sell her hospital stock, if she wanted to, without consulting you?"

"Quite true," replied Merrick, determined not to lose his temper. "She had no occasion to confide in me, and didn't. But if we are interested in her welfare, I should think that might meet with your approval. You've been managing her affairs, haven't you? "

" Yeah! And I don't need any help! "

" I happen to know that you do. That's what I came here to talk about."

" And what makes you so powerfully interested in my cousin? " Brent sneered. " Trying to get your fingers on her money? "

The fingers were restless.

" I advise you not to presume too far on my patience, Brent."

" When you get too impatient, you can leave! . . . You want to marry my cousin, I suppose — but have to make sure, first, that she has plenty to keep you! "

" Just for the moment," cautioned Merrick, " we'll not be talking about Mrs. Hudson. We're going to talk about you! . . . And that Northwestern Copper stock! "

" What do you mean, you low-down, sneaking spy? "

" I mean that in the last twelve months you've lost upwards of one hundred thousand dollars on the ticker and the ponies. . . . That last big flyer in oil — along in May, wasn't it? — wiped out the Northwestern Copper completely! . . . I'm here, as Mrs. Hudson's friend, to find out exactly what you propose to do about it."

Brent's face was livid. He stamped to the door and threw it open.

" Now — out you go, damn you! — or I'll call the house detective! "

Merrick turned to the untidy desk and took up the telephone.

" I'll save you the trouble," he said quietly, lifting the receiver.

"Put that down!" screamed Brent, slamming the door.

Merrick smiled and obeyed.

"You're not anxious to talk to a detective, Brent. But you're going to talk to me! Do you want to come clean on all this, now, and tell me about it — or do I have to break you in two over that table? I can do it, you know; and I'd like to!"

Blind with fury, Brent lunged savagely with his fist. Stepping aside to let it go by, Merrick caught the shaking wrist in a vise-like grip of his left hand. With the other, he gathered up a large handful of Brent's throat, pushed him to the table, and bent him over it — back — back farther, until the purple neck was corded with distended veins, and his labored breathing signed it was a good time to ease up.

"Like to talk business now?"

Brent raised heavily to one elbow, and his hand fumbled in the desk drawer.

"Drop that gun!" Merrick closed down on the wrist until Brent's fingers released their hold on the automatic. It fell to the floor. "That shooting project costs you extra." Once more Brent's Adam's apple and environs were compressed until his breath came in agonizing little whistles.

Merrick stooped and picked up the gun, emptied it, pocketed the cartridges, and waited for his host to recover.

After some minutes he sat up, rubbed his bloodshot eyes clumsily with his fists, and felt gingerly of his neck.

"Well," he croaked, "now you've proved you're bigger than I am, what do you want?"

"I'm no bigger than you are, Brent. Your trouble was that you rushed me with your eyes shut. Just took a long chance that maybe, somehow, your blow would land.

That's probably what ails you, all along the line. You close your eyes and whang away, hoping you'll strike something by accident. . . . That afterthought of yours about the gun . . . you'd be in a nice mess by now if I had let you shoot me. . . . Some little gambler, you are! "

" I'd rather take a chance on the chair than the pen! "

" That proves what I'm saying. . . . And — speaking of chairs and pens, crawl over there to your desk and sit down. I'm going to have you write something for me."

" If you think you're going to extort a confession from me, Merrick, you've another think coming."

" Confession? Nonsense! I've enough evidence in my pocket to send you up for twenty years. . . . I want you to write a letter to your cousin. I'll dictate it. Don't make any mistakes in it, for I'm going to mail it myself."

Brent slumped off the table and sweeping the desk clear of its litter took up a pen.

" Begin with her address and your customary salutation. Continue as follows: In view of the uncertainty of your income from your Northwestern Copper stock, I have disposed of it — "

Flinging the pen down, Brent shouted, " Do you realize you're forcing me to write this letter? "

" Oh, rather! That's why you're writing it! Proceed, please."

" Do you know what that is? . . . compelling me to write this? "

" What is it? "

" Why — it's — it's — "

" You think up the name for it after I'm gone. . . . Pick up that pen! . . . You've got that about your disposal of her Northwestern Copper? Now — go on. . . . I have taken its equivalent for you in Axion Motor Corporation, preferred — "

Brent hesitated and glanced up mystifiedly.

" I don't understand! "

" That's unimportant," said Merrick crisply. " It's none of your business, in fact. You're just acting as my clerk for the moment. You have nothing further to do in your cousin's business affairs after writing this note: — Axion Motor Corporation, preferred; five hundred shares listed today at two hundred and twenty-six. This stock is held by the Trust Department of the Fourth National Bank of Detroit from where your dividends will hereafter be remitted to you regularly."

" How do I know that's true? " growled Brent.

" You don't; but — as I said — it's no affair of yours. Have you written it? Now — one more paragraph: — I find that an important business errand requires me to go immediately to Buenos Aires — "

" But — I'm not going to Buenos Aires! "

" Oh, yes, you are! . . . Sailing on Saturday. . . . You're just packing up, now, to leave for Washington to get the passport I've arranged for you. From there you go to New York where you sail on the *Vigo*. . . . Get on now with your correspondence: — I do not know how long I shall be away; so I am transferring my entire responsibility for your business to the Trust Department of the Fourth National Bank of Detroit. Mr. T. P. Randall will verify this and give you a clear statement of your affairs in a short time. . . . Now add whatever pleasant amenities you may have the crust to write to a woman you have robbed, and sign your name to it . . . and address an envelope."

While he wrote, Merrick took out his wallet, extracted a

steamship ticket, and counted two thousand dollars in bills of large denomination.

"There." He pointed to it, as Brent finished. "That is for you. Take it — and be off! And if you're in the market for any advice, I'd suggest that you quit trying to be a sport, which you most certainly aren't; make some new connections; find a few honest friends; get yourself a respectable job; buck up — and be a man!"

His face distorted, Brent fumbled with the money, and blindly groped out with his hand. Merrick ignored the gesture. He was not fond of the movies.

"You can get out of the country, can't you? . . . I've fixed things for you so you'll have no trouble about the passport, unless you're wanted for some other crime. . . . Sure you'll not be stopped? . . . Haven't been robbing anybody else besides your little cousin, have you?"

"No! No! . . . God — but I've been a rotter!" Collapsing in his chair, Monty buried his tousled head in his arms.

"You don't have to remain a rotter, Brent. . . . Start fresh! . . . Go straight! . . . You can do it! . . . I'm going now. If you have any trouble getting off, wire me. There's my card. And I presume I needn't tell you that Mrs. Hudson is never to know anything about this little transaction of ours."

"You mean," said Brent, looking up perplexed, "that she's not going to know you've given her all this money? What do you expect to get out of it?"

"That's my business! . . . No — I think I'll tell you . . . just to clear your mind of any nasty suspicion that my obligation to her may be somehow to her discredit. . . . Do you recall the story of her husband's death?"

Brent nodded.

" Do you remember that a young man was resuscitated, while Doctor Hudson was drowning? "

" Yeah — I remember . . . some rich guy. . . . By God — it was *you?* "

" Yes! My life was saved, that day, by a machine which might have brought Doctor Hudson around, if he'd had a chance at it. . . . Had Hudson lived, you would not have squandered Mrs. Hudson's money. . . . Do you understand now? "

" Was that why you became a doctor too? " inquired Brent, wide-eyed.

" That would be a good enough reason . . . but — no matter about that. . . . I just wanted you to know the nature of my interest in your cousin. . . . I don't give a damn what you think about me, but I'd prefer you'd think straight about her! "

" So — you figured he had handed your life back to you — sort of — and you had to make good with it; is that it? "

" Something like that."

For a long time Brent sat staring up glassily, and when he spoke his voice came from a distance.

" God! — I never heard of such a thing! . . . And here you've just handed my life back to me! . . . If I were the kind of a person you are, I suppose I'd have to do something about it, wouldn't I? "

" Oh — not necessarily. . . . I was a good while debating whether to do anything about my affair. . . . I was a pretty rummy lot, Brent. . . . I'd have ducked it if I could."

" How do you mean — rummy? . . . Hadn't stolen anything, had you? "

" Never needed to steal anything. . . . Had everything.

. . . Had too much! . . . Corrupted a lot of people with it! . . . You've had too little. I suppose that's the main difference between us."

" D'you think there's anything I could do — to square up for what you've done for me? "

" Perhaps — if that sort of thing interests you? "

" What — for instance? "

Merrick rose and took up his coat.

" You'll have to figure that out for yourself."

" I'd like to, you know," said Brent earnestly.

" You mean that? " challenged Merrick, putting both hands on Monty's shoulders and looking him squarely in the eyes.

" Yes — more than I ever meant anything in my life! "

It seemed to Monty that his athletic young benefactor would never emerge from the brown study into which his words had driven him. He stood, leaning against the table, hands deep in his pockets, oblivious to his surroundings.

" In that case," he said slowly, " I presume I'll have to help you. I don't want to! But — there's just a slim chance that. . . . See here! You shave and dress for dinner. I'll be in the lobby when you come down. We'll eat — and I'll tell you all I know about it. After that — it will be up to you! . . . Better put some iodine on those scratches. . . . Sorry I hurt you."

◇ ◇

They went in a taxi to a down town restaurant. It was somewhat after the dinner hour and their table in the corner permitted them to talk undisturbed. Counseled to forget the experience of the past two hours, Monty had regained his self-confidence and listened with rapt attention to his host. If it was not good soil for the reception of a new idea, it was for no lack of sufficient plowing and harrowing.

"I am going to tell you a strange story, Brent, about a sculptor named Randolph. If it seems incredible to you, I shall not be surprised. It was to me when I first heard it."

It was a long story. Dinner courses came and went. In the hour, Monty had spoken but once.

"He'd quite lost his mind, hadn't he?"

Dessert glasses had now been pushed aside and cigars lighted.

"Of course," Merrick was saying, "if you should decide to experiment with this projection of yourself through investments in other people, you must be prepared for all manner of failures, disillusionments, disgusts. You will frequently go to no end of trouble and expense for somebody who turns out to be a pest and a piker. You will be imposed upon, lied to, lied about! You will run into cases of ingratitude so rank that it will sicken you! But — now and again, you will manage to put the thing over . . . and when you do you will discover it has squared for all the failures you've had!"

He paused, and his mood seemed reminiscent.

"I expect you're wondering," risked Monty, "whether you've been wasting your time and money on me."

"So far as the money's concerned, I'm afraid that wasn't an investment in you. I just wanted to be rid of you. But — you're quite right about my wondering whether it's really been worth while to confide to you this theory of personality projection."

"Do you mind if I inquire whether you think it would

give you additional personal power in your undertakings, if I managed to make good? "

" Oh, unquestionably! "

" And — if it ever got out — that you had started me on the way up — then this whole investment of yours in my behalf would be a total loss to you? "

Merrick smiled and toyed preoccupiedly with his ash-tray.

" Well — no! . . . Randolph was a bit obsessed, you know. He was for breaking people's necks if they told of his investments in them. That was going it rather stronger than necessary. . . . Hudson was careful to caution his beneficiaries against telling, and threw every possible safeguard around his investments to protect them from discovery; but I don't believe he felt they hadn't been worth doing if the facts leaked out. . . . The really important feature of it is here: if you succeed in expanding your personality, I shall come in on the reward by just as much as I've been responsible for it. . . . In the process of expanding yourself, you are almost sure to help somebody else make himself bigger. He, in turn, energizes other people. . . . If you know anything about chemistry, you will be helped by considering this as a process of catalysis. . . . Personality projection is like any other investment. The thing goes on! It earns compound interest. If you were the agent that set it going, the credit's yours. . . . Some of it will be going at full blast long after you have been declared dead. In actual fact, the real *you* may be more alive, as to personality energy, fifty years after you're gone, than when you seem to be at the top of your power! "

" But — if your beneficiary does not succeed in making good on your investment? . . ."

Merrick shrugged.

" In that case, you can see for yourself that nothing comes of it."

" But — you tried! Isn't there any satisfaction to be had of that? "

" Oh, it's good practice, I suppose. . . . But — if you had spent twenty thousand dollars and six months' time sinking an oil-shaft, and got nothing but a dry hole, would you have much satisfaction in reflecting that — at all events — you'd tried? "

When they parted at the curb, Brent said, " May I write to you, sometimes, and report? "

" Glad to have you. . . . But you needn't try to tell me what you're doing for anybody else. That's your affair. Write and tell me if it works — but not what you did to make it work. Do you get me? . . . Good luck! . . . Good-bye! "

◇ ◇

Bobby went to the Ritz-Carlton for the night, stood for a long time at the counter of the Western Union office in the lobby trying to compose a cable to Vienna, gave it up, bought a few magazines and took the elevator.

Having made himself comfortable in a dressing-gown, he drew up to his desk and wrote:

" Dear Marion: I've been racking my brain for a solution to your problem, but nothing comes. You have lost a friend and I see no way for you to regain her at present. I learned tonight that she is in Nice. But I don't want you to go there seeking a reconciliation, for you couldn't do it without making things bad all around. You would be obliged to say that you went to Bellagio as my agent to discover what had happened to her money. I've arranged

— guided by your report — for the complete untangling of her affairs. She has recovered in full. But the machinery devised to effect this restoration of her property without offense to her is frail enough. I believe and hope it will go, but it won't stand any wrenches being tossed into it.

" The postscript to your letter broke me all up. She left Bellagio about four, you said . . . drenching rain . . . heartsick and betrayed . . . by you and me — who would have laid down and died for her! . . . Stuffy little steamer to Como. . . . Probably spent the night there — or maybe caught a train over to Milan . . . wondering where to go . . . what to do next! My dear — was there ever a more pitiful state of things? . . . Consult Jack about this. Ask him if he sees any other way out. If neither you nor he can think of a plan by which you can communicate with her without jeopardizing everything we have tried to do for her, better keep away! I'm devastated over the situation, but — there you are! "

Then he wrote a letter to Helen which he had no intention of mailing, tore it into small bits, undressed, went to bed, tried to read, turned out the light, relaxed.

For a long time it had been his custom, just before dropping off, to attempt an inward look. His corridor — as he called it — was, of course, a mere hallucination developed and encouraged by his own quest of it. He had long since decided that the corridor was but an eccentric property of his own imagination, located somewhere in that No-Man's-Land between fading consciousness and sleep.

It amused him to search for it, and, by practice, he had been able to arrest the clouding of his consciousness at the exact phase where his curious phantom resided.

The clearness of it depended upon his mood; and his

mood — in respect to the corridor — was determined by the projects he happened to be working on in the field of personality projection.

Usually a very thin, faint pencil of promising yellow light streaked down the middle of the corridor's rough flagging — the flagging was always rough as if paved with cobble-stones. There would be but an instant of it. The big doors would part, and the light would shine through . . . just enough to nourish a great hope.

Tonight — perhaps because of the investment he had made, his intense concentration upon the subject he had endeavored to make clear to Brent, and the emotional strain incident to both — his mood, he found, was unusually conducive to a materialization of the corridor.

As he neared that gray twilight of consciousness, it came sharply into focus. The doors, instead of parting a little, slowly, tentatively, were opening! The corridor was flooded with a shimmering radiance.

After that, events moved with bewildering swiftness. The corridor suddenly seemed objectified — a thing apart from himself — and he walked into it! A terrific roar deafened him. . . . Finding the blinding glare at the big doors too painful to face, he turned his attention to the objects against the wall, blinking in his effort to accommodate his eyes to the dazzling light.

All endeavors to recall, afterwards, exactly what he saw there were futile. They belonged to a narrowly restricted phase of half-consciousness, and were not to be reconstructed elsewhere. He was left only with a very hazy impression that he had seen his own laboratory — the oven, the black switch-board, the little vise screwed to the table. His diminutive blast-furnace was at top heat. White flames jutted out about the hinges. Doubtless that accounted for the roar. There was also a nebulous recollection left that the door of the five-foot cabinet, containing all the apparatus he had been at such pains to manufacture over a period of many months, stood wide open. . . . He had almost decided, a few days earlier, to dismantle it and have it carted off before some inquisitive colleague in the hospital discovered what an audacious thing he had had in mind, and chaffed him about. . . .

Well — be he waking or sleeping, sane or crazy — there it was!

In the lowest compartment there was a box containing the vacuum tubes; *but they were not arranged in the order of the tubes in his cabinet!*

He had summoned all his efforts to concentrate on that illusory tube-box, and the exertion aroused him to full consciousness.

Tossing aside the bed-clothes, he leaped out drenched with perspiration and trembling so he could barely stand. For an hour he sat at his desk, drawing diagrams of another experimental hook-up of his tubes. He was unable to shake off the impression that he was on the edge of discovery. A strange sensation of exultancy possessed him.

Mechanically putting on his street clothes, he went down into the deserted lobby and sought the outer air. For miles and miles he walked, neither knowing nor caring where he went; walked with long strides, seeing nothing; utterly absorbed by the curious experience that still clung to him like a garment. . . . When dawn broke, he found himself down at the ferry-docks.

Returning to the hotel, he bathed, breakfasted, and drove to the station. Securing a compartment, he went to bed and slept dreamlessly all day. When he awoke it was dark, and for a moment he was unable to recall where he was. Then remembrance came, and he smiled broadly. A strange sense of mastery exalted him. He laughed, and recalled Randolph. Randolph had laughed. Randolph had found the grass greener; everything tuned up to a higher key; every sensation more intense. He laughed as Randolph had laughed!

"And once I thought him crazy!"

He sat on the edge of his berth and stared hard at the shiny mahogany walls of his compartment, his eyes wide with the interest of his pleasurable self-analysis. He laughed.

"And once I thought Hudson was crazy!"

The jolting of the trucks over the rail-ends, the clank of chains, and the wail of flanges tortured by a sharp curve, stirred him out of his rhapsody. The sound of his own laughter still echoed in his brain. He rubbed his forehead roughly with the back of his wrist, and swallowed with a dry throat.

"My God!" he groaned. "I wonder if I'm going mad!"

XIV

YOUNG MERRICK DISCOVERED, WITHIN A WEEK, THAT when a man begins to suspect he is slipping mentally his disorder fattens on itself.

He became morbidly introspective, exaggerated the significance of his little tricks of manner, caught himself doing things automatically and wondered what else he might have been doing of which he had no recollection.

Then, in the course of two hours, one Friday morning, Pyle had said, " You're not quite par, these days. Something bothering you? . . ." Watson had said, " I'll look after that Weber case, Merrick. She has a notion you're too young. Silly nonsense, but we'll have to humor her. . . ." Nancy Ashford had said, " What is it, Bobby? Tired? "

That settled it. At noon he told Pyle he was going out to the country for a couple of weeks. He spent the afternoon gutting his little laboratory, assisted by an orderly who packed the apparatus into boxes. His first intention was to store the stuff in his suite of rooms near the hospital. On second thought, he shipped the whole of it out to Windymere. Perhaps he might amuse himself if time dragged.

Farmers along the roads near Lake Saginack grew accustomed to the sight of a tall, slender chap, in knickers and white sweater, walking rapidly on the highway; learned who he was; vainly speculated about the cause of his leisure. One tale had it that he was discharged from the hospital for drunkenness, another that he had decided to give up medicine and loaf. Meggs' curiosity, reaching that state of compression which demanded that he either blow off or blow up, ventured to inquire of Bobby why he had come home, and was informed that his young master was recovering from " a slight touch of leprosy."

Old Nicholas aged markedly during that first week, but made a gallant effort to disguise his worry, a well-intended deceit which added to his grandson's anxieties. The old man's excessive solicitude annoyed him. He reproached himself for making wild remarks for the sole purpose of seeing to what ridiculous lengths he might lead his grandpère in assenting solemnly to his nonsense.

" Believe I could persuade him a cloud resembled a camel," thought Bobby, " and then talk him into the notion that it looked like a hawk."

More than two weeks had passed before he had any inclination to rig his laboratory. Somehow it seemed related to his mental dishevelment, and the thought of it had been repugnant. One morning at breakfast, he announced impulsively that he wanted the use of an attic room for a work-shop.

Nicholas was delighted. Carpenters, plumbers, and electricians were in the house before noon, taking orders from a young scientist who obviously knew exactly what he wanted, surprising them with the breadth of his practical information about their trades.

That night at dinner, Bobby was more like himself than he had been at any time since his home-coming.

The farmers who lived near the highway missed him; presumed he had finished his vacation, or he had been reinstated at the hospital, or had gone "gallavanting to furrin parts."

Old Nicholas worried more about him now than before; feared his close confinement in the attic would do him harm.

Bobby rarely came down to the first floor. Most of his meals were sent up to him, and as often as not the tray was returned almost untouched.

◇ ◇

It was on Thursday about nine. The lights in the laboratory had burned all Wednesday night. Bobby was haggard and stubbly with three days' beard. Meggs had tried the door, found it locked; had knocked and been told to go away.

Taking in his left hand the tiny knife, attached to the end of a long green cord, Bobby reached up and slowly moved the lever along the dial of the rheostat.

The little scalpel came alive!

For a long time he sat there on his laboratory stool with the dynamic thing in his hands, too deeply stirred to make a sound, trembling with ecstatic happiness.

Then he switched off the current, put down the scalpel on the bench, rose, stretched his long arms until every fibre was at top torsion, and laughed boyishly.

◇ ◇

Old Nicholas was quite swept off his moorings when Bobby strode into the library, shaggy as a tramp, hollow-eyed, pasty from lack of sleep, and said he wanted to use the telephone.

" Is anything the matter, Robert? " he quavered, rising hurriedly, and taking him by the arm.

Bobby shook his head and smiled. The operator was in the process of giving him his connection.

"I want to talk to Doctor Pyle, Nancy. . . . No! Everything's quite all right! . . . Yes. . . . That you, Doctor Pyle? . . . I wish you would come out here! . . . Yes — very urgent! . . . That's fine! Thanks! Bring your bag along and we'll put you up!"

"What's it all about, son? Feel all right?" Nicholas had dropped into a chair and his face was twitching.

"Very much all right!" shouted Bobby, patting him on the shoulder. "I'll tell you about it after a little! I want to run up and shave first. Then I want my breakfast. . . . Meggs! . . . I'll be down again in a half hour for a thick slice of ham, two eggs turned, a pair of flapjacks, and a pot of strong coffee."

Doctor Pyle was consumed with curiosity when he arrived. Nicholas could not tell him exactly what was wanted. He was to go up to the attic when he came. Robert wished to see him there.

"You can come along, Grandpère!" called Bobby from the head of the stairs.

Nicholas trudged wheezily after Pyle, and they entered the laboratory.

"Hello, Doctor Pyle," greeted Bobby radiantly. "Got something to show you! Wanted you to be the first to see it!"

He held up the gleaming little scalpel, dependent from yards of green-clad wiring, leading to a tall cabinet.

"Take it in your hand! . . . Now look!" He stepped to the switchboard and drew a lever.

"Look out!" he warned, as Pyle lifted the knife for closer inspection. "Don't let it burn you! . . . Know what it is, don't you?"

Pyle slowly nodded his head, eyes still intent upon the glowing blade.

" Humph! . . . Cuts and cauterizes instantly, eh? . . . Hummm! . . . Takes care of the hemorrhage as it goes, eh? . . . Hummm! . . . Well — that means we're to have some new brain surgery, doesn't it? "

He reached out a hairy hand.

" I needn't tell you what you've done, Merrick! . . . Thank you for letting me be the first to congratulate you! "

Then, turning to old Nicholas, who had been standing by, his face puckered with baffled curiosity, he also extended his hand to him.

" Mr. Merrick, your grandson has invented a device that will completely revolutionize brain surgery, and make a new science of it! Operations which have never yet been successfully performed will now be comparatively safe. Within the next thirty days, his name will be as familiar in the clinics of Europe as yours is among manufacturers of motor cars! "

Old Nicholas' chin vibrated spasmodically. All he could say was " Indeed! . . . Indeed! "

He threw an arm around his grandson's broad shoulders, and mumbled,

" Why, Bobby! . . . Indeed! "

◇ ◇

Pyle could not stay the night, but consented to remain for dinner which was called earlier than usual for his convenience. When he had gone, old Nicholas and Bobby, deep in their chairs in the library, talked of the invention.

To the latter's pleased surprise, the old man asked questions which showed with what tenacity he had retained his interest in physics; for there had been a time when Nicholas Merrick had had to know a great deal about electricity.

Bobby was so delighted with the lucidity of his grandfather's queries and the comments, that he drew the small coffee-table between their chairs and proceeded to make a detailed diagram of his coagulation cautery, Nicholas following with keen attention.

" It was the vacuum tubes that had you stumped, eh? . . . And the success of that came, you say, as a sort of bolt out of the blue. . . . How do you mean? "

" Did you ever go to bed, Grandpère, with a problem on your mind, and find in the morning that you'd worked it, somehow, in your sleep? "

Nicholas rubbed his jaw.

" I've heard of such things. Can't say I ever had that experience myself. . . . Was that what happened to you? "

Bobby pushed the table away, and shifted his chair until their knees touched.

" Grandpère," he said, soberly, " I'm going to tell you something that you may have trouble believing. It's a long story, and I'll have to begin at the beginning."

Nicholas' contribution to the conversation, during the next hour and a half, was limited to an occasional " Indeed! . . . Incredible! . . . You don't tell me! "

When finally Bobby had made an end of it, the old fellow sat for a long time in deep meditation.

" I had never suspected, Bobby, that you were interested in religion."

" Not sure that I am, Grandpère."

" But that's what this is! You've been talking about this 'Major Personality' that supplies our personalities with added energy, as we ask for it and obey the rules for getting it. . . . Well — that's God, isn't it? "

" Doubtless. . . . Just another way of saying it, maybe."

" I've always shied off from the subject, Bobby. But, of late, it has been much on my mind. I'm quite disturbed, these days. I'm in a mental revolt against death. It's sneaking up on me, and there's nothing I can do about it. Death holds all the trump cards. . . . It takes me a little longer to get out of bed in the morning than a month ago. It is just a bit harder to climb the stairs than it was last week. The old machine is running down. I don't want to die. I understand that when a man actually faces up to it, nature compounds some sort of an anesthesia which numbs his dread and makes it seem right enough; but that thought brings me small comfort. I have been accustomed to meeting all my emergencies with my eyes open, and I don't get much consolation out of the thought that I'm to be doped into a dull apathy — like a convict on the way to execution — as I face this last one. . . . I wouldn't mind so much if there was anything — after that. . . . Bobby, do you believe in immortality? "

" I wish I was as sure of a few other things that bother me," replied Bobby, instantly, " as I am of the survival of personality. Once you've experienced a vital contact with the Major Personality, Grandpère, you become aware that the power of it is quite independent of material things. . . . To my mind, that's clear. Personality is all that matters! The roses in that vase have no meaning for each other; no meaning for themselves. A tiger doesn't know he is a tiger. Nothing in the world has any reality except as it is declared real by our personalities. Count personality out of the scheme, and there's no significance left to anything! Include personality in the scheme, and the whole business is automatically explained!

"I've thought a good deal about the soul lately, Grandpère. It strikes me that the things one reads about souls are frightfully misleading. They inquire, 'What are you doing to, for, and with your soul?' as they might ask 'When are you going to turn in your old car?' . . . I can't say 'my soul,' as I would say 'my hat,' or 'my canoe,' or 'my liver.' . . . I *am* a soul! I *have* a body! My body is wearing out, and when I can't tinker it back into service any more, I'll drive it out to the junk-pile; but I don't have to be junked with it! I'm tied up to the Major Personality! . . . like a beam of sunshine to the sun! . . . I'll not lose my power unless He loses His! . . . If that's religion, Grandpère, I'm religious! But I'd rather think of it as science!"

"Bobby — are you a Christian?"

"That's what I'd like to know, myself, Grandpère. . . . For some time I have been very much absorbed by the personality of Christ. Here was the case of a man who made an absolutely ideal adjustment to his Major Personality. He professed to have no experience of fear. He believed he could have anything he wanted by asking for it. . . . The story interests me at the point of his bland assurance that anybody else could do the same thing if he cared to. I'm amazed that more people aren't interested in that part of it. . . . Now — if that's being a Christian, I'm a Christian."

"Is that what the churches teach, Bobby?"

"I'm sure I don't know; for I never go to them. From what I gather, they approach this whole subject sentimentally. They regard the soul as a sort of congenital disease that ought to be cured. The soul has been passed along, from one common carrier to another, like a trunk with a bent lock and a broken hinge labelled 'Received in Bad Order.' . . . And as for the things you read in the papers about the churches, either they're campaigning for money to build something, or helping to elect a new prosecuting attorney, or stopping a prize-fight, or panning some other sect's belief, or raising hell with one another inside their own bailiwick. . . . Maybe you and I had better start a church; eh, Grandpère?"

"Very good," approved Nicholas, grinning. "I'll build it and you be the parson."

"It would be just like all the rest of 'em. . . . Nobody would want to go to the bother and expense of making his own connections with his Major Personality. . . . He'd decide to sing about power. . . . Fancy! — singing about power! Watt didn't sing for his! And Faraday didn't produce the dynamo by reciting 'I believe in Volta, Maker of the dry battery and Father of the Leyden jar, and in his successor Ampère, who codified the formulae for electrodynamics, and in Ben Franklin who went at it with a kite.' . . . No, sir! By the Great Horn Spoon — No! . . . Faraday did his in an attic, alone, on an empty stomach!"

He rose with a prodigious yawn and sauntered toward the door.

"I'm off to Brightwood early in the morning. . . . Think I'd better turn in!"

Old Nicholas struggled heavily to his feet.

"Bobby, I'm not physically able to go around trying to nose out some opportunity to experiment with your theory. Keep your eyes open and let me know if there's anything I can do. You arrange for it: I'll furnish the money."

"That wouldn't get you anywhere. . . . You can't do

this with a check-book! . . . By the way — did you know that old Jed Turner, up the road here, had to kill seventeen of his Holstein cows, last week? The State Vet condemned them as tuberculous. . . . Jed's all broken up about it."

"I wonder if he has a telephone."

"Oh, you can easily send for him to come over."

Nicholas' eyes brightened. He rubbed his hands.

"Thanks for telling me, Bobby. I'll let you know how it comes out!"

"That you won't! I never want to hear about it again!"

"Maybe you were thinking of doing it yourself," said Nicholas. "If so, I'll not get into it."

"No, Holsteins are not in my line. That's your job. . . . And Grandpère — while you're over in that neighborhood — I noticed, the other day, that Jim Abbot's ten year old boy is dragging a leg in a brace that didn't look right to me. . . . Why don't you hop into your car tomorrow, and have Stephen drive you about through the district? You'll be amazed what it does to you to make connections with people who need you! . . . Oh, I know you've done a lot. It was big stuff when you contributed a hundred thousand to the hospital in Axion; but you couldn't do it without getting your name on a bronze tablet in the main hall. You drop in at Jim Abbot's and inquire all about the boy. If they ask you to stay for noon dinner — corned beef and cabbage — you stay! I know you can't eat boiled cabbage at home, because it isn't good for you; but you'll be able to eat it at Abbot's, and it won't hurt you a bit. I'll guarantee that on my honor as a medic!"

"Run along to bed!" Nicholas slapped him vigorously on the back. "Glad we had this talk! Glad your worries are all over! Now you can be happy again!"

" I'm not looking for happiness, Grandpère. . . . She's out of my reach! "

" Since when was happiness a she? "

" Mine is! "

" Going to tell me about that, too? "

" Sometime, maybe. . . . Good-night, Grandpère."

XV

THE *AQUITANIA* HAD CREPT UP THE RIVER THAT MORNING with exasperating caution. It was the day before Christmas. The more impatient compared tedious experiences in customs; hoped good-will toward men might have percolated through to the baggage inspectors; wondered if they could get Pullman space on the two-forty-five in case they missed the one-twenty.

Her furs muffled high about her throat, Helen Hudson ventured to the frosty rail of B-deck as they passed the Battery, and found the stinging breeze a bit strenuous. She had avoided three consecutive winters, and the fast trip from Nice to New York had not been free of discomfort.

A spluttery scrawl from Joyce accounted for her sudden decision to return. She had read the letter on a stone bench by the sea wall, a stone's throw from the Casino pier, one week ago this morning. . . . It had been that kind of a journey.

"All packed and waiting for the taxi," Joyce had begun. "Going back to Detroit. Why Detroit, I don't know unless because it seems to offer something like anchorage. I'll try to find some employment there — anything to occupy my mind. . . . The past month has been a nightmare! Quite unendurable! Last night, Tom struck me a savage blow on the breast with his fist . . . deeply penitent afterwards . . . wailed his remorse like a little child. . . . But I told him I'd had enough. . . . I'm through! . . . He left, early this morning, ashamed and glum. He thinks I'll be here when he comes home tonight, though I made it plain enough I was leaving. . . . I wonder, darling, would it be asking too much of you to come back and be with me for a few weeks. I do need some good counsel, and I'm bitterly lonely. . . . It's a shame to drag you back to Detroit in mid-winter — but could you? I've nobody but you! I need you desperately! . . . Cable me at the Statler. . . . I'll be wild with joy if you say you'll come!"

It had taken only an hour to decide. Creasing the letter with puzzled fingers, she had risen and walked mechanically along the Promenade des Anglais for fully a half mile; had slowly retraced her steps, past the Negresso and the Ruhl, so deep in her problem she barely noticed the strollers recruited from a dozen nations. By the time she had reached the little park fronting the Jettee, Helen was ready to concede that Joyce had won her case.

She had called the roll of all the alternatives to a return trip. Why not cable Joyce to come over? But no — Joyce had set her heart on finding some employment. She would find none along the Riviera. Joyce wanted to begin life again. She couldn't do it lounging in Nice. Joyce was bitterly lonely. Well — Nice wouldn't help that very much. . . . After all — she did owe Joyce some attention. She must go! . . . It was almost as busy an afternoon as the one on which she had impulsively migrated from Bellagio.

Slowly the big ship warped into her slip; sleety, salty hawsers were wound upon huge rumbling spools somewhere deep in her vitals; the covered gangways were hauled up from the dock and opened to the swarm of restless homecomers. Almost everybody had located wide expectant eyes in the steam-breathing crowd that huddled at the openings of the wharf-shed.

Helen felt very much alone. She exchanged tentative good-byes with the few friends she had made on board;

doubtless she would be bumping into them again in the customs.

Already a nervous little caucus had convened under the big H, half-way down the drafty warehouse where a pile of luggage was rapidly accumulating. Some sat on their trunks with the resigned despair of the shipwrecked on a desert island; some — less experienced — squatted before their gaping bags contemplating last minute amendments to their declaration slips.

Young Mrs. Hudson had done a minimum of collecting in Europe, but it was amazing how many things one unwittingly came into possession of in the course of a mere three years of foreign travel. As she neared her letter, she met a pair of officials headed also in that direction and told them she was hopeful of spending at least part of Christmas day with relatives in Detroit. She led them to her belongings and indicated which pieces they were to put the stickers on. She could have brought in the crown jewels, that morning.

To her delight, the three o'clock train was not crowded; but why should it be? It was Christmas Eve! Normal people were at home. The thought depressed her. For a little while, as the train roared through the tunnel, she missed a home as she had never before.

There was a pleasurable excitement however in this return to Detroit. She and Joyce had been very close. Whatever of constraint had come upon their comradeship, in that last trying winter when she had attempted so unsuccessfully to keep the girl from utterly ruining herself, Joyce's urgent need of her drove all that into oblivion.

And there were many other friends in Detroit she would be happy to see again. . . . The Byrnes. . . . Should she go out to see Mrs. Ashford? Why not — indeed? Mrs. Ashford had been good to her. . . . It might be thought strange if Doctor Hudson's widow returned to Detroit and failed to call at Brightwood. . . . Perhaps it would serve the purpose if she invited Mrs. Ashford down town for luncheon and a matinée. . . . It wouldn't be necessary to go out to the hospital. . . . Doctor Pyle would be glad to see her, of course; but she could call on the Pyles at their home. . . . Besides — it would be awkward meeting people one scarcely knew any more, and being expected to remember their names. . . . And as for that glass-blower, who meddled in people's affairs and sent spies about to report on their movements, one would be almost sure to encounter him! . . . Why should he want to blow glass, anyway? . . . Imagine! — a brain surgeon spending his time in such silly business!

The sky was the color of wood-ashes. Big snow-flakes flattened against the pane, crumbled, edged toward the lower corner of the sash. No matter where they struck and spattered, or how slowly they made their way, sooner or later, quickly or slowly, they eventually arrived in the corner and packed themselves down hard against the others. . . . Her thoughts were like that. Let them strike where they would — they all contrived to bring up at one spot. She was impatient about it, tugged herself free of her reveries, returned to the magazine story and reread with utter disinterest the page that had failed to register. . . . Would it pay to take the coupé out of the storage garage? She had not driven on icy streets for so long. Had she lost her nerve? Skidding was dangerous. . . . She watched a snow-flake creep across the pane. . . . Her eyes grew reminiscent, tender. She bit her lip. Her cheeks were flushed. . . .

Then, vexed with herself, she shifted her position and took up the magazine with resolution.

Had Joyce been effectually cured of her drinking? Would she drift into her old habits, once she had renewed connections with her Detroit set? . . . And be brought in, at all hours, maudlin and stupid? . . . An unusually big snow-flake went scudding across the glass, clawing for a hold, but unable to stand out against the rule for all snow-flakes on this pane. . . . For a brief instant, she was in his arms, and she felt his lips pressed hard against her own. . . . She threw down the magazine and rang the bell for a table. A game of solitaire might divert her.

◇ ◇

It was pleasant to be back in an American dining-car. . . . And, all things considered, it would be better to invite Mrs. Ashford to take an afternoon off and come down town. . . . Our diners were so much nicer than the European ones where the passengers were organized into platoons and given so many minutes to devour each course. . . . What a pity she had felt she had to sell her Brightwood stock. Would it make any difference in her relations with Mrs. Ashford?

It was bitterly cold that night as the long train clanked and creaked and screamed along the east bank of the Hudson, and, crossing the bridge at Albany, thrust its black muzzle into the face of a blinding blizzard; but the scurrying landscape, blurry with snow, did not seem so bleakly inhospitable as she had feared. In her berth, she raised on one elbow, drew aside the blind, and watched the sleet-trimmed trees and fences skimming by, half glad she was returning. She snuggled down with her furs against her cheek, and drifted off into an extended debate with somebody, whether she wasn't under a sort of obligation to call at Brightwood, if only for a moment.

◇ ◇

Joyce was at the gates, dancing gleefully, arms outstretched, as she sighted her beloved emerging from the concourse tunnel, pursued by two porters staggering under bags plastered with foreign labels. There were some murmured tendernesses, and a moment later they were careening around the circle, tire-chains rattling merrily. Bubbling with excitement, Joyce tried to tell half a dozen stories at once.

" First thing I did, darling, when I arrived — week ago — I went out to see Nancy Ashford. Isn't she the dearest thing? But you hardly knew her. Well — she's regular! . . . I went out to Brightwood and told Nancy all about it; how I couldn't stick it another minute and had had to leave him; and could I possibly find anything to do, just to keep from going crazy. . . . And, what do you think? They had just lost a file-clerk, and would I like to do that for a week or two, to find out how I would react to the discipline of office hours; and, meanwhile, we could all be thinking and inquiring for something permanent. . . . But, I don't mind if nothing turns up for a while. Really — it isn't dull work, at all; and I quite like it! "

" Oh, you've begun it already? "

" Umm-humm! . . . That same afternoon! . . . Just took off my hat and went to it. Honestly — it's a lark. Of course, I knew several of the people — Doctor Pyle and Doctor Carter, and the red-headed Watson boy, who's grown a moustache and glasses since I saw him last; and fully a dozen of the older nurses. . . . And — my dear — you should see the Merrick person! . . . Don't frown that way! . . . I know you never liked him."

"You mean I never knew him."

"Of course! That was the whole trouble! You never met him but once, on that awful night! Ugh! . . . that night!"

Helen patted her hand.

"Forget it! We'll never mention it again!"

Joyce brightened and resumed her monologue.

"Well, as I was saying, all you ever knew about him was that he had a sentimental notion he must study surgery and try to take dear dad's place. . . . And you thought it a piece of impudence, didn't you? . . . Listen! He's going to come near doing it! Do you know what Bobby Merrick's up and done? He's invented a thing —"

The taxi scraped against the curb, and the door-man was reaching for the baggage.

"Look! Isn't this foxy?" prattled Joyce, as they entered the lobby. "All done over! . . . Let's go straight through to luncheon. I'm starving! . . . There's a place — by the window. . . . Umm! Duck! That's Christmasy!"

"What were you saying about your work at the hospital, when I interrupted you?" asked Helen, as the waiter moved away, scribbling on his card.

"What was I saying? . . . Oh, yes — about Bobby! He's made an electrical thing that's bringing head surgeons here from all over. I don't know exactly what it is — some sort of a charged knife . . . awfully complicated. . . . They're doing operations with it at Brightwood that have never been done anywhere before. . . . Something that prevents hemorrhages, or something. Nancy Ashford told me about it; but she couldn't explain it very well. I saw it — a big, tall, wooden case full of the most intricate machinery you ever saw. . . ."

"Glass things?"

"Umm-humm! . . . How did you know?"

"Well — they always do have a lot of — of things made of glass whenever they use electricity, don't they?"

"Naturally. . . . Have some of that wonderful celery, darling. . . . Only celery in the world, you know. . . . And handsome? My word! Honestly — I wouldn't have known him! And he always was good-looking! . . . But the change in him is simply marvelous! I'm half afraid of him. . . . Oh — very professional! Crisp! No nonsense — no — sir-ee! And the nurses are all wild and crazy about him — and he doesn't know they're existing. . . . He's doing some of their most important cases out there, now. . . . Calls me 'Mrs. Masterson!' Isn't that idiotic? Nancy says it's because I'm employed there. . . . Funny — don't you think?"

Helen thought it was funny; thought the whole speech funny.

"Really — " Joyce leaned forward and dropped her voice. "If I had the teeniest right to, I'd lose my heart — utterly! You know I always was a little bit soft about him!"

"I hope you'll not be indiscreet, Joyce."

"Oh, I'll take pains not to let him know I think he's nice," she reassured. "But — I don't want you feeling unkindly toward him. You really can't avoid meeting him, you know."

"Why not?"

"Well — you'll be out at Brightwood, more or less, now I'm there. . . ."

"I don't see how your work at Brightwood would require my presence."

"But — you're going out, aren't you? . . . Honestly, darling, you'll just have to be pleasant toward him — for my sake!"

"For *your* sake?"

Helen experienced a momentary wave of disappointment. . . . In her long absence from Joyce, she had idealized her somewhat; but — she was the same Joyce, whom no blunders could chasten; the same unchanged Joyce who couldn't forget anything, or learn anything; hopping gaily out of the frying-pan into the fire.

"Yes," repeated Joyce dramatically, "for my sake!"

"Then," said Helen slowly, "I'm sorry I came back."

They ate their duck; but it wasn't very good.

◇ ◇

That night they saw "The Hypotenuse." It was a rollicking comedy employing a small cast and simple materials. A young widow and her contemporary step-daughter furtively concealed from each other, throughout the first act, that the late Judge Haskins' junior partner was of larger interest than was demanded by his professional service as their attorney and business counsellor. Act Two developed some delicious situations, adroitly handled. The audience was delighted.

When the curtain had finally settled, after several trips in response to warm applause which brought them all back together, and then reconsidered them in relays, finishing with mama and Polly, hand in hand, Joyce turned animatedly to offer comment and surprised an abstracted look on Helen's face. She, apparently, had not been quite prepared for the sudden onrush of lights.

"You're tired, aren't you?" inquired Joyce solicitously. "It always takes a day or two, I think, to recover from a long journey."

"Awfully jolly show, don't you think? Fancy such a mess! You and I — for instance! We'd be honest with each other, at least! I suppose we'd just cut the deck to see which one was to get him."

"Stuffy in here, isn't it?" said Helen. "Let's go out and prowl in the foyer. Want to?"

◇ ◇

Joyce's incapacity for understanding the operations of her own mind was spectacularly displayed, early next morning, as she dressed to go to Brightwood, babbling about herself as a "woiking goil."

Breakfast had been served in their rooms. Helen, exquisite in a dainty lounging-robe, was lingering over her coffee and the morning papers.

"I think it's simply marvelous," enthused Joyce, into the mirror, "that I've been able to adjust so quickly to office routine, don't you? . . . After all these years of indulging myself, sleeping late, pottering, lazing about! I'm happier than I ever thought I could be again. I know now I'll never be contented, any more, without a regular job."

"Glad you like it," said Helen, deep in the theatre advertisements. "What do people say about this new musical comedy, 'Jasmine'?"

"Very tuneful, I hear. . . . Like this hat?"

"Cute! . . . Suppose Mrs. Ashford might like to come

down town, tomorrow, and have dinner with us and see 'Jasmine'? "

"Oh, I'm sure she would love it! I'll ask her. And, darling — she and Bobby Merrick are such pals. Wouldn't it be nice to ask him, too? "

"Not a bit nice! I don't know him! I don't want to know him! " Helen's tone was frankly impatient.

"Well, you could get acquainted with him. *I* know him! Couldn't you consider my wishes a little? " Joyce savagely flicked probable dust from her coat.

"Hand me my pocket-book . . . there . . . on the mantel. Thanks! "

Helen opened it and unfolded a letter.

"Oh — it's the one I wrote you! . . . Well, what about it? "

"Read it. . . . You will see that you asked me to travel five thousand miles to give you some good advice. Now that I've gone to the bother of humoring you, I hope you'll not resent it if I say that your present state of mind in regard to Doctor Merrick is absurd! . . . If you want to be silly about him, don't annoy me with it! I won't have him thrust down my throat! "

"Well — what's come over you? I hadn't heard that residence in France and Italy made people so squeamish! . . . And it seems to me that a person with your admiration for people who do really valorous things — at a lot of cost to themselves — would take a little human interest in Bobby Merrick, slaving himself almost to death, when, if he wanted to, he might be lounging on a yacht somewhere in the Mediterranean! . . . I heard one of the nurses say he had come into a million dollars' worth of Axion Motors when he was twenty-five, and is due for another million when he is thirty! I tell you he deserves some credit! . . . Good-bye. . . . Don't be peeved! . . . See you about five-thirty."

Helen rose, after the door had slammed, and stood looking down upon the street. . . . Axion Motors! . . . A million dollars' worth of Axion Motors! . . . *Axion!*

XVI

MR. T. P. RANDALL WAS EXTREMELY SOLICITOUS IN HIS attitude toward his charming client. She had telephoned him at ten, and they had agreed on a business conference at one-thirty.

He was tall, fifty-five, well fed; grizzled at the temples. The tailor who had made his waistcoat might have succeeded as a sculptor. He rose, as she entered his padded leather and dark mahogany sanctum, dignifiedly offered his hand, bowed to the top of her close-fitting gray hat from his considerable altitude, helped off the gray fur coat from the gray gown, drew out the throne-like chair for her, seated her, walked around the table majestically, sat down in his swivel-chair, folded his big, pink, newly manicured hands on the bare desk, and said again that he was glad to see her. He mentally doubted his assertion however and looked more than a little troubled.

Considering it highly important that he should lead the conversation into safe channels, he talked of Paris, where he had once spent a fortnight, and of Venice, where, he declared, he would like to live; but it was obvious, from the restlessness with which she chafed the backs of her gray gloves, that she hadn't come to hear his impressions of Europe.

At the first semicolon, she leaned forward in her big chair.

"You had a long talk with Mr. Brent about my affairs."

T. P. — he was known as T. P. throughout the Fourth National organization — drew an anxious smile. Now, why the devil hadn't he been told that he was supposed to have talked with this rapscallion Brent? He had been under the impression that Brent was to be presumed as having had all his business with him by correspondence.

" Umm! " murmured T. P., deep in his throat. He gave it just that quality of indeterminateness which might make it pass either for an affirmative, or a mere receipt of information already in hand, or a promise that presently he would discourse at more length about the matter when she had quite finished her remarks.

But she was not going to be contented with his " Umm." He saw that at a glance.

Mrs. Hudson smiled — a bit roguishly.

" There was one man you had to look up to; is it not so? "

Her syntax was unfortunately under continental influence. It made the query difficult to evade. . . . My Eye! — was this innocent child with the wide blue eyes leading Detroit's most resourceful side-stepper into a trap? . . . Well, he'd follow along, and see what came of it. Of a sudden he remembered; he brightened; he tossed up an outspread hand.

" Rather! . . . Uncommonly tall! . . . Your cousin, I think."

" Yes," agreed Mrs. Hudson.

T. P. took a long breath, exhaled it luxuriously, and felt relieved.

" Must be six feet three, isn't he? "

" About my height," said Mrs. Hudson. " But — he is my cousin."

" Oh — of course! " T. P. laughed, boisterously. " Of course! You knew I was jesting, of course! "

She did not join in his merriment.

" Odd that you should have forgotten! " she said meaningly.

When in doubt about what next to do, T. P. always fell back on the didactic style. He could stun and bewilder with his voluminous vocabulary of technical terms relating to the upper ether of large finance. He settled sternly to it, ignoring their brief exchange of exploratory thrusts, and discoursed of stocks. Most industrials were good now; motors especially; Axion most assuredly. She could be confident that her money was prudently placed. Moreover, she could sleep soundly o' nights while the Fourth National looked out for her interests. . . . And — by the way — he wanted to show her about through this fine new building before she left, if there was time. . . . Not quite satisfied with her expression, he launched upon an oration of some length, rumbling wisely of economic trends, cycles, the periodicity of financial mutations now happily stabilized by the Federal Reserve. At the first full stop, she said:

"I would like to see my stock certificates."

"To be sure, Mrs. Hudson! Of course!"

T. P.'s tone was paternal. Inwardly he chuckled. If this amazingly good looking young widow had hopes of learning how she had become possessed of her Axion Motors by inspecting her stock certificates, she was about to be disappointed. She had caught him napping in respect to his relations with her ne'er-do-well cousin, and it was up to him to take the next trick in this little game. Well — she would discover nothing new, bearing on the question, from these certificates. Hadn't he told Riley to hustle those shares of Doctor Merrick's back to the Axion office to be re-issued in the name of Mrs. Hudson? Of course!

However — just to make doubly sure. He quite distinctly remembered having written to Blair, the transfer agent of the Axion Motor Corporation, notifying him that, beginning at once, all future dividends on that block of stock were to be forwarded to the address of Mrs. Hudson, who now owned them, and that the certificates would be brought over to him for re-issuance. Surely he had remembered to tell Riley about that. To be on the safe side, he'd inquire.

" I'll send for them," continued T. P., beaming amiably. " Excuse me, please."

He was detained in the adjoining office for fully five minutes, and when he returned he was mopping his expansive brow with a large, monogrammed handkerchief. Resuming his chair, he smiled, not very happily, and said:

" It may take quite a little time. Had we known you would want to see them, they would have been ready for you. We have such things pretty carefully stowed away, you know."

" Yes," said Helen, comprehendingly, " you would have, of course."

" It's rather a pity to keep you waiting so long," regretted T. P. Why the devil couldn't the woman say, " Oh — never mind about them, then."

" I can wait," she replied, settling comfortably in her big chair.

T. P. drummed on the desk with anxious fingers.

" You know we have them, of course, or you wouldn't be getting your dividends."

" Oh — certainly."

" They're just like any other. . . . You've seen stock certificates, haven't you? " He was still amiable, but he was growing desperate.

" Yes . . . and I would like to see these! " She glanced at her watch.

There was nothing more that T. P. could do about it. He pushed a button, gave an order, tried to be cheerful, tried to be nonchalant; but the conversation was unsatisfactory. Neither of them had the slightest interest in it.

At length the certificates arrived, and he pushed them across the desk.

She slipped the top one from under the broad rubber band, spread it out, turned it over, and noted the endorsement whereby it had been transferred from Robert Merrick to Helen Hudson.

"Thank you!" she said, rising. "That will be all, I think. I shall be in again tomorrow to talk further with you."

T. P. did not waste time, immediately his client had left. He took up the telephone, and in his best bank manner told the switchboard to get him Doctor Merrick at Brightwood Hospital. The contact was no sooner made than T. P. went off the deep end, without ceremony, and reported what had happened. The answer he received consisted of a few words not properly used over the telephone, which really has to draw the line somewhere.

"Now — Doc — you've got to keep your shirt on! I tell you it absolutely couldn't be avoided! It was either that — or tell her we didn't have the stuff at all! Would that have improved the situation any? . . . Hell! . . . She's suspected all along. You might 'a' known she would! That woman's no ninny! . . . What say? . . . Why — damned if I know, Doc. She left here — pronto — shot out of a gun — a bit flustered, maybe. . . . No — I don't know, I tell you. Perhaps she was. If so, I suppose you'll soon find it out! . . . Well, I'm sorry as you are, Doc; but you might 'a' . . . "

There was a metallic click that made T. P. wince. He laid the instrument back on its rack, opened the left lower drawer of the desk, took out a bottle and a glass; poured, swallowed, sizzled and shuddered; replaced the bottle, shut the drawer, lighted a cigar, pushed a button.

"Riley — put those certificates back where you got 'em . . . and if anybody wants me importantly, call me at the Athletic Club. I've a headache."

◇ ◇

Not often was Helen Hudson a victim of emotional stampede. Her poise was not a pose; neither was it arrived at by effort. It was native to her.

This afternoon she simply tossed the reins of discretion upon the neck of her indignation and abandoned herself to the tempestuous rush of it. Mentally at full gallop, she hurled herself at Brightwood.

It was as if a huge, ugly cauldron of anxieties, perplexities, forebodings, misgivings and suspicions, which had been simmering and bubbling for all the dragging months, had suddenly reached that stage of the brewing when it was time to pour.

A taxi waited at the door of the bank as she emerged, half-blind with humiliation. She walked swiftly to it, gave the driver an order, and sat tense throughout the journey.

This abominable Merrick had placed her in an impossible position. . . . No matter about the intent. . . . He had doubtless enjoyed his Galahading. . . . But he had made her his pensioner; treated her like an irresponsible child; helplessly loaded her with an obligation she would probably be unable to discharge. . . . Well, she could disavow her willingness to accept anything further at his hands! She could return the capital of it, at once; and set to work toward a replacement of what she had spent.

Exactly what she was going to say to Bobby Merrick when she saw him, Helen had not yet determined clearly. Of one thing she was sure: she would denounce his officious meddling with her affairs, and let him know exactly where he stood in her regard. . . . He should have it all back! . . . Oh! . . . She pressed her shaking fingers against her eyes and tried to cool her cheeks with the back of her gloves.

Barely conscious of the journey, the unhappy girl stepped out of the cab as it stopped in front of the hospital, ordered the driver to wait — she would not be long — and quickly pattered up the broad concrete walk between masses of formal shrubbery coated with glistening ice.

At the desk in the snug little lobby, she inquired for Mrs. Ashford, and was shown into her office, where she quite took that pretty lady's breath away with her exotic beauty.

"Why — what a joy!" cried Nancy, putting forward both hands in greeting. "I knew you were in town, and have been so anxious to see you!"

"Yes," said Helen breathlessly, and with an effort to steady her voice, "I do want to have a good visit with you — and I shall — soon. But not — just now. . . . I find I have a rather sudden errand with Doctor Merrick. Could I see him? . . . Is he here?"

He was here, and she could see him. Nancy believed he had just now finished an operation, and would probably be at liberty. She would send him in, and they could talk in her office.

Nancy went out, her own heart beating rapidly, and closed the door behind her. For a while, Helen fidgeted on the little divan, fumbled with her pocket-book, latching and unlatching and latching, tapping her little gray-shod toes impatiently on the rug; then, unable to sit still another instant, she rose, walked to the window, and stood gazing preoccupiedly at the street, her fingers busy with her coral beads.

At length, the door was quietly opened and as quietly closed, and she was aware of his presence in the room. She knew he was standing there, just inside the door, expectant, waiting for her to turn and face him. . . . Why in the world didn't she? . . . Would he cross the little room, and approach her — speak to her? . . . Perhaps not. . . . But why didn't she turn quickly and confront him? . . . She had asked for this interview, hadn't she? . . . She had sent for him to come to her, hadn't she? . . . What ever ailed her, anyway? . . . The difficult thing about it was that she had delayed turning about to face him! . . . Every second that passed made the situation more trying. . . .

After a young eternity, he spoke — rather unsteadily.

" You wanted to see me? "

His quiet query broke the spell for her. She turned quickly, and, leaning against the window, put her outspread hands upon the sill, in a pose that Bobby sorrowfully interpreted as a sort of back-to-the-wall defense; but not defiance. Her head was bowed; her eyes to the floor. It was so thoroughly against his wish and hope that whatever he had done for her should put her into this attitude.

Helen was dismayed at her own sensations. Ten minutes ago, she had been ready to do violence. When she had stepped to that window, she had been aflame with a passionate anxiety to call him hard names; to hurt him, somehow; to let him taste a little of the humiliation he had put upon her. . . . What had happened to her? . . . She felt deserted even by her own rage. . . . Well — she could not stand there silently any longer.

She lifted heavy eyes to meet Bobby's.

"I must have a talk with you," she said, in that throaty contralto he so keenly remembered; a timbre that seemed to set up all manner of curious vibrations in him.

"Won't you shake hands?" he begged.

"No need!" she said, with a little gesture of futility.

"Then — will you sit down?"

"Thank you — no. I think I can say it — quickly!"

Bobby leaned against a corner of Nancy Ashford's desk, folded his arms and listened.

"I have just discovered that everything I have in the world is — is yours. I have been living, for some time, as your dependent. . . . I didn't know. I'm sure you will believe I didn't know . . ."

"Of course you didn't know! You have nothing to blame yourself with — in this matter."

She went on as if she had not heard.

"The very clothes I have on me . . ."

She lowered her head and covered her eyes with her outspread fingers.

Bobby could stand no more. With his heart furiously pounding, he stepped quickly to her, and took her hands in his. For the tiniest instant, she permitted his impulsive gesture of sympathy, and then withdrew from him, shaking her head.

"No! No! I didn't come here to be pitied!" Her voice was firmer now, and there was a note of rising impatience in it. "I've been pitied — quite long enough! All I came to tell you is that all your money at the bank I am going to turn back to you; and, as fast as I can possibly earn it, I shall pay you every dollar I have spent."

Bobby drew a deep sigh of regret, stepped back, and leaned his weight against the desk, his eyes brooding.

"I'm so sorry," he said slowly. "You see — the circumstances were very strange. I wanted to spare you, if I could, a misfortune that would bring you some unhappiness. I guess I went about it the wrong way — but I meant it all right. Won't you believe that?"

◇ ◇

For a second, their eyes met in a look that each remembered later, when, that night, the episode was reviewed, inch by inch, and word by word, on sleepless pillows — Bobby solemnly wondering whether, had he taken her in his arms at that moment, their difficulties might have been solved — Helen remorsefully chiding herself for what she feared was a serious disclosure of a feeling she had tried to batter into submission.

"Perhaps you did," she admitted, tugging herself loose from his eyes. "But it doesn't make my position any more endurable. I don't propose to be pensioned by you! I'm going to give all your money back — the capital, tomorrow — the amount I have used, at the earliest moment I can earn it!"

"You mustn't do that!"

Bobby's voice was stern, commanding. He stood erect and faced her determinedly.

"There's more to this than you are aware of . . . more than I dare tell you! The lives of many people would unquestionably be affected! Whatever you may decide to do with that money, you can't give it back to me! I won't take it! I can't take it . . . because you see, *I've used it all up!*"

Helen glanced up quickly, her eyes wide with amazement. She swallowed convulsively.

"W-h-a-t?" she whispered. "What is that you say?"

"*I've used it all up!* . . . Do you know what that means?"

"No! Tell me! What *does* it mean?"

"Sit down," he said gently. "I'll try to explain. . . . It's not easy, though."

She walked with some reluctance to the little divan and sat.

"Perhaps you never had it called to your attention," — Bobby was feeling his way with caution — "that there is sometimes a strange relation between the voluntary, secret bestowal of a gift, without expectation of any return or reward, and certain significant results that accrue from it in the experience of the giver. . . . Now I am not sure that this money I was so happy to put at your disposal is not that kind of an investment. Shortly after I arranged for it, something of quite tremendous importance occurred — something that dares not be trifled with by either of us. . . . It's almost hopeless to try to make it convincing to you, I know. . . . Can't you just take my word for it — and trust me — dear?"

Helen flushed deeply, and rose — her eyes flashing.

"No — you're not dealing squarely with me!" she retorted hotly. " And I'm not — your — dear! You have humiliated me! There are many things I have wanted to know, and you seem to be able to clear up some mysteries; but you are plainly not disposed to do so. I'm going now. I shall arrange at the bank about the money. And — the rest of it — the part I've spent — I shall pay that back! You can depend on it! " She was at the door, her hand on the knob.

Bobby stepped swiftly to her side and covered her hand with his own.

" Listen! " he demanded soberly. " It is quite important, both for your sake and mine, that we do not set every tongue in this place wagging with the gossip that we met here to have a row. You're ready to go stamping out through the office, rosy with rage. Much curiosity will be aroused and explanations will be in order."

" Then you can make them! I do not feel that I owe anybody an explanation. If you think you do, that is your affair! Let me go, please."

Bobby did not remove his detaining hand.

" My dear," he said, scarcely above a whisper, " I appeal to your good sportsmanship! Granted — that you have cause to be indignant. Granted — that I have blunderingly placed you in an awkward predicament. Let us at least keep our misunderstanding to ourselves. Please! Compose yourself — and we'll go out to face these people as if there were no trouble between us. Wouldn't that be ever so much better? "

She hesitated for a long moment; looked up searchingly into his eyes, like a bewildered little child, and finally replied:

" Agreed."

He released her hand and she walked to the window, took out a tiny vanity case and consulted her reflection, Bobby regarding her with repentant eyes. How wretchedly he had bungled everything — everything!

Presently she turned and faced him calmly, like a stranger.

" I'm quite ready, if you are."

Bobby hesitated.

" But — really — don't you think — " he stammered shyly, " that a wee bit of a smile might help to — to . . . "

" I'll attend to that when we need it! "

◇ ◇

He opened the door and signed for her to precede him. At that instant, she became another person, gracious, smiling.

Nancy Ashford, who had been hovering about, with curiosity and some anxiety, met them. She drew a quick breath, apparently of relief.

" I'm so glad you two have found some occasion to become acquainted at last," she exclaimed, searching their faces eagerly.

" Yes — isn't it? " responded Helen, slightly confused over her cue. " Doctor Merrick and I have been talking of so many interesting things — some of them quite mystifying, I'm afraid."

Ah! . . . Good! . . . So that was it! . . . Mystifying things! . . . Mrs. Hudson had been asking questions. . . . Somehow she had learned — by a chance word, perhaps — that Bobby Merrick was in a position to clear up some of the strange riddles bequeathed to her by her husband. . . . So — that was what had brought them together. . . . Good! . . . Nancy was radiant.

"I hope I may soon have a little visit with you, Mrs. Ashford," continued Helen rather breathlessly. "Today — I'm in something of a rush. . . . Important errands."

At the sound of the familiar voice, just outside the door of her little filing-room, Joyce came bounding into the circle with a shrill exclamation of surprise and delight and a torrent of questions.

"Why, whatever brought you here, darling? Why didn't you tell me you were coming so soon? And you and Doctor Merrick have actually met! How jolly? Oh — now we can have that dinner we talked about! Let's do it tonight! We four! My party! And I'll get tickets for 'Jasmine!' What do you all say? Can you come, Mrs. Ashford?"

Nancy swiftly sought Helen's eyes, and thought she detected a faint expression of annoyance. Should she encourage the dinner project? It was an awkward moment.

Suddenly sensing her own obligation to take a cordial interest in Joyce's proffer of hospitality, Helen smiled, inquiringly, and Nancy replied, "I should be very happy, Joyce. Thank you."

"And you can come, too, can't you, Bobby?" persisted Joyce.

He studied Helen's face for a brief second, and found his heart pounding when she glanced up unmistakably interested to hear his reply.

"I'll be very glad to come, Joyce."

Helen glanced at her watch.

"I must be going," she said determinedly. "I'll see you all this evening, then."

The three of them accompanied her to the big, glass-paneled doors — Bobby at her elbow, obviously proposing to see her to the waiting taxi. The pair descended the snowy steps, his hand on her arm, both conscious that Nancy and Joyce were still standing just inside the door, observant.

◇ ◇

"We must talk," said Bobby cheerfully. "This game isn't over yet."

"True," agreed Helen, turning toward him with a smile that fairly dizzied him. "And from all indications, you've let us in for a whole evening of this delightful recreation! Whatever made you say you would come to that wretched dinner Joyce contrived to plan? Some more of your good sportsmanship, I suppose!"

Bobby was contrite. His face was overspread with it.

"Don't look like that!" she commanded, her tone oddly out of step with her smile. "They'll think we are quarreling!"

"Well —" glumly, "aren't we?"

She laughed.

"As a dramatist, you seem to be better as a producer than an actor!"

"But, really, I was going to refuse the invitation. And then, when I happened to glance at you, you seemed so — so friendly about it . . ."

"What had you thought I might do? Scowl at you? It was your own suggestion that we appear to be on good terms. And now — well, you have taken advantage of me — as usual." She was still smiling. They had reached the curb. The taxi-driver was churning his engine.

"I'll contrive some excuse," decided Bobby weakly. "I'm sorry."

"No! You can't do that. We're in for it, and we'll see

it through; and I can promise you that my own feelings will not be apparent to anybody." She hesitated for a moment, and added, "Not even to you! I'll guarantee not to spoil your dinner."

Bobby opened the door and helped her in. The warm grasp of his hand on her arm vexed her — thrilled her. Safe in her seat, she no longer felt under compulsion to make further show of amiability. The smile had vanished. He held out his hand, and she, annoyed, was obliged to accept it. He held it tightly.

"Good-bye, dear," he said tenderly. "Please don't think too badly of me. I have blundered, terribly, but — my dear — I do love you so!"

XVII

When merrick arrived at his apartment shortly after midnight, he slipped out of his dinner clothes and into a dressing-gown, and told Matsu to toss another chunk of pine on the fire and go to bed.

The evening's entertainment had been a gusty symphony set to every key and tempo; brief passages of ineffable tenderness, momentary measures of hope, drably padded intervals of maneuvering and modulation, spiced with occasional breath-taking crescendos that went ripping shrilly up the chromatic scale precariously freighted with anxiety. The finale, unfortunately, had brought up on a most disquieting diminished chord. . . . Considering the evening, in total, its moods were as fitful and erratic as Sibelius' *Valse Triste*.

He had hoped to bring to it the sportsmanly spirit of an athlete entering upon a vigorous contest. His dear antagonist had promised that nobody — not even he — should be aware of her irritation and resentment, and he knew she would keep her word. If hers would be a difficult part to play, his would be more so. All she had to do was to register cordiality. Whoever, with any social experience at all, had not learned how to dissemble in pretense of amiability when thrown with persons whom one disliked? As for him, the part he had drawn called for a cool casualness; not the stiff restraint of renunciation, or a show of ascetic indifference, but the calm courtesy of a man toward a woman he had barely met. It would be his task to carry this off convincingly — this with a heart aflame.

As he gave himself a brief inspection in the cheval glass

before starting down town, he seriously pledged his own reflection that he would maintain an attitude of dignified chivalry toward the woman whose promised pretense of friendship, for an evening, would probably be little short of torture. And he had seen it through, almost valorously — all but to the end.

And yet, remorseful as he was over that one brief but utter breakdown of self-discipline, which now made their relations more difficult than ever, he tingled to his nerves' ends with memories of those few enchanted moments when, even fully aware that she but kept her contract, her comradeship had seemed sincere.

In the mood of a miser, eager to be alone to finger his gold, he impatiently dismissed the solicitously lingering Matsu, lighted his pipe, and eased himself into a deep chair before the crackling fire, determined to live the evening over, item by item, and recover its most stirring sensations.

◇ ◇

Pursuant to instructions from Joyce, he had called for Nancy Ashford. Regally stunning in crimson, with her youthful face, glistening white hair, superb figure and resilient step, Nancy was worth all the pride he had in her. He told her so, and she thanked him — for that, and the flowers.

Nothing ever escaped her eye. She remarked, as he helped her into the limousine, that Richard had a new cap and puttees.

"You haven't had him in uniform before, have you?" she inquired. "I thought you had some democratic convictions on the subject."

" So I had," he admitted, " but I've changed my mind. He's part of an institution, with his uniform on, and it helps him keep out of mischief. At least, that's the theory. Besides, he likes it."

There had been a lot of rambling chatter like that, to which he had contributed with unusual animation; but Nancy dodged from under the fusillade of inconsequential talk presently, eager to be enlightened.

" Bobby," she said, as his beautiful new car had swung into the current of boulevard traffic, and lengthened its stride, " something tells me this is to be a rather difficult event."

" You always were a keen observer, Nancy," he conceded.

" One didn't have to be gifted with occult powers to see that the atmosphere at Brightwood, this afternoon, was heavily charged."

" Pardon the interruption, but — I like you tremendously in that color. You are very beautiful tonight, dear."

" Meaning that you don't want to tell me about it? "

" Well — perhaps. . . . Something like that."

" Very good, then. I shall shut my eyes, ears, and mouth. I am the three wise monkeys. I'll pretend I don't know that you two have had a quarrel."

" That's a dear! "

" And I shall also pretend I don't know that you silly things are so deeply in love you're afraid to exchange glances for fear your secret may be discovered."

" I still think you are beautiful, Nancy."

" But dumb! "

" No, no! Not that! . . . Quite exasperatingly to the contrary! "

At this she had forgiven him, squeezed his hand, called

him her dear boy; and, for the rest of the trip, discussed hospital affairs in a most business-like manner.

They stepped out, at the Book-Cadillac, into a big-flaked snowstorm, and hurried to cover through the revolving doors. Joyce and Helen were awaiting them, by appointment, on the mezzanine, Joyce almost boisterously gay, swishy and sinuous in some green taffeta confection, wearing the corsage he had sent her; and, unless he was much mistaken, she had tucked a cocktail or two under his orchids for there was a taut nervousness in her canary gestures and a strident overtone in her voice hardly to be had for less bother than the embarkation of about three jiggers of gin. . . . If Helen observed it, she was apparently resolved to ignore it. Seeing it was an occasion for the wholesale ignoring of unpleasant facts, there was probably no reason why she should cavil at this one. . . . What an adorable creature she was . . . in the black velvet . . . and the pearls . . . and his orchids. So she had actually consented to wear them! . . . Score one against the beloved enemy!

Curiously enough, Joyce, from the first moment, had seemed bent upon hurling them at each other, almost violently. . . . Maybe it was the gin. . . . Perhaps her instinct told her there was some unspoken bond between them which it was her duty to make articulate. . . . Of course, it was always difficult to guess what, how, or whether Joyce was thinking. . . . But, whatever her motive, if she had one, she was at no pains to disguise her intention to make this little party the occasion for a rapid development of their budding acquaintance . . . as if it were some fungus that must mature now or never.

Indeed, she had been utterly ruthless. Over the salad, she had chinked a momentary gap in the conversation by murmuring to herself, in an exaggeratedly stilted style, "Mis-ses Hudson! . . . Doc-tor Merrick! . . . Dear me!" — with a shrug and a sigh — "I had hoped they might be Bobby and Helen by this time!" To which Helen had replied, leaning toward her, in an apologetic, maternal undertone, "Drink your milk, little one. There's a good child!" . . . They had laughed, their merriment in the nature of applause.

The hotel was suffocatingly crowded. Some big trade convention was on, and the public lounges and foyers were swarming with fussy fat men, wearing long blue and gold badges on their lapels, beads of perspiration on their foreheads. Dozens of them were milling about, bound in as many directions, teetering themselves crabwise athwart the current, begging pardons, right and left, in the tone of "Gangway!" Their corrugated brows certified that unless they managed to squeeze through, the whole enterprise, after all this trouble and expense, would be futile.

Their weary wives sagged in every available chair, conscious of their redundant knees, pecking at fresh marcels with nervous fingers. A few of the more intrepid attempted a languorous indifference toward their unaccustomed cigarettes which, however, they regarded gingerly and at arm's length, as foolhardy urchins hold sputtering firecrackers — nonchalantly, but with secret concern at the tail of the eye.

Joyce had impetuously taken Nancy's arm and led the way.

" Keep close, you two," she shrilled, over her shoulder, " and don't get lost. We must hurry, so we will not be late for the theatre! " — and had swept Nancy along into the squirming pack.

Bobby had offered his arm to Helen and she had taken it; not perfunctorily, but as if she wished to do so. . . . She really needn't have done it. . . . Neither Joyce nor Nancy could observe them. . . . She might have ignored his gesture. . . . It was not necessary she should play a part at that moment.

They were jostled in the crowd. He had drawn her closer to him, and she had responded. . . . No — it was not merely that she had been pressed against him from without. . . . She had responded. . . . There was a difference. He had drawn her closer to him, and she had responded! . . .

He relighted his pipe, mechanically, and absently held the match until it nipped his fingers.

She had responded so generously that he could feel the warm, soft contours of her against his arm. . . . She needn't have done that. . . . It was not in the book of her play. . . . Yet, it was what she would have done if there had been no estrangement between them; or would she? . . . Probably not. . . . It was hard to think straight about this affair.

Until now, no words had passed between them except their brief salutation at meeting, and Joyce's patter had sent even that into eclipse. He felt he should be saying something to her. He despied dull commonplaces, but the silence must not be permitted to grow any longer.

Of a sudden, he had become audacious.

"I led you this way, once, through a very dark lane," he heard himself saying.

"Oh — was it?" she laughed. "I thought, we went hand in hand. I felt like a little girl being led to her first day in the kindergarten."

"So — you do remember!"

"Rather! I don't know what I should have done that night without you." And she had looked up into his face and smiled. He wondered if she could feel the pounding of his heart. . . . They were entering the dining-room. . . . Joyce waved a hand from a table halfway the length of the room.

"Tell me something, while we're thinking about that," continued Helen, confidentially. "Why didn't you let me drive you home, that night, or at least put you down as we passed your gate?"

"Because I preferred you shouldn't know me. I thought that if you knew, you might —" He had broken off, lamely, groping for a word.

"That was a very appropriate way to begin a friendship like ours," she said crisply, "seeing it was destined to be full of little deceits and riddles."

"I am sorry," he said. He must have appeared appallingly so.

"Well — don't be, then!" she commanded hotly, with a savage little tug at his arm. "You look like Hamlet! Grin, I tell you! Your Nancy Ashford knows well enough we have been quarreling! I saw it in her face, this afternoon. I'm not going to do this farce all by myself!"

He had looked down into her big blue eyes, amazed at this outburst so startlingly out of keeping with her serene expression, and laughed aloud. As he reviewed it, now, he laughed again. It had been absurd . . . beyond belief!

◇ ◇

"What's the joke?" demanded Joyce, as the waiters drew their chairs.

"Long story," said Helen briefly, "and the good man laughed at it once. I can't have him hearing it over again."

Nancy looked puzzled. He was secretly pleased over her bewilderment, and amused to see that the little episode had put a crimp in her omniscience.

"Your curriculum is all prescribed," Joyce was saying, as the waiters hurried away, "all but the dessert. That's an elective. Otherwise, you take what the institution thinks will be good for you. No, darling," she added, turning to Helen, "it isn't veal. I remembered that you had already worked off your credits, majoring in veal."

"Do tell us some of your other experiences abroad!" Nancy had begged. "I'm hoping to go over, for a summer, presently, and I'm awfully keen on travel tales."

How graciously she had complied! And how charmingly she talked of her impressions. Most of the larger cities he knew almost as he knew his own, but she had seen things that he had missed — intimate glimpses up narrow streets and into quaint shops where, it seems, she had frequently made the acquaintance of a whole family. . . . How tenderly she talked about little children! . . .

◇ ◇

" In Assisi, I once made some wonderful friends that way, in a little shop," she was saying. " I'm afraid I began visiting the Bordinis, at first, to improve my colloquial Italian. Of course, I always bought some trifle to pay my tuition, or brought along something for the children; but after a while, I found myself going there because I liked them and really needed their friendship. And, one day, little Maria, about three, took dreadfully ill. For three weeks, she just hung on to the mere edge of life. They were all so terribly worried. And, not having anything very important to do, I was in and out, frequently, through those days — "

She interrupted her story to unfasten from within the neck of her gown a little silver cross.

" Maria's mother insisted on giving me this when I left Assisi."

The trinket was passed around the table. When it came to him, he had inspected it, with a feeling of reverence. It was holy — for many excellent reasons.

" I did not want to take it," pursued Helen, " for I am sure it was the most treasured thing she owned. It had been blessed by the Holy Father, himself, when, as a young girl, in nineteen hundred, she had accompanied a pilgrimage to Rome."

" So that's why you're wearing that cheap little cross! " exclaimed Joyce. " Does it bring you good luck? "

Helen smiled.

" Perhaps," she answered. " At least, I like it better than any other jewelry I have."

" Very naturally," commented Nancy understandingly.

Joyce was quite attentive.

"You must have been the family's main prop, during their trouble, to earn their enchanted cross. Let's have the rest of the story. What all did you do for them while Maria was sick? Help keep store? Were you the nurse? Go on, darling! Tell us all about it!"

At that point, he had been unable to restrain himself. Quite to his own amazement, he had held up a protesting hand.

"No, no, Joyce! We really daren't ask Mrs. Hudson to tell us that!" Instantly he had felt embarrassed by his own remark.

"How funny! Why shouldn't she tell us?"

He had turned to Helen, at that, and asked soberly, "Did you ever tell anybody that story?"

"No! Now that you ask — I don't believe I ever did."

"Then I wouldn't, if I were you. This is a very valuable little keepsake, and its chief charm is in the fact that nobody knows but you what all you did to earn it."

"How perfectly ridiculous, Bobby!" shouted Joyce. "Did you know he was so superstitious, Nancy?"

"I had suspected it — a time or two."

Helen was regarding him with perplexed, wide eyes as he put the little fetish into her palm with a gesture that had been perilously close to a caress, for his finger-tips had lingered there.

"Sometimes I have thought of sending it back to her. You seem to have ideas on this subject, Doctor Merrick. Perhaps you will tell me; should I?"

"By no means. It wouldn't be valuable to her any more if she accepted it. She really can't take it back now, you see, because — because . . ."

Helen's lips were parted, and she was a bit breathless as she urged, insistently, " Yes? — because — because what? "

" Well — because — by this time she has possibly — probably — used it all up, herself."

She stared at him steadily for a moment, as if she had seen a ghost. Then, half-articulately, and for his ears only, she murmured, " So — that's — what — that — means! "

" Yes — exactly! That's what it means! "

Her eyes were misty and her fingers trembled as she refastened the little cross inside the neck of her gown.

" I'm glad you told me," she said, under her breath. " I have so often wondered."

◇ ◇

Joyce put down both hands with a sudden gesture of impatience.

" What on earth are you people talking about? . . . Do you know, Nancy? "

" Oh — vaguely, I think," she replied. . . . " You liked the little towns best, didn't you, Helen? Let's hear some more about them. There was Bellagio. Tell us about that."

" Oh, do! " echoed Joyce. " You wrote such wonderful letters from there. What was the name of that little hotel — on top of the hill? "

" The Villa Serbelloni? " Helen grew moody. " Yes — I quite liked it, at first; but I grew very lonely there. I became so unhappy I left, one afternoon, on a moment's impulse — in a drenching rain."

" Why — what was the matter, darling? " inquired Joyce solicitously.

"Just sheer loneliness! The season was over, really, and almost everybody had gone away. There was a young woman I had found congenial, but she turned out to be a writing person, and seeing that was what she was there for I couldn't impose myself on her when she needed all her time for writing; so, one dreadfully lonely, stormy day, I left."

"Ever see any of her work?" Nancy wanted to know.

Helen shook her head.

"Perhaps you should make some inquiries," suggested Joyce. "Maybe you figured in some of her tales, yourself. Wouldn't it be odd to pick up a story and find oneself cavorting about in it?"

During all this Bellagio talk, Helen had addressed herself chiefly to the others. As she replied to Joyce's comment, however, she turned her eyes slowly in his direction.

"It's quite possible I may have qualified for some minor part in a story; for I had been as garrulous as a high school girl before I discovered her occupation."

"I am sure you were the heroine of the piece," he had declared stoutly. "I would swear to that!"

"You seem as certain as if you really knew." She had leaned slightly toward him. Her nearness gave him a chance to mutter, in an undertone, "I do!"

◇ ◇

The talk had drifted, then, to ships. Nancy was anxious to know all about voyages; what to wear, how much and whom to tip, how long in advance one should book passage to insure good space.

"Helen had hers on a day's notice, coming back," remembered Joyce.

"But it's not always that way," Nancy argued. "I recall a quite hectic experience we had in getting accommodations for some friend of Bobby's who was suddenly required to go to Buenos Aires."

He had glanced apprehensively at Helen, and found her staring into his eyes, her brows knitted in perplexity. Quickly collecting herself, she said:

"Perhaps the season had something to do with the congestion. When was it?"

"When was it, Bobby?" queried Nancy. "You ought to remember. You were no end excited over getting him off by that boat. It must have been about a year ago; possibly a little earlier than this."

"Something like that," he had agreed disinterestedly.

The waiters had handed them menu cards. Joyce and Nancy had their heads together in consultation over parfait flavors. Helen had raised her card until it screened her face from them.

"That was very good of you," she said softly. "I never guessed — until now."

"I didn't intend you should. I hope you will never give it another thought. I'm sorry the matter inadvertently came up."

Her face was studious for a moment; then brightened, suddenly, with illumination.

"Oh — I see!" she murmured.

"I wonder if you do."

She nodded her head vigorously.

"It's something like — like my Bordinis — and my little cross, isn't it?"

"Yes — exactly like that!"

Joyce had put an end to their cryptic by-play with a

demand for light on the dessert problem. . . . It had been a very tender moment. As he mulled it over now, analytically, it occurred to him that had he been called away, on some emergency duty, at that juncture, he might at this moment be exulting in the hope that their misunderstanding had been definitely cleared. . . .

◇ ◇

He rose and paced the room, digging his finger-tips into his temples, paused at the little table, re-filled his pipe, replenished the grate, and sank again into his chair. A small cathedral clock on the mantel wearily tolled the first quarter.

Those four strokes, when, on occasion, they caught his attention, invariably sent a momentary cloud drifting across his mood. It was not so at the half. The clock seemed to have cheered up, noticeably, by that time. It was almost reassuring when it came to the third quarter. But, always, that jaded, resigned, mocking, Omarish da — de — di— dum at the first quarter impressed him with the solemn asininity of whatever he happened to be doing and the futility of everything he was planning to do. It was exactly as if Eternal Destiny stretched its long arms and yawned. He could never be sure precisely what it said. Sometimes the strokes were but four gradations of an articulate sigh of inexpressible fatigue.

The vibrations still lingered. He glanced up. It was fifteen minutes past two. . . . He resumed his reflections, moodily, realizing that his memories, from this point, would be disturbing.

◇ ◇

The short trip to the near-by theatre had been uneventful, made in his own car. As it drew up at the curb, he had heard Helen exclaim to Nancy, "What a beautiful car! What is it?" . . . He had not caught Nancy's reply; but she knew.

They were very late, having lingered long at dinner. . . . Gropingly following the usher's little electric torch, they had dodged guiltily into their seats which fortunately were on the aisle.

A nimble chorus marched mincingly across the stage, single file, in close formation, like a garish caterpillar; coquetted, shrieked a piercing blast, broke ranks, and were joined by the male contingent which sauntered in from the wings. There was a stormy repetition of the theme song, a final deafening screech, with arms aloft, and the lights burst on as the curtain fell.

Joyce, who had insisted on leading the way, leaned to the left, across Nancy and Helen, to hand him the seat checks. . . . How vividly every trivial incident stood out now, chiseled in high relief. . . . He had reached for the ticket-stubs, his movement pressing him close against Helen's bare shoulder. His hand had lightly brushed her arm. Every chance contact swept him with a suffocating surge of emotion. It was only by the sternest resolution that he resisted the urge to touch her.

He could not remember what the chatter was about at this first *entr'acte*. Joyce seemed to have provided most of it — some amusing incident of 'Jasmine's' opening night in New York. Nancy was her best listener; Helen smilingly half-attentive, half-preoccupied.

The orchestra trailed in, twitched its E-string; the director raised both hands, swept his crew fore and aft with a final inspection; and they were off at full gallop in the descending darkness.

He had wished he was not quite so acutely conscious of her beside him, fearing she might sense the psychical outgroping of himself toward her. Nancy's experienced observation recurred to him. He had told her how keenly aware he had been of the girl in the car beside him, that night in the country. Nancy had pooh-poohed his naïve notion that Helen was, of course, ignorant of his sensations.

"Nonsense!" Nancy had scoffed. "Do you imagine she could have that effect on you without sharing it? . . . How little you know about women!"

It was near the close of the second act that the catastrophe occurred.

He had not been following the silly, threadbare plot with enough attention to realize what, if anything, it was aiming at. His mind had been concentrated on the magnetic presence beside him, what time he was not day-dreaming of the happiness he would find in surrounding her with the things she ought to have. It was not until he had irretrievably blundered that he came awake to the fact that he had unwittingly insulted her.

The dashing ingénue had returned — it was a colorful scene of a country house party — in a luxurious limousine. The fact that she was penniless; that the car was the property of the brazen broker who had been pursuing her throughout the play with gifts and attentions obviously to be credited on account; that the imported gown she wore was his by purchase — all this was of no significance to him. . . . At that moment, the only fact of any interest to him was the quite good-looking limousine.

Impetuously, he had turned to Helen — their heads had touched, lightly, for an instant — and whispered, " I heard you say you liked my new car. I'm not using it much. I'd like to lend it to you for the time you're here."

Perhaps, even then, the most serious blunder of all might have been avoided had she been quick with an emphatic refusal. . . . Unsuspecting that her silence meant nothing more encouraging than that she had been stunned by his raw audacity, and heartened by that misinterpreted silence, he had groped shyly, his heart pounding, for the hand that he knew lay, palm up, very white against the black velvet.

Perhaps she had intuitively divined his intention. . . . Perhaps the slight movement of his arm gave her warning. . . . Or, did she choose that exact second to toy with her strand of pearls? . . . He would probably never know how it had happened. . . . The warm velvet stirred uneasily under his brief caress.

The curtain was falling. The house was flooded with light. He glanced apprehensively toward her. Her cheeks were flushed, and her little fist, tightly clutching her handkerchief, was pressed hard against her lips.

On Joyce's suggestion, they strolled in the lobby. On the way up the aisle, Helen had taken Nancy's arm, and Joyce, observant, had tarried until he fell into step with her. Animatedly, she had carried the full responsibility for their desultory talk. He was glad, for his mind was in chaos.

When the signal summoned to the last act, they returned

in the order in which they had made their exit, and when their seats were reached, Helen led the way in, leaving Joyce beside him.

What a beastly cad she must think him! . . . But — surely her own good sense would tell her he had not meant it! . . . Not that way!

He hadn't the faintest idea what the last act was about; sat through it suffering every imaginable torture. After a few eternities, the wretched thing was done.

Their parting was brief, conventional, without one single understanding look into each other's eyes.

In the morning, he would find her and attempt an explanation. . . . The clock tolled the four quarters and struck three. . . . He had an operation to do at nine.

Wearily he flung off his clothes and went to bed. As he relaxed on his pillow, sick at heart, the chimes offered a cynical comment on his adroit handling of the evening's complicated problem.

Upon his arrival at the hospital, in the morning, the desk notified him he was requested to call Mr. Randall at the Fourth National Bank, to which he paid no attention.

Having finished his operation, he called the Statler and asked for Mrs. Hudson. She had checked out.

XVIII

THE BRUCE MCLARENS WERE ENTERTAINING DR. ROBERT Merrick at luncheon in their cosily furnished apartment. It was Sunday, and the three of them were just back from Grace Church where the appearance of the distinguished young surgeon in the minister's pew, in company with Mrs. McLaren, had excited a genial buzz of pride and satisfaction.

Bobby Merrick's recent spectacular contribution to the cause of brain surgery had been made much of by the press, somewhat to his own dismay; for he had the honest scientific worker's shyness of publicity. It had been quite embarrassing to see his invention described in the argot of journalistic ballyhoo, and he was not nearly so grateful as he would have liked to be for the well-intended eulogies on the editorial pages of the dailies, and the sentimental twaddle which embellished his biography in the digests and reviews.

Of course, it really had been a corking story, well worth its two-column head on page one. The scribes had left nothing out. Young Doctor Merrick's utter abandonment of the leisure to which he had access by virtue of his large fortune, to give himself tirelessly to the most difficult and discouraging specialty known to surgery, was played up for all that the traffic would bear. Had he not promptly barricaded himself against the fleet of feature writers who bore down upon him, the matter would unquestionably have been worse.

" You really owe something to your public! " one of them had twittered, as if she were talking to some movie-struck flapper who had won *The Times'* beauty contest.

It was even recalled that Doctor Merrick's life had been

saved, some years ago, at the same hour when another eminent brain surgeon, the late Dr. Wayne Hudson, had drowned in Lake Saginack. One paper (pink) had broadly wondered if the wealthy young Merrick's immediate decision to enter a medical school where he trained to espouse brain surgery might have been influenced, if not indeed directly caused, by that tragedy; but, lacking the details, and unable to twist them out of the unhappy hero or his associates, it had been content to toss out the hint and let the public draw its own conclusions.

Within eighteen hours after the news broke, Bobby had decided that if the liabilities of front page publicity were pitted against the assets accruing therefrom, his account with Fame was already in the red. It was obvious that a new star was better off for a low visibility. His mail was crammed with importunities from every known species of beggar; appeals from alleged philanthropies ranging all the way from foundations guaranteeing international understanding to wildcat altruistics for the relief of hectored bluejays. He was the recipient of home-brewed poetry extolling his merits, slobbering songs hymning his praise and hopeful of publication at his expense, saccharine love letters, many of them enclosing photographs. He was besieged for luncheon talks. He became a fugitive, darting from cover to cover.

Even out at Windymere, where he sought seclusion for a week-end, shortly after the persecution set in, he was exasperated to find his grandfather proudly and — for him — garrulously accommodating a severely tailored young woman who required some intimate knowledge of Bobby's boyhood to adorn a magazine story.

"Ah — Robert — surprised to see you!" exclaimed old

Nicholas. "We were just speaking of you. This young lady . . ."

"Yes, I see," Bobby had responded icily. "I dare say she will pardon us if we change the subject."

"That I will not!" giggled the visitor.

Nicholas had looked very foolish and helpless over the situation until Bobby came to his relief by summoning Meggs.

"Tell Stephen to drive this lady down to the station, Meggs. She is anxious to make the 4:16."

As for his colleagues in the profession, their gratitude and generous felicitations had been a source of much pleasure. Every day brought dignified encomiums from well-known men of his own specialty, thanking him for the unselfish manner in which he had promptly made his find available to his fellows. He had had letters from every civilized country of the world.

Now that sufficient time had elapsed for his sudden fame to jellify, Bobby had shyly crept out into the open to resume his normal schedule of activities and recreations. He had not yet become accustomed to the stares, whispers, and nudges, which singled him out in public places; but, seeing he couldn't sneak about forever like a hunted thing, he masked his self-consciousness the best he could and took his punishment with an assumption of nonchalance. Today he had even risked going to church.

Doctor McLaren had preached a scholarly sermon to a large audience of good-looking people — fully half of whom were under forty — on a topic he hoped would be of special interest to his important guest.

Indeed, what Dr. Robert Merrick was going to think of that sermon had loomed so large in the popular young preacher's mind, while preparing his discourse, that it was with much difficulty he had restrained himself from the use of a scientific phraseology quite beyond the ken of his customers — albeit, as church audiences went, they intellectually registered A-plus; and freely admitted it. Grace Church was quite conscious of its modernity.

"Really, the most forward-looking — indeed the only forward-looking church in town!" — Mrs. Sealback was remembered to have said in prefacing her suggestion of Doctor McLaren as the proper person to invoke the divine blessing on that session of the Social Congress which had programmed a discussion of Birth Control.

"As to what?" President-of-the-Social-Congress Mrs. Cordelia Kunz of Grand Rapids had inquired drily, tapping her notes with a cunning little lorgnette. "Forward-looking on economic questions, social problems, political issues — or merely posing as the last outpost of orthodoxy?"

Mrs. Sealback, slightly dizzied and not a little nettled, had replied that she was sure she didn't know exactly how far or in what direction Grace Church led the way to freedom — and snapped her purse several times, quite noisily, to emphasize her disclaimer of further interest in the matter — unaware that the brusque gavel-swinger from up state had indeed touched a mighty live wire.

◇ ◇

Obedient to the necessary precautions however, Doctor McLaren had made a few last-minute substitutions for certain erudite terms he feared might overshoot his congregation; but, even with these begrudged alterations in the cause of clarity, the address was as one scientist to another, and the people who heard it were at once flattered and befuddled by its charming inexplicability. They too wondered what Dr. Robert Merrick thought of it, and were glowingly proud of their wise young pastor.

And they had every right to be proud. The Rev. Bruce McLaren, Ph. D., was by no means an intellectual coxcomb or a solemn blatherskite with a fondness for big words and an itch to achieve the reputation of a savant. His scholarship was sound, and the sermon that morning was a credit to it.

Deacon Chester, warmly gripping his pastor's hand, shouted above the shrill confusion of the metal-piped postlude that he guessed it was the most profound sermon ever delivered in Grace Church! The statement was entirely correct; nor was the word " guess " used in this connection a mere colloquialism. Had Mr. Chester been a painstaking stylist — he was a prosperous baker of cookies by the carload lot, and not averse to admitting that he had left school at thirteen — he could not have chosen a word more meticulously adequate than " guess " to connote his own capacity to appraise the scholarship disclosed by that homily. Had a photographic plate been exposed to Mr. Chester's knowledge of the subject which Doctor McLaren had treated, it could have been used again, quite unimpaired, for other purposes.

The warm friendship which had arisen between Doctor McLaren and Doctor Merrick dated from a raw March evening when the rangy, bronze-haired preacher had been brought into Brightwood, unconscious and breathing stertorously, with an ugly and dangerous smash in the right squamous temporal. He was muddy, bloody, and limp. It had looked bad for him, that night; and the only recesses Doctor Merrick had permitted himself, from the time he finished the necessary repairs at nine until the next morning at seven, were brief pacings up and down the corridor in front of his important patient's door, tugging nervously at cigarettes, and disinterestedly accepting the sandwiches and milk brought up by a nurse at three.

Bobby Merrick had liked McLaren from the first moment; liked the length and strength of him as he lay on the operating table, subconsciously making his good fight for life; liked the shape of his broad forehead, the cut of his ears, the cleft of his chin, the hardness of his well-tennised right forearm, the texture of his hide, the elliptical curve of his thumb. All these things were significant. Had Doctor Merrick been required, he could have written a two thousand word paper on the character of Doctor McLaren before ever he had heard him speak.

He had liked his patient, next day, for the inherent poise he exhibited when, rousing for the first time to a vague consciousness of his surroundings, he had taken in the situation at a glance, and, apparently considering it as all in the day's work, had dropped off to sleep, at the nurse's suggestion, without bothering to ask questions. Bobby had liked him even more, a few days later, for his quite superior capacity to take his punishment — and there was a lot of it — without flinching or grousing. And, finally, he had liked Doctor McLaren's state of mind when, a week after the accident, he had spoken calmly and without rancor of the drunken insolvent who had run him down in a safety zone.

" He probably feels bad enough about it," remarked McLaren, in his deep bass, mellowed by an ancestral Scotch burr. " Anyway, I'm not going to press the matter, or make myself wretched by mulling it over."

" That's amazingly good sense! " Merrick had commented, privately resolving to see more of this man when he was up and had his boots on. He had never known a preacher before. His rather nebulous opinion of the clergy had been collected from cartoons, the quips and jibes of paragraphers, and satirical sideswipes at the profession roughly projected from the stage and screen. He had lately thumbed, scowlingly, a nasty novel vilifying men of this vocation. He was not conscious of an active dislike for them, but shared what seemed to be the unchurched public's general belief that preachers were — to put the matter laconically — a bunch of saps.

Every day, the young surgeon found himself more and more pleasantly attracted by his patient, enjoyed his droll comments offered in moments when drollery came high, admired the adroitness with which he parried the friendly raillery of doctors and nurses — chaff invited by his own whimsical humor. Almost everybody in the organization at Brightwood was in to see him, at one time or another, during his convalescence; and it was quite unanimously held that he was a good sport.

And no less cordially interested had been the Brightwood household in the brown-eyed, deep-dimpled Mrs. McLaren who had appeared, anguished but admirably controlled, a half hour after her husband's arrival. They had telephoned her that Doctor McLaren was seriously injured, suggesting that she come at once. When she came, there was no hysteria. . . . Would Doctor McLaren recover? They couldn't say. It was too soon to tell. He was very, very badly hurt. . . . She took the blow standing, and they rejoiced in her pluck. She was invited to stay the night, and they were at pains to give her every scrap of available information about her husband — both good and bad.

From the first, Mrs. McLaren was adopted at Brightwood on unusual terms. When Doctor Merrick told her, at noon, that her husband was putting up a very encouraging resistance, and had at least an even break in the decision, she did not stage a scene. There was a momentary tight closing of her eyes, a quick breath of relief, and a misty smile; but no theatricals. She had herself well in hand. Bobby liked her for that. He was glad to have her about. Sometimes, when her husband was asleep, she would read to other convalescents. On several occasions she offered first aid to hysterical next-of-kins, who waited while operations of interest to them were in progress. One day, upon invitation of Doctor Pyle, she went into the operating-room to see "some interesting surgery" — from which entertainment she hastily excused herself, however, when a diminutive saw began making noises that played the deuce with her digestion.

The McLarens were, by popular suffrage at Brightwood, "all to the good."

◇ ◇

One afternoon, the Reverend Bruce said to Doctor Merrick, as the latter sat by his invalid chair, visiting — not very professionally, but with a hope of hearing a few more Scotch stories: "Beloved, I'll soon be out of here, and I'm just a bit anxious about my bill. My income is small, and my present balance at the bank, if there is one, would amuse you. Of course, I know what the hospital charges are, and I can manage to pay them. But I have been afraid to ask about your fee, thinking perhaps the shock wouldn't be good for me. Speaking of the Scotch — what are you going to charge me? "

" Well — I'll make you a proposition, dominie. You have given me a chance to patch your head. I'll give you a chance to do something for my soul. And we'll call it square. I'll take it out in trade. How's that? "

" It's mighty generous," rumbled McLaren, in a tone at least three added lines below the bass clef. " I'll expect you to come in and attend my church, soon as I am in the running again."

" Oh — do I have to go to your church for this treatment? "

" Well — I came to your hospital, didn't I, for mine? "

" You win! " said Bobby submissively. " I'll be there! "

Pursuant to his promise, he had gone to Grace Church on that fine May morning, after having telephoned the McLarens he was coming, and having accepted their invitation to return with them to their apartment, afterwards, for luncheon. Betty McLaren had quite enjoyed the sensation of presenting him to many of their friends. She had been very proud of Bruce's performance in the pulpit. She was having a good day. . . . Would Doctor Merrick have two lumps or three; cream or lemon; and wasn't he surprised to see so many young people in the congregation? . . . Doctor Merrick would have one lump; neither cream nor lemon; and was it anything to be surprised at that young people went to church?

"Oh — quite!" replied Doctor McLaren, helping his guest to a portion of a delicious omelet. "That's our one great satisfaction! You see — the students and the young business and professional people have outgrown the old traditions and are eager for an — shall I say an intellectual approach to religion. We have been trying to give it to them."

"I noticed that," said Bobby. "Your sermon was very scholarly; and they liked it, I am sure."

"Well, doctor — if you don't mind being helpfully candid with me, exactly how did it strike you — as a scientist?"

"Oh, I'm not much of a scientist. A surgeon doesn't have to be a scientist — just a good mechanic."

Betty McLaren protested with a laugh.

"Come now, Doctor Merrick! The very idea! You — not a scientist? We know better than that!"

"At all events, you have the scientific outlook — the scientific approach," insisted Doctor McLaren. "Perhaps you noticed at what pains I was to avoid the old stock phrases of theology."

"I fear I wouldn't recognize them as such," confessed Bobby. "But — what's the matter with the old terminology?"

"Obsolete! Misleading! We'll have to evolve a new vocabulary for religion, to make it rank with other subjects of interest. We've got to phrase it in modern terms; don't you think so?" Doctor McLaren was eager for his guest's approval.

"Perhaps," agreed Bobby tentatively. "I don't know. Whether people could learn any more about religion by changing its names for things of concern to it, I'm not sure. It just occurs to me — casting about at random for a parallel case — that the word 'electricity' means 'amber.' All that the ancients knew about electricity was that a chunk of amber, when rubbed with silk, would pick up a feather. Now that it has been developed until it will pick up a locomotive, electricity still means amber. They never went to the bother to change the name of it. Maybe they thought there was at least a pleasant sentiment in retaining the name. More likely, they never thought about it, at all. Too busy trying to make it work, I suppose."

"Humph! That's a new idea. Then you think it doesn't make much difference about the phraseology of religion?"

"It wouldn't — to me," replied Bobby, hoping he had not too ardently objected to a pet theory of his host.

"Well — there seems to be a demand for a more adequate interpretation of theology. We are trying to be a little less dogmatic in our assertions and a little more honest. For instance — I think it's ever so much better to say frankly that God is an hypothesis than to attempt to offer proofs which fail to stand up under their own ponderosity."

Bobby was tardy with a rejoinder, and both McLarens silently quizzed him out of the tails of their eyes. Surely he ought at least to believe in the Deity as an hypothesis! . . . He observed that they waited.

"I'm afraid I don't accept that," he said at length, rather shyly.

"Oh — Doctor Merrick!" reproved Betty disappointedly. "You don't mean to say that you do not believe in God, at all!"

"I mean that I do not think of God as an hypothesis."

"But — my dear fellow," exclaimed McLaren, "we really have no hard and fast proofs, you know!"

"Haven't you?" asked Bobby quietly. "I have."

The two forks in use by the McLaren family were simultaneously put down upon their plates.

" Er — how do you mean — proofs? " queried his host.

◇ ◇

Bobby wished then that he had smilingly deferred to the minister's theory. He had no relish for controversy. And this was no place for it, had he been no end a debater. Moreover, he knew he was not in a position to explain what he had called his proofs. Lamely he admitted that what he had considered sufficient evidence for the existence of God might satisfy no one but himself. He privately hoped the conversation might soon find safer going.

" You're probably arguing from ' design '," McLaren suggested bookishly.

" Oh — probably," said Bobby, with a gesture of dismissal.

" The whole business of institutionalized religion," resumed McLaren, didactically, " demands reappraisal! It appalls me to contemplate what must be the future of the Church when all the people who are now fifty and up are in their graves! This oncoming generation, now in its adolescence, is not in the least way concerned about organized religion. Religious enough, instinctively, I dare say; but out of sorts with the sects; weary of their bad-mannered yammering at one another over matters in which one man's guess is as good as another's, and no outcome promised either in faith or conduct, no matter whose guess is right! "

" Is it that bad? " commented Bobby. " I hadn't known the churches were losing ground. There seems to be such a lot of them."

" Yes — too many! " grumbled McLaren. " Too many

— of the wrong kind! . . . Take so important a matter, now, as the nature and mission of Christianity's author, himself. A Christ who can help us to a clearer perception of God needs to be a personality confronted with problems similar to ours, and solving them with knowledge and power to which we also have access — else he offers us no example, at all.

" But here we have a majority of the churches trying to elicit interest in him because he was supernaturally born, which I wasn't; because he turned water into wine, which I can't; because he paid his taxes with money found in a fish's mouth, which — for all my Scotch ingenuity — I can't do; because he silenced the storm with a word and a gesture, whereas I must bail the boat; because he called back from the grave his friend who had been dead four days, while I must content myself with planting a rosebush and calling it a closed incident! What we want is a Christ whose service to us, in leading us toward God, is not predicated upon our dissimilarities, but upon our likenesses!

" In our church, we're trying to offer a Christ who is not a mere prestidigitator — a magician who feeds an acre of people from a boy's lunch-basket — but a great prophet and an understanding friend! Don't you think a man can accept that, and still be a sound scientist? "

Bobby accepted a light from his hostess' hand, and slowly nodded.

" I know very little about the conflict between the traditional estimate of Christ and the more recent theory. Viewing it superficially, I should say that neither system would appeal very strongly to this age. Isn't the modern school just substituting a new metaphysic for the old one? Our generation is doing all its thinking in terms of power, energy, dynamics — the kind you read about, not in a book, but on a meter! Why not concede the reality of supernormal assistance, to be had under fixed conditions, and encourage people to go after it? "

" That sounds a little as if you believed in prayer, Doctor Merrick," said Betty wistfully.

" You mean — getting down on your knees to wish you had something? "

" Oh, it's more than that! . . . Asking God to give it to you! "

" Well, that depends on your credit."

" Agreed! " nodded McLaren.

" I'm afraid I don't quite understand," said Betty.

" Why, he means that unless one has been living up to one's best ideals, it's useless to ask for God's approval and assistance. That's obvious."

" No," said Bobby. " That is not what I meant. If you're interested, I'll tell you a story."

◇ ◇

For the next two hours — they had moved to the library on Bobby's hint that they had let themselves in for an extended tale — the McLarens sat scarcely daring to trust their own hearing.

Eager to give them all the steps of his spiritual progress, in their exact sequence, he had begun back in Randolph's studio. Carefully picking his way with a care to the avoidance of any act of his own, performed in pursuance to the Galilean theory of availing prayer, he laid the facts before them in a dispassionate recital.

He finished as he had begun. He could hardly expect

them to believe it, he said. He hadn't believed it; had been disgusted by it; intellectually offended by it; in violent revolt against it; but — well, there it was!

"How utterly trivial," said McLaren humbly, "my whole program of preaching seems in the face of such astounding possibilities! Why — we've been trying to teach religion without — without knowing what it's about!"

"Oh, I shouldn't go so far as to think that!" consoled Bobby. "You've inspired people to take stock of themselves. They can't help being better for every serious thought you've given them about life and duty. That's ethics. And ethics is decidedly important. This thing I've been talking about is not in the field of ethics. It belongs rather to science. We have been at great pains to construct devices and machinery to be energized by steam and electricity and sunshine; but haven't realized how human personality can be made just as receptive to the power of our Major Personality."

"I feel, today," said McLaren, "as if I'd been doing nothing — exactly nothing!"

"By no means! You have been doing some highly necessary work in clearing away the old superstitions; the old irrelevancies. That's not labor lost, you may be sure! Only — as I listened, this morning, I couldn't help wishing that this new interpretation of religion which you are so splendidly equipped to offer might go further and show how soundly scientific religion is. You counseled us, today, to accept the evolutionary hypothesis. You said — if I recall correctly — that we could explain everything we have and are by that theory. . . . Now — I don't agree with you. Perhaps our bodies derive from some pre-human type of life. Perhaps all romantic literature is but an elaboration of the animal's urge to reproduce itself. Perhaps our brains are but refinements of elementary nerve ganglia that used to respond, automatically, to the necessity for food and shelter. . . . It hasn't been proved. You were ever so much more sure of it, in your pulpit, than my biology professor was, in his classroom. . . . But — assuming a physical evolution, biology has no explanation to offer for human personality. You ask old man Harper how he accounts for aspiration, penitence, inquisitiveness about our origin, concern about our future — and he'll say, ' I'm not a theologian, sir! I'm a biologist! ' "

" And I suppose you're hinting," smiled McLaren, " that my chief business is to account for aspiration, penitence, and man's passion to be a time-binder — and if anybody inquires what I think about evolution, I'd better reply, ' I'm not a biologist, sir! I'm a theologian! ' "

" Something like that," agreed Bobby.

" I wonder if we modernists," said McLaren, after a considerable pause, " are not somewhat in the predicament of Moses, who had enough audacity to lead the slaves out of their bondage, but lacked the ingenuity to take them on into a country that would support them. We've emancipated them; but — they're still wandering about in the jungle, dissatisfied, hungry, making occasional excursions into paganism and experimenting with all manner of eccentric cults, longing for the spiritual equivalent of their repudiated superstitions — sometimes even wishing they were back in the old harness! "

" It's worth while to have fetched them out of that," said Bobby. " It ought to be equally interesting to lead them on. They mustn't go back! But they will — if they're not pointed to something more attractive than the jungle you say they're in."

◇ ◇

As he left the house at four, McLaren followed him out to his big coupé parked at the curb.

" Merrick," he said rather timidly, " would it be asking too much of you to come to my church again next Sunday? I'm going to have something a little more constructive to offer — and I'd like your reaction."

" I would gladly, but I shall be on the briny deep. Sailing Saturday to France, en route to Vienna to see a colleague. I'll be happy to come when I return."

He stepped on the starter and the powerful engine hummed.

McLaren gripped his hand.

" Merrick — just a minute! . . . We modernists have been trying to show how religion is not at odds with science. What we've got to do now is to show how religion *is a science!* Isn't that what you mean? "

" Exactly! Nothing less or else than that! You have it! More power to you! See you in September! "

XIX

MAXINE MERRICK, POURING THEIR COFFEE IN THE SUNNY breakfast room of her over-Louised apartment in Boulevard Haussmann near the Étoile, glanced up shyly at her distinguished guest, finding it difficult to identify him as her son.

His mouth was somehow different. Ungifted with any capacity for character analysis, she was unable to define the change, but some dormant instinct told her it was other than merely functional; it was organic, structural.

It was not an austere mouth, neither was it pessimistic; but it had put off its adolescent wistfulness. It no longer entreated or anticipated, or even inquired; it accepted. The mouth had none of the tight-buckled smugness of self-imputed infallibility; none of the haughty protrusion of authority in repose; but it looked as if it were concerned only with facts, and had learned to be very particular about them. If they had really been shown to be facts, the mouth accepted them — let the facts be fair as a May morning or ugly as sin.

And his eyes were somehow different. They seemed deeper set, not as if they had winced but retreated from sights they had found disagreeable — experienced eyes that were used to looking at suffering, but not without great cost to themselves. They were not sad or weary eyes, but one felt they had seen so much they would not again widen readily with surprise. They did not cynically defy you to startle them; but you knew there was nothing you would be likely ever to say or do that would make them blink with amazement.

There was a difference in his hands; same long, slender,

artist fingers — but they had left off groping uncertainly for things. They had achieved a sureness, a poise, a confidence not to be had at less expense than the honest, tireless, discriminating experience of dealing with facts — let the facts be no end unpleasant.

In short, they were the mouth, eyes, and hands of a surgeon.

Bobby's decision to go in for a profession had failed to impress her favorably. Beyond a feeling — which she tardily and peevishly expressed — that he was enslaving himself unnecessarily, she had been left unstirred by his resolution. His completion of his medical course evoked only a request that now he was finished with school she dared say he would be able to run over and spend the summer with her. Later, when he had settled to the routine of an occupation demanding a devotion all but cloistral, she confided to her intimates how unfair it was that he should give his life to strangers when his own widowed mother stood in such desperate need of him. Her infrequent notes, in purple ink and big sprawling letters, blubbered with self-pity and petulant accusations of indifference; but her mileage was about as good as ever, and she was rarely alone except when asleep.

When however it had been called to her attention — she never read the journals or reviews herself — that a young Doctor Merrick of Detroit — could it possibly, her informant wondered, be her own Bobby? — had been making himself famous by the invention of a remarkable surgical instrument, her pride knew no limits. Suddenly aware that she had sacrificially offered him, years ago, on the altar of humanitarian service, and had been waiting hopefully for the day when her unselfish renunciation of her maternal claims on him might be publicly recognized, Maxine hastened to collect the tribute due her valiant and uncomplaining martyrdom, inviting all and sundry to view the stake whereon she had sizzled through the long-drawn days when her faith and hope were under fire.

For the space of a week she romped about among her acquaintances, accepting with happy tears their high-keyed chirps of felicitation, and cabled a mawkishly sentimental message to her son which fervently thanked the good God for making all her wonderful dreams come true, and cost her four hundred and fifteen francs.

This morning, Maxine lacked but a decade of looking her age, and felt even closer to it than she appeared. At no little cost she had planned the brilliant luncheon she was giving today at two when Bobby was to be triumphantly exhibited to a half dozen young old ladies — mostly self-exiled Americans who had either outlived, outgrown or outworn their relatives — and as many modish and musty old gentlemen with gray moustaches and ginny breaths. She had been bland with her statement that they were exceptionally favored by this invitation to meet her boy prodigy, and privately hoped he had matured sufficiently to justify the story of his wide distinction. It had not occurred to her that he would return to her with that kind of a mouth, those eyes, those hands, which accused her of being not a day under fifty-six.

Accustomed to playing rôles on short notice, suggested by her own volatile caprices, she determined to meet this awkward circumstance on its own ground. She would enjoy being the mother of a lion, even if the fact that the lion was no longer a cub would make it difficult for her to be quite so kittenish as usual. She was giving herself a dress rehearsal, this morning, of the new part, and was almost matronly.

"You'll love them, Bobby! . . . Such dears! . . . And — Bobby." She held up a warning finger and twinkled it mysteriously. "— I've asked my adorable Patricia Livingstone to come with her mother. We've been so anxious to see you two together. You'll be enchanted with her!"

Bobby grinned amiably and said he was going to be happy to meet them all, especially someone his mother considered adorable. It was obvious she was preparing for this event as if it were a coronation, and he was resolved to humor her. God knew it was little enough he had ever been able to do for her pleasure. He would today atone for all his failures to be what she wanted him to be by going cheerfully into an affair which, he suspected, would establish his utter asshood as a fact beyond controversy in the opinion of any sensible person present.

Considering the will — in this instance — equivalent to the deed, he later scored up the party to his credit; though he was unable to attend it.

Bobby Merrick's decision to request a four months' leave had been based ostensibly upon an extended correspondence with Dr. Emil Arnstadt of Vienna. Arnstadt had been long at work on the coagulation cautery project before the Merrick invention was announced. Immediately he had sought full information about it which was promptly and cheerfully given. Then had sprung up the warmest attachment between them, leading to Arnstadt's ardent hope that Doctor

Merrick would come to Vienna for a leisurely conference on their mutual interests.

" We have much to give each other," wrote Arnstadt. " It is well we should meet."

In the scales alongside Arnstadt's intriguing invitation was an importunate letter from Jack Dawson, down on all fours in supplication.

" No small matter, I tell you, to be asked into conference with Arnstadt! You've got to come. It's equivalent to a command! You've got to come for my sake! You must realize I've never felt decent about the way I came here as the winner of a prize you tossed into my lap. You shouldn't have done it. Of course, as it has all turned out, you've more achievement to your credit than had you written that exam in full for old Appleton and taken the persimmons you so jolly well deserved. I never had any illusions, old chap, about my winning the first honors and this prize. You handed them over to me because you thought I needed them more than you. I never felt easy about it. But — now that Arnstadt wants to do you this honor, don't refuse. It will make me a heap more comfortable, I can tell you! "

But these pressing invitations to Vienna were not the actual driving reasons why Bobby Merrick had decided to spend the summer in Europe. The real tug, he was bound to admit, resided in the fact that Helen Hudson was conducting a small party of tourists through Italy and France. He had a hope of meeting her. She was interfering with his work, disturbing him in his sleep, making him restless, absent minded, distraught. However she might regard him, he must see her again, if to no better purpose than to change the torturing mental picture he carried of her, shamed and hurt by his unintended impudence. Some kind of reconciliation must be attempted. He had accepted his expulsion from his Fool's Paradise, and no longer cherished the notion that he could reinstate himself with Helen; but it would be worth the trip to see her — let her be indignant, indifferent, or contemptuous. He must dispose somehow of this haunting picture of her, hurt and humiliated.

He had kept track of her movements through Joyce, who had quite voluntarily confided the essential facts of Helen's sudden departure from Detroit the next morning after the execrable theatre party. It was apparent that Joyce had not been informed — and equally apparent that she very much wanted to know — what business had drawn her young step-mother impulsively out to Brightwood, that winter afternoon. In Joyce's mind there seemed an inevitable sequence relating that event to Helen's sudden departure for New York, early next day, on some unexplained errand.

Short of actually putting a thumbscrew on him, Joyce's inquisitiveness to learn how much Bobby knew about it was persistent, ingenious, desperate; but she received small pay for the news she offered as bait.

Exactly why Helen Hudson wanted or needed employment badly enough to become a routing agent in the office of the Beamond and Grayson Travel Bureau, Joyce couldn't imagine. It was so unlike her. She hated routine. She wasn't used to taking orders or keeping hours. She was about as practical as a Persian kitten on a satin pillow.

Bobby had had to listen to an inordinate amount of this, astounded at his own patience, though in his honest moments he reflected that had Joyce not prattled so volubly of her own accord he would have been obliged to prime her to it.

He was thankful enough for her gift of garrulity the day she told him Helen was about to leave the New York office for Cherbourg, as the conductor of a small party.

"Does Joyce annoy you, Bobby?" demanded Nancy Ashford one afternoon, with her disconcerting directness.

"Oh — not at all!" he had replied, feeling a bit silly.

"As I thought! . . . She has just been offered an interesting position as a home visitor with the Juvenile Protective League. I shall press her to take it."

Duly pressed, Joyce accepted the new job. On her last day at Brightwood, she cornered him as he was leaving the hospital at five.

"I won't be seeing you any more, will I," she said. "I'm leaving, you know."

"Why — that is true," he replied, as if it had not occurred to him before. "You'll be busy, and you know how this ties me up here. I do hope you like your new work. You must let us know how you get on with it, Joyce."

"You couldn't come and see me sometimes? I'm going to be horribly lonely." It was evident that the speech cost her something. She forced it with an effort.

"Oh — I don't go anywhere. . . . Unsocial as an oyster. . . . This business is cruelly confining. Some day I hope to have a little more time for — "

She laughed, nervously, mirthlessly.

"Don't say any more, Bobby. It's plain you don't want to. . . . Good-bye! I may not see you for a long time."

He took her cool hand and repeated his good wishes. The episode left him uncomfortable. It had been a decidedly awkward situation. Maybe, if old Tommy could be bucked up, somehow, Joyce might be willing to give him another try. It was worth looking into.

◇ ◇

Arriving in New York that Friday morning, the twenty-second of May — he was sailing on the *Majestic* the next day at four — Bobby had hunted his old friend down and was startled at the change in him. Tommy was seedy, shiny, spiritless, and had skipped patches under his jowls in shaving. . . . Not much wonder Joyce wanted some other employment besides looking after Tommy.

They had lunch together and tried heroically to recover their long lost collegiate mood, but it was rough going. Too much water had gone under the bridge. . . . Too little water had gone into Tommy.

"Sometimes —" Masterson furtively pushed a soiled cuff back into his coat-sleeve, and attempted to steady his leaky spoon. "Sometimes, I've had a notion to end it. If I wasn't such a damned coward, I'd have done it long ago."

So — there being at last a definite motion before the house, Bobby discussed it. Masterson was of the artist type that required a deal of encouragement and adulation. It couldn't be laid on too heavily. Tommy had always possessed an almost infinite capacity for absorbing glory, laud, and praise. Unquestionably Joyce could have kept her man on the rails had she been a little less frugal with his necessary rations of ambrosia. Well, it was high time he had some. Bobby fed him on the rich confectionery of appreciation all day and left him hilariously drunk with it at midnight — drunk as ever he had been on whiskey. He was going to perk up and show 'em, by the Eternal, that he had the stuff! He'd been temporarily depressed, but — as Bobby had said — that was naturally to be expected of any man gifted with so sensitive a creative imagination! And he'd been drinking too much; but he could stop it. He would stop it! And there was his hand on it! The worm had turned! . . . And a good deal more like that.

Before he turned in, Bobby wired to Nancy.

JOYCE URGENTLY NEEDED IN NEW YORK STOP TOMMY HAS FINISHED WITH J BARLEYCORN STOP IS FULL OF REVIVED AMBITION STOP DEMANDS REGULAR MEALS ENCOURAGEMENT COMPANIONSHIP STOP STRONGLY COUNSEL HER TO HELP HIM MAKE GOOD STOP PUT IT UP TO HER AS IMPORTANT SOCIAL SERVICE STOP SHE WILL STILL BE WORKING IN INTEREST OF JUVENILE PROTECTION STOP YOU NEED NOT TELL HER THAT STOP AFFECTIONATELY MISTER FIXIT P S AND HERE IS HOPING FOR BETTER LUCK THAN USUAL IN MANAGING SOMEBODY ELSES BUSINESS R M

Sunday afternoon he was roused from a nap in his steamer-chair to receipt for a radiogram. He smiled with pleasure.

JOYCE LEFT FOR NEW YORK AT NOON

◇ ◇

" Patricia paints beautifully! " continued Maxine, passing Bobby his cup.

" Does she, indeed? "

" Batiks."

Bobby's eyes wandered disinterestedly over the head-lines on the front page of *Le Matin* at his elbow.

" Any news? "

" No. . . . But — what's this? . . . Seven Americans hurt in a railroad accident near . . . *Oh, my God!* "

Maxine rushed after him as he dashed from the room and

found him telephoning for a taxi. For the next five minutes, while he frantically tossed a few necessaries into a bag, she hovered at his elbow, extracting broken phrases from him. . . . "Terrible accident . . . my best friend . . . have to go . . . awfully sorry. . . . No! . . . No! . . . Have to go — at once!"

"But — Bobby! . . . My party! . . . Surely, you wouldn't do such a thing to me! . . . Be reasonable! . . . You can start tonight, just as well! . . . Oh! I think this is just too cruel — too cruel!"

He wasn't hearing her. . . . Luncheon? . . . Ridiculous! . . . He kissed her wet face and rushed out. . . . There was no time for the sluggish automatic lift. He ran down the stairs.

Ordinarily, the deafening roar of the propellers exasperated him; gnawed the insulation off his nerves, bit by bit. Today he was barely conscious of the racket. He had seen nothing on his way to Le Bourget field, and was equally indifferent to the receding landscape as Pierre Laudée tilted up his ship's nose and climbed a steep grade into the clouds for what he boasted, that afternoon, was the record flight from Paris to Rome.

Bobby still clutched the newspaper in his hand; unnecessarily, for he could recite every word. . . . Late last night . . . Naples-Rome express . . . wreck near Ciampino . . . open switch . . . seven Americans among the injured . . . Mrs. Helen Hudson, conductor of a touring party . . . fatally hurt . . . removed to the English Hospital on Via Nomentana, in Rome.

He remembered the place . . . little hospital . . . Ardmore — good man — chief of staff . . . throat specialist. He knew of him.

The day dragged on. Sometimes he relaxed from his tension, sank back into the cushions, limp, and wondered how much of the quiver of him was due to the ship's tremor. Then his anxiety would sweep over him, drying his throat, nauseating him.

It was an interminable grind. And it seemed almost as long again to creep in, at a thirty-mile snail-pace, from the landing-field to the hospital.

The taxi turned in at the hospital gate and slowed down as it followed a graveled driveway hedged with masses of shrubbery. It drew up under the porte-cochère. He had not remembered it to be such a gloomy, taciturn, forbidding place as it appeared today. He wondered if that was the way Brightwood looked to people who came, heart-sick with anxiety, to inquire whether their beloved still breathed.

XX

YES — DOCTOR ARDMORE WAS IN, ADMITTED THE DESK IN the lobby, but it was to be doubted if he could be seen. . . . Yes — so very busy today. . . . Mrs. Hudson? . . . She was still living. . . . Would he sit down? . . . The desk was sympathetic.

Bobby nervously scribbled a message.

" Take that card to Doctor Ardmore," he commanded, " and make sure he gets it! "

In a few minutes a stocky, graying man of forty-five came quickly down the corridor and reached out his hand.

" Yes — I'm Ardmore. Only today we were speaking of you, Doctor Merrick. This is indeed a great pleasure. . . . Now — you have come about your countrywoman, Mrs. Hudson. . . . My friend, I fear we are not to save her. . . . No — nothing has been done yet. . . . Too soon — you will understand. . . . Cerebral concussion. . . . Donelli must wait a little. . . . He thinks tonight it may be safe to try . . . but he has no hope. . . . Conscious? Oh — fitfully; partially. We have had her quieted, you know. . . . She is aware that she is totally blind — I am sure of that."

" Then the contusion covers the occipital lobes! "

" Exactly! Squarely on the back of the head! Very deep lesion! . . . Then there are the fractured ribs. That's bad too. Lowers the resistance. . . . Donelli had decided at noon that it was useless to attempt the head operation, but now he's going into it. . . . He does not see too many of these cases. . . . I could wish — But — my God, man! *You're* here! You shall do it! Donelli will be very grateful! "

Bobby's heart was pounding.

"You really think he might want me to?"

"Want you? He'll say you're a godsend! Donelli's an excellent surgeon, but he does not specialize. You'll win his everlasting appreciation! . . . Come — we will go to your patient. . . . I shall be responsible for Donelli's full approval. . . . Come — please."

"Just a moment, Doctor Ardmore," said Bobby, tugging loose from the arm that was propelling him down the corridor. "I have something to say to you before I see Mrs. Hudson. Let us go some place where we may talk privately."

Ardmore led the way into a small parlor.

"I think you ought to know," said Bobby, "that this young woman's life is more to me than of professional concern; more than might be implied by the fact that we are fellow countrymen and acquaintances. . . . I have had hopes of making her my wife."

"My word! — What a situation!"

"Yes, isn't it? Now, I'll tell you the rest of it. We have had a very serious misunderstanding. That is to say — she is misunderstanding me. That being the case — perhaps it would be much better, in the event she has an interval of consciousness, that she be left unaware that I am her surgeon."

"But," objected Ardmore, "might not that fact put a little more resistance into her?"

"Not the kind we want."

"Well — you ought to know. . . . I shall tell the nurse and endeavor to keep your identity secret."

◇ ◇

It was the droop of her mouth that brought the scalding tears to Bobby's eyes. For a moment he thought he couldn't bear it.

Ardmore, observing how deeply he was affected, felt some concern. This was not an affair into which an operating surgeon dared to fetch his emotions. He gripped the visitor's shoulder with five vise-like fingers and muttered, "Steady! You're her doctor; not her lover!"

He motioned the nurse to follow him out into the hall and left Bobby alone with his patient. She roused slightly, drew a short, painfully interrupted sigh that made her wince; the lips tightened momentarily, and relaxed again into the pensive droop.

Bobby took the hand that lay on the white counterpane and held it in both of his. There was the very faintest imaginable pressure in her fingers. Dear little chap! She was at least vaguely aware of a friendly handclasp, no matter where it came from. That was that much — anyhow!

The door opened and Ardmore returned with the nurse whose eyes sparkled. She shared an important secret.

"Perhaps you would like to make an examination, doctor," said Ardmore.

Bobby nodded. The nurse led him to a wash room and found him a smock and gloves.

The patient was placed in position and the temporary bandages were removed. Bobby stood stunned at the sight. It was, as Ardmore had said, very, very deep. He gave a quick, almost articulate intake of breath as he touched it. . . . Again the English doctor's strong fingers gathered up a large handful of his young colleague's shoulder and growled, "Remember! She's your *patient!*"

"There's nothing to be gained by waiting," said Bobby. "Send for Doctor Donelli, please. We will go into this as soon as he arrives."

It was six o'clock when Helen was laid upon the operating table, and seven-thirty when she was transferred again to the wheeled bed on which she had come.

During that hour and a half, Bobby Merrick, by a supreme effort of his will, was a brain surgeon, and Helen Hudson was a patient — a case — a precariously difficult occipital contusion.

When they had wheeled her in, he feared for a moment he would be unable to achieve that professional attitude. He hesitated, before making his first incision, as he might have hesitated had the scalpel been aimed at his own heart. Once that deft stroke had been accomplished, he was all surgeon.

Donelli stood by, attentively, gently sponging away the blood; marveling at the uncanny accuracy with which the veins were clipped with forceps almost before they had a chance to signal their location; regarding with envious admiration the swiftness and sureness of those slim, strong, experienced fingers.

Twice Merrick had glanced up anxiously into the eyes of the anesthetist — it was no small matter to be conducting ether into those pummeled lungs — but, apparently satisfied with what he read there, applied himself with renewed concentration to his task.

It was a terrific strain, and the little group in the operating room was strangely silent. By common consent it was understood that a moving drama was being enacted here — a tragedy, perhaps. Any breath might be her last. That would depend upon the skill of the surgeon. Life and death here were to be determined by the promptness and accuracy of decisions in the removal of the clots. Too deep meant death; not deep enough meant blindness for life!

When the operation was all but finished, Donelli inquired, with an entreating look and a hand outstretched for the needle, if he might not do the scalp stitches; but Merrick shook his head.

The little procession crowded through the door. Bobby walked shakily into the adjacent dressing room; sat down on a white enameled stool, his shoulders slumped; and contemplated his hands. . . . Her blood! . . . Donelli and a nurse helped him off with his rubber gloves and out of his smock. The impulsive Italian himself insisted on mopping his guest's face with a cold towel, eager to show his sympathy. It had been the most stirring event of his experience in a vocation singularly exposed to dramatic situations.

They tried, a little later, to persuade Merrick to eat something, but his dinner consisted of a stiff drink of brandy which he gulped greedily as a toper. It was useless to argue with him. He was determined to go at once to his patient's bedside and wait results.

"But — there's nothing you can do," expostulated Ardmore. "It will be hours before you can determine anything more than you know now, unless — of course . . ."

"Exactly!" muttered Merrick. "It's the *unless* that concerns me! . . . That — and the threat of a quick pneumonia."

Donelli and Ardmore went to dinner. As they parted at

the hospital gate, the Italian said, " It's too much to hope for. Our young friend will be deeply grieved. But — it was a masterful piece of work! "

◇ ◇

Her room was in semi-darkness, but Merrick's eyes, once they were accustomed to the gloom, caressed the loveliness of her face. He had not bandaged her eyes. They were closed; and the long black lashes — incredibly long lashes — made heavy shadows on her darkly flushed cheeks. Her breathing was regular, quiet — almost too quiet, at times, and he would rise from his chair by the window and move anxiously toward the bed, his nerves keyed to the breaking point.

Mostly he sat resting his elbows on his knees with his chin in his hands, staring at her face, occasionally rousing when a longer breath, exhaled shudderingly, would bring him to her side, his stethoscope intent.

About midnight, he took a turn up and down in the corridor, and upon reëntering the room, whispered into Julie Craig's ear:

" Is her clothing in that closet? "

" Yes, doctor. . . . Can I help you? "

He shook his head, stepped to the wardrobe, and after some search brought out a soiled and torn blue gown, fumbled at the neck of it, and, having found what he sought, restored the garment to the closet and closed the door.

Julie Craig watched him interestedly as he sat toying with the bit of jewelry he had abstracted from his patient's clothing. Doubtless it was one of his gifts to her. There was some delicious secret connected with it. She wished she knew.

After a while, he rose, and, bending over her, whispered:

" You may go out and take a bit of exercise. I shall call you if you are needed."

◇ ◇

Dawn was breaking. The little clock ticked energetically on the bureau. Birds twittered sleepily, outside the window. Bells tolled matins.

There was a weary sigh from the bed. Julie Craig bent over it, solicitously.

And then, in that dear voice, curiously like a muted 'cello, between hysterical little sobs, Bobby Merrick's patient murmured:

" Oh — Blessed God — *I can see!* "

XXI

JULIE CRAIG WAS A ROMANTIC LITTLE THING, AND THE drama in which she had been assigned a rôle was quite to her liking. It was not a fat part as to voluminosity of lines, but it kept her almost continuously on the stage in the thick of action.

Very thrilling it was to feel herself the chief custodian of so valuable a secret. She had resolved to safeguard it against any hazard until the impressive moment arrived for its sensational release.

As for Doctor Ardmore's attitude toward the matter, he was so hilarious, that morning, to learn of the complete success of young Merrick's operation that it mattered little to him when or how his attractive patient should discover the identity of her benefactor. Ardmore was British. It occurred to him that whatever misunderstandings might have estranged these two interesting young Americans, the machinery of reconciliation was now in good running order. If they couldn't execute some kind of a treaty in the face of this theatrical life-saving event, they deserved to go their separate ways without expectation of sympathy.

Donelli, by race and temperament cordial toward the grand opera aspects of the situation, rather hoped the fair patient's identification of Merrick might not be brought about until she was at least sufficiently clear of mind to get a real emotional wallop out of the occasion, and sincerely hoped he might find some good reason to be present when it happened.

Julie was for postponing the great moment as long as possible. To her active imagination it was a situation to be nibbled at appreciatively; toyed with — cat and mouse fashion; savored, rolled about on the tongue. She could not conceive anything more bitterly disappointing than a prosaic anticlimax, now that the dramatic materials were all in hand for a perfectly whopping curtain! It made her shudder to contemplate the possibility of his popping into the room while his idol was in the throes of nausea, as she was almost sure to be, a dozen times before the day was out. The whole affair, Julie decided, should be insured against a commonplace outcome, and dedicated herself to that movement with almost as much concern as if she were one of the principals.

Pursuant to that determination she had left word at the office that she wished to communicate with Doctor Merrick as soon as he returned from breakfast and the brief nap he had promised himself. When the message came up that the young American surgeon was in the building, Julie went to the stairs to meet him. He greeted her warmly, told her she had been very faithful, suggested she would be better off for a few hours' sleep. He would see to it that she was relieved at once.

She shook her head.

"I am not sleepy. I shall wait until this afternoon. Doctor Ardmore told me my patient was not to know who was treating her. So — I have restored the bandage to her eyes. I told her they should not encounter the strong light for several hours. I hope I haven't done wrong, sir."

"You are very resourceful," said Bobby, endeavoring to keep a straight face. "Is there, by any chance, something else I ought to know before looking in?"

She colored with conscious pride.

"Yes, sir. If you don't mind, I have told her that since

she does not speak Italian fluently, whatever conversation she may have with you is to be interpreted by me. . . . And Doctor Donelli can be asked in, this morning, while you make the examination. Is that agreeable?"

"Miss Craig," said Bobby solemnly, "you're wasting your talents here. You should belong to the diplomatic corps."

"I hope you're not making fun, sir. . . . Doctor Ardmore said she wasn't to know — and I saw no other way of keeping it from her."

"You have done very nicely," commended Bobby. "I'll wash up and change my coat."

◇ ◇

Helen had been creeping out of her etherized torpor, at closer intervals of full consciousness, since seven; had even smiled gratefully under Julie's little tendernesses.

"So glad!" she had murmured when Julie assured her she was going to be well and sound as ever.

"And — I can see!"

She raised a white hand and tugged weakly at the edge of the bandage over her eyes. Julie hastened to restore it.

"Tomorrow, perhaps," she promised. "He wants them protected today."

"Very well," with an obedient sigh, "he ought to know, I suppose."

Julie was a tense little figure when Doctor Merrick came in, arrayed in his borrowed surgical gown, accompanied by the volatile Donelli who greeted her with a bombardment of praise for having contributed so much to this happy eventuality. She returned a volley warning him against an accidental disclosure of their secret. Donelli nodded vigorously and chuckled.

Doctor Merrick stepped at once to the bedside table, consulted the chart, and proceeded to verify the latest pulse-count.

" Please tell the doctor," said Helen slowly, " that the bandage around my chest is so very tight. Could he make it more comfortable? "

Julie dutifully relayed the request in a swift Italian sentence composed of one word of two hundred syllables — mostly vowels.

Seeing that the surgical bandage around her chest had been Donelli's affair, it was only a natural courtesy for Doctor Merrick to permit his colleague to decide whether or not he wished it changed. Stepping back, he silently signed to Doctor Donelli that this matter was up to him. But Donelli vehemently protested, with outspread fingers, that he was only too eager to discover his guest's technique.

The opportunity for a debate not being favorable, Bobby turned down the sheet, examined the broad bandage, unpinned it, unfolded it down to the creamy-white satin skin, carefully inspected the discolored field of the fractures, and expertly replaced the bandage.

" Oh — that is ever so much better," sighed his patient, gratefully.

Julie shook loose a cascade of musical Italian, and the doctor grunted his receipt of it.

" He has very gentle hands," murmured Helen sleepily.

" Shall I tell him that, madame? " asked Julie, her eyes brightly searching his face.

" No. . . . Tell him I am thankful he has made me see again."

Impulsively Bobby entertained a foolhardy notion. In a clumsy Italian phrase, remembered from boyhood, he mumbled something about the pleasure being all his own — and, dismayed by his own audacity, walked to the window to write a prescription.

Julie's eyes were intent upon her patient's half-covered face. She was about to interpret the doctor's remark when she noted that the full lips parted; then, that the lower lip was gently pinioned between an even row of white teeth, while the dimples deepened ever so little and a slow flush crept across her cheeks.

With agitated fingers, Julie refastened the smock at the throat, her sentimental little heart beating wildly. . . . She knows! — thought Julie. . . . Bending over her, she said gently:

"But perhaps you understood what the doctor was just saying. Is it not so?"

There was no reply. She had drowsed off again. But the smile lingered on her lips, and the flush lingered on her cheeks.

As they went out, Doctor Merrick beckoned Julie to the door and said, in an undertone:

"You might remove that bandage from her eyes while she sleeps. It will be more comfortable."

◇ ◇

Two hours later she roused again. Having soberly regarded Julie for some minutes, she fumbled at the neck of her smock and drew out the little silver cross. Holding it tightly in both hands and pressing it to her heart, she inquired:

" How did you know I wanted it? "

" I did not know, madame; or you should have had it from the first."

There was a long pause.

" When did you put it on me? I just now discovered it."

" I did not put it on you, madame."

There was another long silence.

Observing that her patient was dabbing clumsily at her eyes with the corner of the sheet, Julie hastened to restore her handkerchief; then turned and walked thoughtfully to the window.

" Did you see him do it? "

Julie did not turn from the window as she replied, unsteadily:

" No, madame. He invited me to leave the room."

" The — poor — dear! "

◇ ◇

At nine that evening Marion Dawson arrived and Bobby met her at the station.

Immediately upon reading the news of the accident, she had been fortunate in making connections with the best westbound train of the day. Her frantic telegram of inquiry, addressed to the hospital while en route, had been handed to Merrick who had wired reassuringly to her train. She had received the message at ten. It did not greatly surprise her to have a telegram from him, knowing that he would have been likely to see the account of the disaster while in Paris.

" Oh, Bobby — how wonderful! " she exclaimed tearfully, when he told her that everything was favorable to a prompt recovery. " Can I see her? "

"Better not tonight. She will be brighter in the morning."

"And I suppose you two blessed things have found that you're necessary to each other, haven't you?"

"Well — not yet," he said, hesitatingly. "You see, I have her at a rather awkward disadvantage. I performed the operation, myself. I don't wish to make capital of any obligation she might feel toward me. In fact — she doesn't know I'm here, at all."

Marion was pink with indignation. The taxi-driver stood by the open door of the cab waiting for them to step in; but she ignored the gesture and blazed at her compatriot angrily.

"Bobby Merrick — I think that's simply disgraceful! You've always kept the dear soul in the dark and made her feel irresponsible. And here you are again with some more of your wretched secrets! Well — we'll see if you're going to use her that way, this time! When I see her in the morning, I mean to tell her! You don't need to think I'm a party to any more of these mysteries!"

He rather suspected that she meant it. On the short ride over to the Quirinal where he had reserved a room for her, he told her as much as he could explain of the operation, attempting to divert her attention from her annoyance over his attitude toward Helen.

"I am leaving in the morning for Vienna," he said, after making sure she was receiving proper attention at the hotel desk. "Doctor Donelli can do the dressings as well as I. There is no danger now, and no reason for my staying on; especially since you seem bent on informing her."

"It's the only decent thing to do," retorted Marion obdurately. "She has a right to know. . . . Well — give my love to Jack and tell him I'll be back when Helen doesn't need me any more. I wonder if she'll forgive me!"

"I hope so, my dear; but I wouldn't bet much on it. . . . Good-bye!"

◇ ◇

Later in the evening he had a consultation with Donelli and felt confident he was leaving his patient in competent hands. He stepped into Helen's room, found her sleeping, took her hand and held it for a moment, and walked out with only a nod for the nurse who had relieved Julie. At the desk he scribbled a note to her, thanking her for "exceptional faithfulness and originality," and enclosed a substantial tender of gratitude (part of which she used to defray a three months' vacation in Switzerland).

Reconciliation was effected promptly and silently, the next morning, when Marion called. They kissed each other and wept a little. Julie excused herself and left them alone together.

"Helen, dear," whispered Marion, the moment the door had closed, "you could never guess who did your operation?"

"Oh yes, I could," drawled Helen, smiling.

"Good! He thought he had such a secret! When did you find out?"

She laughed — with a little wince of pain.

"He talked some Italian for me, yesterday."

"And you recognized his voice?"

"Instantly."

"He doesn't know it; I am confident."

"Well, he probably will before the day is over."

Before Marion had a chance to reply, Doctor Donelli

came bustling in, trailed by Julie, and smilingly approached the bedside.

Helen looked up inquiringly.

" Isn't Doctor Merrick coming, this morning, Miss Craig? "

Julie shook her head.

" He left for Vienna at seven, dear," said Marion. " I told him I intended to tell you he was here, so — off he goes! "

" How like him! " said Helen, smiling.

XXII

DOCTOR MERRICK'S UNUSUAL CAPACITY FOR PIN-POINT concentration upon problems of scientific research was not quite up to par during his collaboration with Doctor Arnstadt. The Viennese surgeon seemed every way satisfied, and rejoiced in his close association with his young American colleague, but Bobby was too restless and distracted to make the most of his opportunity.

Jack Dawson had been quick to understand his friend's mood.

"Bobby," he advised, one early August night, as they were finishing their dinner in the low-ceilinged grill room at Hangel's, "I don't want to meddle, but I believe you really ought to run over to the Imperial City and do your stuff. You're getting to be damned poor company, and I think you have something weighty on your conscience."

Bobby nodded soberly.

"You're right! . . . I'll go — tomorrow!"

◇ ◇

Marion had stayed on in Rome. Jack's daily letter from her constituted the log of Helen's rather tedious trip through convalescence.

It was a great day in Vienna — demanding a bit of celebration that night — when the news came that she had sat up for a half hour.

Now she had been wheeled out into the shady patio. . . . Now she had taken a short walk. . . . Now they were both at the Quirinal, and every afternoon Helen was down in the garden, in the hotel court. . . . Now she was taking drives in the evening. . . . You could hardly find the scar, any more. . . . Helen was so happy.

◇ ◇

On the morning of the sixth of August, Jack and Doctor Arnstadt saw Bobby off. After the train had slipped quietly out of the station, Jack went to the telegraph booth and wired to Marion. He did not tell her it was a secret that Bobby was on the way. She would not have kept it, in any event. She was all done with riddles.

" Who do you think's coming? " she cried, romping into Helen's room waving her telegram.

" When does he arrive? "

" Tomorrow afternoon — about six! . . . Isn't it wonderful? "

" I'm going, dear! I don't feel I'm quite up to it."

" Why — the very idea! . . . You can't! . . . When you know he's on the way? . . . He'll be wretchedly disappointed! "

" But — I don't know he's coming — that is, not officially. . . . He probably didn't want me to know, or he would have informed me."

There was no talking her out of it. She was going! That night they paid a farewell call at the hospital. Julie Craig shyly inquired of Mrs. Dawson if Doctor Merrick was still in Europe, and was appalled to learn that he was arriving in Rome tomorrow.

" But — you will have gone, madame! " exclaimed Julie, looking reproachfully at her patient. . . . Surely this affair was being badly managed by somebody.

◇ ◇

All that the concierge at the Quirinal seemed to remember at first about the whereabouts of the two young American women was that they had left, that noon, for Paris. Upon further reflection, and in appreciation of the color of the bank-note which Doctor Merrick was twisting in his fingers, he recalled that Madame Hudson's heavier baggage had been expressed directly to Le Havre. He had himself seen to it. Yes — she was sailing on the *Île de France* on Thursday. At all events, her trunks were.

Bobby spent an hour, pacing up and down the flagging in the garden of the Quirinal, planning his next move. This game of hide and seek couldn't — mustn't go on any longer! He resolved to corner her and take her by force!

He sent a long telegram to Jack Dawson, confiding the full particulars of the enormous audacity he had decided to commit. He had made his reputation with her by various acts of impudence. This would be the crowning deed which would make all his former impertinences seem bland. He was very nervous as he prepared for it.

Events moved very swiftly, once he had come to his decision. He engaged an aeroplane and flew to Paris. Between the racket of the triple engines and the furious pounding of his heart, it was a noisy trip. There was a hasty half-hour with his mother, in which he persuaded her to forgive him on the strength of a promise that he would return and be with her at Christmas.

At the down town office of the French Line, he engaged the most luxurious suite on the *Île de France*. Next morning, he flew to Havre, arriving an hour before the boat-train from Paris.

It was a long and anxious hour. Never had he been so utterly stampeded by his own emotions.

Seeing to it that his light luggage was in his quarters, and having strolled about through the commodious suite to make sure it was ready for occupancy — he had retained enough presence of mind to order the place filled with flowers — he went up to the captain's cabin, renewed acquaintance, and asked a favor.

Then he went down and took up his stand at the foot of the first-class gangway, waiting with an impatience almost too urgent to be borne.

Whatever would she think?

Slowly the train crept into the shed, across the way, and the passengers swarmed in little groups about their hand baggage. Presently the procession began to move stragglingly toward the ship.

Bobby saw her coming, tripping smartly along with two porters attentively close behind her.

Mauve — this time. . . . Snug, saucy, cloche hat — mauve. . . . A tailored suit of mauve that sculptured every curve of her.

She sighted him waiting for her. He knew she had seen him. Now her eyes widened and her lips parted as their gaze met. She advanced steadily toward him with a tread almost martial.

As she neared him, he did not extend his hand, as she had thought he might. He held out both arms; and, to his inexpressible delight, she walked confidently into them, shyly laid her slim fingers on his coat lapels, looked up into his face, and smiled.

" Put madame's baggage in Suite B," said Bobby, in a proprietorial tone to the porters.

" You are traveling with me! " he explained rather unsteadily. " The captain is marrying us, this afternoon! "

" Yes, dear," she said softly. " I know."

Bobby's arms tightened about her.

" How did you know? " he grinned, boyishly.

" Well — let's see. You wired it to Doctor Dawson, and he wired it to Marion, and she wired it to me. . . . Awfully roundabout way to learn one was being married, wasn't it? "

" But — but — you're for it, aren't you? " he pleaded, searching her eyes.

She smiled.

" Perhaps we should go aboard, Bobby. We're blocking the traffic."

CPSIA information can be obtained
at www.ICGtesting.com
Printed in the USA
LVOW07s0119190817
545577LV00001B/130/P

9 780395 957745